GOURMET
HIDEAWAYS

GOURMET
HIDEAWAYS

Text by Lannice Snyman

Photography by Andrzej Sawa

Project co-ordination by Tamsin Snyman

Gourmet Hideaways is dedicated to the rising stars of Southern Africa's
hospitality industry: the charming hosts and talented cooks whose splendid
establishments and delicious recipes we have captured for posterity.

ACKNOWLEDGEMENTS

The generosity and skills of many people are incorporated in this important book. In particular:
The hotels, guesthouses, country lodges, private game reserves and restaurants whose special charms and recipes fill these pages and who are listed in full on page 150. We treasure the memories of their warm hospitality and cheerful participation in the photo-sessions in far-flung corners of the country.
Tamsin Snyman, who efficiently co-ordinated this multi-faceted project, liaised with the chefs, hoteliers and restaurateurs involved, and who helped so enthusiastically with the recipe testing.
Ninety Six Inc, our brilliant and patient book designer.
The team at Disc Express for the masterful reproduction of our photographs.
ISO Photo for sponsoring the Fuji Film used to capture the special images in this book.
Fotoquip, stockists of Hasselblad cameras – used exclusively for the food photographs – for their assistance in obtaining the Broncolor lighting system.
Giovanni's Deliworld in Green Point for tracking down the more unusual ingredients called for in the recipes.
Friends with healthy appetites and analytical taste buds who clustered gleefully around Lannice's dinner table for regular recipe testing sessions during the years that *Gourmet Hideaways* was in production.
Our wonderful and patient families – Dana Sawa, and Michael, Courtenay and Tamsin Snyman – who have survived yet another publishing collaboration.

LANNICE SNYMAN AND ANDRZEJ SAWA

Front cover photographs: Terrine of Tomatoes, Red Peppers and Basil with Sultana and Caper Dressing, The Cellars-Hohenort page 55.
Ostrich Steaks with Country Mushroom Duxelle, Ginger Crisps and Port Jus, Rosenhof Country Lodge page 81.
Poached Fennel and Strawberries in Vanilla Syrup, Savoy Cabbage page 91.
Gametrackers' Eagle Island Camp, Xaxaba Island, Okavango Delta, Botswana, page 46.

First Published in 2000 by
S&S Publishers
PO Box 26344, Hout Bay 7872, South Africa
E-mail: lannice@iafrica.com

Text and Photographs © Lannice Snyman and Andrzej Sawa. All rights strictly reserved.

No part of this book may be reproduced or transmitted in any form, or by any means, electronic or mechanical,
or by photocopying, recording or microfilming. Nor may it be stored in a retrieval system without prior permission
of the copyright owners and publishers.

Author and Stylist Lannice Snyman
Photographer Andrzej Sawa FRPS FPSSA FPPSA
Project Co-Ordinator and Food Styling Assistant Tamsin Snyman
Design and Typesetting Ninety Six Inc.
Editor Elaine Hurford
Colour Separation Disc Express, Cape Town
Printed and Bound in Singapore by Tien Wah Press (Pte) Limited

ISBN 0 620 25924 8

CONTENTS

INTRODUCTION ◆ 6

MENUS ◆ 8

GOURMET HIDEAWAYS & THEIR RECIPES ◆ 12

THE GOURMET PANTRY ◆ 134
STOCKS & OTHER BASIC RECIPES ◆ 134
COLD SAUCES, CHUTNEYS & PRESERVES ◆ 137
HOT SAUCES ◆ 140
SALADS, VEGETABLES & SIDE DISHES ◆ 141
BREADS & PASTRIES ◆ 145
SWEET THINGS & ICE-CREAMS ◆ 146

METRIC CONVERSION CHART ◆ 149

CONTRIBUTORS' CONTACT LISTING ◆ 150

GLOSSARY OF COOKING TERMS, EQUIPMENT & INGREDIENTS ◆ 152

RECIPE INDEX ◆ 157

INTRODUCTION

THE AFRICAN RENAISSANCE has brought tourists flocking to our shores, revitalising the hospitality industry, rekindling national culinary pride and providing the perfect reason for producing *Gourmet Hideaways of Southern Africa,* a book that showcases the special pleasures of exploring this spectacular yet largely undiscovered corner of the world.

Creating this book took several action-packed years and took us to far-flung corners of the country – a dream project for any writer and photographer. Establishments were carefully selected to fulfil the criteria of the title; all are gourmet hideaways with fascinating historical links and impeccable culinary reputations.

Menus represent their chefs' most inspired work, creating a platform for astonishingly talented cooks whose work is informed in equal measure by classic foundations, modern international influences, an empathy for ingredients of the highest quality and freshness – and an innate sense of Africa. The magic thread that binds it all together is the creative use of bountiful crops, livestock, seafood and wild game, and exotic fruits and vegetables.

Unsurprisingly for such a wide-ranging collection, recipes range from simple yet stylish to fabulously formal. However, although professionally founded, the dishes aren't difficult to make, as each has been meticulously edited and retested in a domestic kitchen to make them absolutely foolproof. *Gourmet Hideaways*, therefore, appeals to cooks with a passion for creativity, as well as those who prefer to keep things simple.

We thank all those who so generously shared their recipes and hospitality when we photographed destinations and recipes in their home environment to capture this stunning pictorial overview.

As our other books have shown, our intention is not to produce 'just another cookery book'. *Reflections of the South African Table* and *Rainbow Cuisine* are books to browse through and travel by, as well as to learn and cook from. *Gourmet Hideaways* proudly joins the line-up.

We trust you'll treasure it for many, many years to come.

Lannice Snyman

Andrzej Sawa

MENUS

96 WINERY ROAD 28

Sweet Potato and Tomato Tarte Tatin with Chilli and Basil Dressing

◆ ◆

Caramelized Onions with Biltong and Pecorino

◆ ◆

Strawberries Steeped in Merlot and Black Pepper

AUBERGINE RESTAURANT 38

Aubergine Scallopine and Tomato Compôte with Pine Seed Vinaigrette

◆ ◆

Grilled Tuna in Lemongrass-Spiced Vegetable Minestrone with Coriander Pesto

AU JARDIN AT THE VINEYARD 104

Marinière of Seafood

◆ ◆

Pan-Roasted Fruit Kebabs with Vanilla Rice

BARTHOLOMEUSKLIP FARMHOUSE 12

Salad with Smoked Meat and Spiced Pickled Pears

◆ ◆

Braised Lamb Shanks with Peppers, Onions and Tomato

◆ ◆

Maize Meal Wedges

◆ ◆

Chocolate Marzipan Layer Cake

THE BLUE TRAIN 40

Timbale of Smoked Fish with Cucumber Zest

◆ ◆

Chicken Breasts with Macadamia Nut Stuffing and Spiced Apricot Sauce

◆ ◆

Springbok Steaks with Chilli-Roasted Onions

◆ ◆

Pears in Red Wine with Cinnamon Mousse

BOSCHENDAL 94

Smoked Snoek Pâté

◆ ◆

Curried Butternut Soup

◆ ◆

Venison Pie

◆ ◆

Bobotie

◆ ◆

Mille-Feuille Cheesecake

BUSHMANS KLOOF WILDERNESS RESERVE 30

Black Mussel and Potato Salad with Roasted Garlic-Mustard Dressing

◆ ◆

Duck Bobotie

◆ ◆

Venison Steaks with Cranberry Apricot Chutney

◆ ◆

Little Malva Puddings with Rooibos Crème Anglaise

CAPE MALAY RESTAURANT AT THE CELLARS-HOHENHORT 44

Smoorsnoek

◆ ◆

Cape-Malay Chicken Curry

CARRIGANS COUNTRY ESTATE 64

Smoked Trout Salad with Papino and Chilli Salsa

◆ ◆

Quail with Fennel, Mushroom and Macadamia Stuffing and Port Sauce

◆ ◆

Chocmint Ice-Cream

THE CELLARS-HOHENORT 52

Roasted Springbok Fillet, Sweet Potato Tatin and Pickled Beetroot

◆ ◆

Terrine of Tomatoes, Red Pepper and Basil with Sultana and Caper Dressing

◆ ◆

Crème Brûlée Espresso with Seed Biscuits, Vanilla Ice-Cream and Butterscotch Sauce

CLOETE'S AT ALPHEN   118

Tartare of Fish with Olive Oil and Lime Juice

◆ ◆

Provençal Lamb Racks with Tomato and Rosemary Sauce

◆ ◆

Orange Blossom Crème Brûlée

THE COACH HOUSE   120

Mango and Prawn Bava

◆ ◆

Butter Fried Trout with Macadamia and Mushroom Stuffing
and Pecan Lemon Butter

◆ ◆

Rare Roast Beef with Yorkshire Pudding and Mango Salsa

◆ ◆

Macadamia Pie

CYBELE FOREST LODGE   98

Tomato and Olive Tarte Tatin with Feta and Basil Pesto

◆ ◆

Seared Beef Fillet with Parmesan and Rocket

◆ ◆

Hazelnut Meringues with Berries and Cream

DENNEHOF KAROO GUEST HOUSE   110

Chicken with Green Olives and Preserved Lemons

◆ ◆

Karoo Vetkoek Schwarmas

EMILY'S BISTRO   76

Baked Beetroot with Harissa and Mustard Foam

◆ ◆

Pienangvleis

◆ ◆

Wine Jelly

FANCOURT HOTEL AND COUNTRY CLUB ESTATE   66

Spiced Semolina Wedges with Oriental Vegetables

◆ ◆

Ostrich Carpaccio with Peach Chutney and Avocado Parfait

◆ ◆

Plaited Salmon Trout with Two Sauces
and Ribbon Vegetables

◆ ◆

Bread and Butter Pudding with Van der Hum

GAMETRACKERS   46

Ostrich Carpaccio with Pickled Ginger and Wasabi Oil

◆ ◆

Tandoori Chicken Salad

◆ ◆

Spiced Fish on Pasta with Olives and Tomato

◆ ◆

Sticky Chocolate Pudding

GARONGA SAFARI CAMP   126

Poached Fruit Flavoured with Lemongrass and Star Anise with
Cinnamon-Honey Yoghurt

◆ ◆

Bread with Roasted Vegetables

◆ ◆

Fish Baked in Banana Leaves with Chilli, Lemongrass and
Coriander with Red Pepper and Coconut Cream Sauce

GLENSHIEL COUNTRY LODGE   72

Sweet Potato, Coriander and Buttermilk Soup

◆ ◆

Ostrich Medallions with Dijon Mustard Crust
with Cape Velvet Sauce

◆ ◆

Chocolate Avocado Mousse

GRANDE ROCHE   16

Almond-Crusted Fish with Coconut Lemongrass Sauce

◆ ◆

Banana Samoosas and Cape Velvet Ice-Cream
with Coconut Foam

HAZENDAL ESTATE   74

Roast Baby Chickens with Mango-Coriander Sauce

◆ ◆

Russian Blinis with Smoked Salmon

HIGHGROVE HOUSE   130

Smoked Salmon on Crisp Noodle Cakes with Avocado
and Horseradish Cream

◆ ◆

Roasted Breast of Duck on a Warm Salad of Tomatoes,
Beans and Peas

LE QUARTIER FRANÇAIS   34

Double Baked Blue Cheese Soufflé with Fried Watercress
Gnocchi and Red Pepper Compôte

◆ ◆

Lamb Burger on Foccacia with Creamed Avocado,
Marinated Tomatoes and Pickled Cucumber

◆ ◆

Butternut Risotto Cakes with Roasted Vegetables,
Smoked Mozzarella and Sage Butter

THE MARINE   82

Parfait of Chicken and Duck Livers with Grape Chutney and
Rooibos Jelly with Toasted Brioche

◆ ◆

Roast Rack of Lamb with Ragoût of Mushrooms,
Liver and Kidneys

◆ ◆

Berry Soufflé with Passionfruit Coulis

THE MOUNT NELSON HOTEL   56

Spicy Chickpea Battered Prawns with Lime and
Coriander Vinaigrette

◆ ◆

Cape-Malay Spiced Fish with Coconut and Lemongrass Broth

NGALA PRIVATE GAME RESERVE   18

Lavosh Flatbread with Avocado Dip

◆ ◆

Sesame-Chilli Breadsticks with Smoked Trout

◆ ◆

Karilinah's Bush Scones

◆ ◆

Apple and Date Crunch Cake

◆ ◆

Mango and Peanut Shortbread

OLD JOE'S KAIA   50

Angel Hair Pasta with Avocado and Bacon

◆ ◆

Old Joe's Oxtail

◆ ◆

Sparkling Mango

PARKS   22

Goats' Cheese Soufflé with Red Currant and Apple Preserve

◆ ◆

Venison on Red Cabbage with Black Currant
and Apple Sauce

PHINDA PRIVATE GAME RESERVE   106

Sausage Stacks with Corn and Cheese Cakes

◆ ◆

Mango and Chilli Relish

◆ ◆

African Banana Chutney

◆ ◆

Pawpaw Daquiri

◆ ◆

Warm Beef Salad with Bacon and Blue Cheese Dressing

◆ ◆

Marinated Tomato with Chilli, Mint and Mozzarella

◆ ◆

Roasted Butternut and Corn Salad

THE PLETTENBERG   24

Seafood Soup

◆ ◆

Lobster Tempura with Jasmine Rice and
Stir-Fried Fine Greens

◆ ◆

Chocolate Amarula Truffle with Raspberry Coulis
and Almond Ice-Cream

THE PRUE LEITH SCHOOL OF FOOD AND WINE   58

Tuna Brix with Harissa Mayonnaise

◆ ◆

Ostrich Fillet with Pesto and Beetroot and Spinach Salad

◆ ◆

Grilled Pineapple with Buttered Mint Glaze

RHEBOKSKLOOF   124

Trio of Rösti with Ratatouille and Camembert,
Smoked Salmon Tartare and
Chicken and Mushroom Ragoût

◆ ◆

Fish Tournedos with Mussel Risotto Dumplings

ROGGELAND COUNTRY HOUSE   60

Caramelized Onion and Tomato Tarte Tatin

◆ ◆

Roast Duck with Oriental Sauce

◆ ◆

Cream Cheese Soufflé

◆ ◆

Chocolate Mousse Cake

ROSENHOF COUNTRY LODGE   80

Ostrich Steaks with Country Mushroom Duxelle,
Ginger Crisps and Port Jus

◆ ◆

Poppy Seed Orange Cakes with Liqueur Oranges

ROZENHOF RESTAURANT   112

Tomato and Bocconcini Salad with Herb Pesto

◆ ◆

Baby Chickens with Roasted Garlic and Pancetta,
and Rosemary Demi-Glace

◆ ◆

Lemon and Basil Mousse
with Strawberry Salad

SAVOY CABBAGE   88

Black Mussels with Smoorsnoek-Filled Cabbage Roses
in Ginger Broth

◆ ◆

Roast Spiced Loin of Lamb with Apricots and Rooibos

◆ ◆

Poached Fennel and Strawberries in Vanilla Syrup

SELATI LODGE AT SABI SABI   92

East African Breakfast Kuku with
Tomato Chutney

◆ ◆

Chilli Beans

SHANGANA CULTURAL VILLAGE   86

Spicy Peanut Chicken

◆ ◆

Coal-Roasted Corn

◆ ◆

Maize and Cheese Bread

◆ ◆

Traditional Sweet Peanut Snacks

SINGITA PRIVATE GAME RESERVE   114

Sesame Beef Salad

◆ ◆

Cumin Grilled Pork Fillet on Peanut Samp and Beans,
Buttered Spinach and Ginger Glaze

◆ ◆

Potato, Spinach and Feta Pie

◆ ◆

Sweet Potato Pudding

SPIER   100

Fish Frikkadels with Chilli Tartare Sauce

◆ ◆

Mutton Breyani

◆ ◆

Date Salad

◆ ◆

Boeber

VERGELEGEN   132

Spicy Black Mushroom Soup with Pesto

◆ ◆

Vegetable Tower Topped with Camembert,
and Red Pepper Sauce

◆ ◆

Iced Dark Chocolate and Hazelnut Parfait with
Orange Crème Anglaise

THE WESTCLIFF   70

Honey-Lemon Chicken with Sweetcorn Pancakes

◆ ◆

Fish with Scalloped Potatoes and Lime and Tomato Confit

◆ ◆

Lemon Tart

 Past, present and future meld harmoniously at this charming Victorian farmhouse tucked snugly below the towering Elandsberg mountains between Wellington and Tulbagh on the edge of the Swartland.

Bartholomeus Klip epitomizes the freedom of open spaces and the joy of quality time out at a gentler pace. Part historic working farm, part nature reserve – entirely enchanting – there are barnyards to explore, fynbos to hike through, mountains to climb, a lake-sized dam to windsurf on, sun-dappled wheatfields to cycle through, birds to watch and game to view. Gardens are filled with agapanthus, lavender, heliotrope, old roses and oak trees planted by the earliest Cape farmers.

The farm was named after the massacre of French Huguenots on St Bartholomew's Day in France in 1572. However the first owner wasn't a refugee from Catholic persecutions, but an elderly immigrant from Holland, Frantz Joosten van der Lubstadt. In 1705 he and his young wife, Maria Mouton, chose this tranquil fynbos-covered place to raise cattle and sheep. One day, on his return home from searching for cattle after a leopard attack, Frantz was butchered by farm workers, Titus and Fortuijn, who hid the body in a porcupine den. It transpired that the deed was masterminded by Maria, who had taken Titus as her lover. All three were thrown into the Cape Town Castle. Maria was sentenced in 1714, becoming the first white woman to be condemned to death in the fledgling colony. With her two accomplices, she was publicly executed on the corner of Buitenkant and Darling Streets.

Bartholomeus Klip is the name of a high rocky outcrop near the guesthouse, from where past owners watched for smoke signals from Signal Hill next to Table Mountain which would indicate the arrival of ships in Table Bay. They would hastily round up livestock and herd them to Cape Town to sell.

BARTHOLOMEUS KLIP FARMHOUSE

HERMON,
WESTERN CAPE

The farms have been in the Parker family for over sixty years, having been acquired from Lord de Villiers, a former chief justice of the Cape. In 1964 Dale Parker set about an ambitious project of reintroducing game and preserving the natural habitat. The reserve land has been declared a Natural Heritage Site. Antelope once again roam mountain foothills where once cattle grazed.

Through the years the original stone farmhouse was changed to a Victorian homestead. In 1994 the Parkers transformed it into a small guesthouse, revitalizing neglected, time-touched buildings. Much has changed; many things remain as they were in ages past. Porcupines still ferret around the farmhouse at night for acorns dropped from free burghers' ancient oaks. The endangered geometric tortoise, one of the world's rarest reptiles, hides in renosterbos, safe in this small corner of the world. Wild gladioli and other exquisite flowers bloom in profusion amongst the fynbos each spring. The custodians of this special place take pride in sharing it with their guests.

ABOVE *Quagga roam free in the foothills of the Elandsberge. Extinct since 1878, they form part of an important rebreeding programme.* OPPOSITE PAGE TOP *Chocolate Marzipan Layer Cake (page 15).* BELOW *Hosts Nic Dupper (manager, ranger and conservationist) and his wife Nicole, the chef.*

SALAD WITH SMOKED MEAT AND SPICED PICKLED PEARS

assorted salad leaves and herbs
200 g finely sliced smoked meat
Vinaigrette (page 137)
SPICED PICKLED PEARS
6 firm pears, peeled, cored and quartered
125 ml brown sugar
300 ml cider vinegar
15 ml balsamic vinegar
15 ml black peppercorns
4 whole cloves
6 juniper berries, slightly crushed

SPICED PICKLED PEARS Set the oven at 190°C. Arrange the pears in a wide baking dish. Place the remaining ingredients in a medium saucepan and heat gently, stirring until the sugar dissolves. Bring the syrup to the boil, pour over the pears, cover with the lid or foil and bake for 15 minutes. Turn the pears, cover once more and bake for a further 15 minutes until tender. Cool at room temperature and chill.
TO SERVE Arrange salad leaves and herbs on a large platter, or on individual serving plates. Garnish with smoked meat and finely sliced pears. Offer the vinaigrette separately. SERVES 8

Afternoon tea served on the front stoep with views of the sheep farm and barnyards.

BRAISED LAMB SHANKS WITH PEPPERS, ONIONS AND TOMATO

As Bartholomeus Klip is a working sheep farm, lamb is often on the menu. It is even better prepared a day ahead and reheated.

3 kg young lamb shanks (10-16 shanks)
cake flour, olive oil
salt, milled black pepper
30 ml chopped fresh oregano
2 yellow and 2 red peppers, quartered
24 pickling onions, peeled
5 garlic cloves, peeled and chopped
1 kg ripe tomatoes, blanched, skinned, quartered and seeded
750 ml Beef or Lamb Stock (page 134)

Set the oven at 180°C. Dust the lamb shanks liberally with flour. Heat oil in a heavy casserole (it should be large enough to accommodate the shanks in a single layer) on the stovetop and brown the meat well all over. Season with salt and pepper, and scatter over the oregano, peppers, onions, garlic and tomato. Pour over the stock, cover and braise in the oven for about 1½ hours. Check for tenderness, and continue cooking if necessary. (Larger shanks from older animals could take 3 hours. To avoid overcooking the peppers and onions you may like to remove them from the casserole when they're tender, and return them later.)

Serve immediately, or allow the casserole to cool, then chill for 8 hours (overnight is even better) for flavours to develop.
TO SERVE Set the oven at 180°C. Remove and discard all traces of fat from the surface of the casserole, cover and place in the oven for about 45 minutes to heat through. Serve with maize meal wedges. SERVES 8

> **WINE** With the salad select any easy-drinking white wine such as chenin blanc, colombard, Cape riesling or unwooded sauvignon blanc. Ensure that it's assertive enough to balance the vinegar in the dressing and the spiciness of the pears, like Buitenverwachting Buiten Blanc. The perfect accompaniment for lamb is a fine French bordeaux, but any hearty red such as claret, shiraz or cabernet sauvignon would do the honours. We suggest Hartenberg Shiraz or La Motte Millennium, their flagship Bordeaux-style blend.

MAIZE MEAL WEDGES

Maize meal is as popular in South Africa as polenta is in Italy. Maize was introduced to South Africa's table by ancient black tribes from plants brought from central America by Portuguese navigators at the start of the 16th century.

1 litre water
5 ml salt
2 ml turmeric
500 ml maize meal or polenta
50 g butter, melted

Bring the water to the boil with the salt and turmeric in a large, heavy saucepan. Tip in the maize meal or polenta, mix and stir briskly. Cover and cook undisturbed over very gentle heat for about 20 minutes.

Spread the maize meal onto a buttered baking sheet to a thickness of approximately 1 cm and allow to cool.
TO SERVE Cut the maize meal into neat wedges, brush liberally with melted butter and place under a preheated oven griller until hot, crisp and golden. SERVES 8

CHOCOLATE MARZIPAN LAYER CAKE

2 eggs
250 ml plain yoghurt
125 g soft unsalted butter
250 ml castor sugar
125 ml cocoa powder
5 ml bicarbonate of soda
250 ml cake flour
1 ml salt
750 g marzipan
45 ml brandy
fresh or glacé cherries to garnish
CHOCOLATE MOUSSE
300 g dark chocolate, roughly chopped
500 ml cream
CHOCOLATE GANACHE
300 g dark chocolate, roughy chopped
60 ml water
60 ml cream

Set the oven at 180°C. Grease and flour a 22 cm springform cake tin. Whisk the eggs with an electric beater until pale and fluffy. Stir in the yoghurt.

In a separate bowl cream together the butter and castor sugar until pale. Sift in the cocoa and bicarb, then add the egg mixture. Sift in the flour and salt and mix in. Pour into the cake tin and bake for 45-50 minutes. Turn out on a cake rack and cool.
CHOCOLATE MOUSSE Melt the chocolate in a bowl over simmering water. Cool slightly. Whip the cream stiffly and fold in. Cover and chill in the fridge.
CHOCOLATE GANACHE Combine the ingredients in a bowl and melt over simmering water until smooth and well blended.
TO ASSEMBLE Roll out the marzipan and cut three circles the same size as the cake. Slice the cake into three layers. Place the bottom layer back into the tin and sprinkle with 15 ml brandy. Top with marzipan, then with half the chocolate mousse. Repeat the layers, ending with marzipan. Freeze until firm.

TO SERVE Release the springform and place the cake on a serving platter. Smooth the chocolate ganache over the top and sides with a palette knife and garnish with cherries. Slice and serve, with cream or Vanilla Ice-Cream (page 147). SERVES 12

> **WINE** Chocolate and wine has never been considered a marriage made in heaven, but this rich cake would go rather well with a ten-year old tawny port, or red muscadel. Perfect partners include Die Krans Estate's new Cape style Vintage Reserve Port or Mossops Axe Hill Cape Vintage Port.

Dinner is presented on an antique sideboard. Salad with Smoked Meat and Spiced Pickled Pears; Braised Lamb Shanks with Peppers, Onion and Tomato; and Maize Meal Wedges.

GRANDE ROCHE

PAARL, CAPE WINELANDS

ABOVE *Horst Frehse, General Manager of Grande Roche.*

THE GRANDE ROCHE, SOUTH AFRICA'S ONLY FIVE-STAR ESTATE HOTEL, is set on a gentle slope overlooking vineyards and rugged mountains. The highly acclaimed hotel and its restaurant, Bosman's, has won a formidable array of awards and culinary accolades since its opening in January 1992.

The magnificent 18th century buildings have a proud history. In 1707 two morgen of farmland named Nieuwe Plantage (later known as Nieuwe Plantatie) was granted to Pastor Hermanus Bosman, who preached from a mud-walled church in the valley. The old church was demolished in the same year and a new one was built where Paarl's Strooidak Church stands today. Hermanus built a T-shaped house and surrounded it with orchards, vines and vegetable gardens. Old manuscripts mention the existence of a slave building, bakery, shop, horse stable, coach house and wine cellar. Sadly, no written record has been found of the old mill, thought to have been used as a slave church, which has been restored for intimate chapel weddings.

Hermanus' eldest son Abraham, a trader and wine grower, inherited the farm and built a kraal and shepherd's cottage which are still in evidence today. Two more generations of the family made this their home. In 1876 Jan Daniel Victorianised the house and altered its interior, changes probably prompted by a visit to Nieuwe Plantatie by Prince Alfred, second son of Queen Victoria, who later became the Duke of Edinburgh. Jan Daniel's wife, Catherina Sophia, and her sons inherited the farm. In 1929, after 214 years, Nieuwe Plantatie was transferred out of the Bosman family to Albertus Johannes du Toit. In 1953 a spark ignited the old thatched roof, burning the house to the ground.

Nieuwe Plantatie was rebuilt in its present form and in 1991 transformed into the luxurious Grande Roche, restoring it to its former glory as it was between 1869 and 1876. Today, the manor house and its collection of individually decorated suites are a gentle alternative to the hurly-burly of city life.

ALMOND-CRUSTED FISH WITH COCONUT LEMONGRASS SAUCE

6 x 160 g pieces filleted, skinless fish
salt, milled black pepper, cake flour
2 eggs, lightly beaten
200 g flaked almonds
butter, vegetable oil
fresh coriander leaves to garnish
COCONUT LEMONGRASS SAUCE
6-8 spring onions, finely sliced
5-6 garlic cloves, peeled and finely chopped
15 ml crushed green ginger
sesame oil
15 ml coriander seeds
30 ml finely chopped lemongrass
500 ml coconut cream
250 ml milk
ORIENTAL NOODLES
250 g oriental egg noodles
5 ml finely chopped garlic
5 ml crushed green ginger
5-6 spring onions, trimmed and finely sliced
250 g vegetables (carrots, leeks, baby corn, courgettes), cut into fine strips, blanched and drained

COCONUT LEMONGRASS SAUCE Gently sweat the spring onion, garlic and ginger in a little sesame oil in a covered medium saucepan until soft. Add the coriander seeds, lemongrass, coconut cream and milk. Cover and simmer for about 45 minutes until slightly thickened. Purée and sieve into a clean saucepan. Season with salt and pepper and reheat.

Season the fish with salt and pepper. Dust with flour, brush with egg and roll in flaked almonds. Fry in butter and oil over medium heat until golden. Turn the fish and finish cooking over medium-low heat.
ORIENTAL NOODLES Cook the noodles in salted boiling water until done. Drain. Heat a little sesame oil in a frying pan and fry the garlic, ginger and spring onion for 2-3 minutes until soft. Add the cooked noodles and vegetables, and heat through, adding a little of the sauce to moisten.
TO SERVE Pile noodles in warm soup bowls. Place fish on top, and spoon sauce around. Garnish with coriander. SERVES 4

WINE Lemony-spicy L'Avenir Chenin Blanc will complement the flavour of the fish and balance the slight acidity of the sauce. Fruity Lievland Noble Late Harvest Reserve will be delicious with the banana samoosas, gently underscoring the tropical flavours.

BANANA SAMOOSAS AND CAPE VELVET ICE-CREAM WITH COCONUT FOAM

4-6 bananas, peeled and finely chopped
45 ml lemon juice
60 ml icing sugar
60 ml toasted sesame seeds
3 x 250 mm square sheets springroll pastry
COCONUT FOAM
4 egg yolks
100 ml sugar
60 ml white wine
30 ml Malibu liqueur
15 ml desiccated coconut
TO SERVE
Cape Velvet Ice-Cream (page 147)

Mix together the banana, lemon juice, sifted icing sugar and sesame seeds.

Cut each sheet of pastry into 3 long strips. Cut one end of each on the diagonal and fold over twice to form a triangle. Fill the pocket with a little filling.

Fold the pastry across the top of the triangle, moisten with water and pinch to seal. Cover and set aside in a cool place for about 30 minutes.
COCONUT FOAM Whisk together the egg yolks, sugar, wine and liqueur in a double boiler over simmering water until thickened and creamy. Remove from the heat and stir in the desiccated coconut. Chill.
TO SERVE Deep fry the samoosas in hot vegetable oil for 2-3 minutes until crisp and golden. Drain on kitchen paper. Serve warm with coconut foam and Cape Velvet ice-cream frozen, if preferred, in a chocolate cone. SERVES 4

 NGALA, A ROMANTIC 42-BED LODGE WEST OF THE KRUGER NATIONAL PARK, has been designed to recreate the elegance of bygone Africa. It lies on a beautiful tract of land, the early hunting grounds of the Shangaan people, and is named "lion" in their language.

The Shangaan-Tsonga moved here from what is now southern Mozambique more than 100 years ago, and are said to have been the first permanent inhabitants of the area. The Shangaan have a proud tradition of hunting and are renowned trackers of wildlife. Many of Ngala's staff are descendents of this important cultural group and, as rangers and trackers at the lodge, use their ancestral skills to fine advantage.

Ngala has a proud history. The land was bought at an auction by the Hoheisen family in 1933. The same auction was attended by Mrs Eileen Orpen, who bought the adjoining land and donated it to the Kruger Park, giving the well-known Orpen Gate its name. Sixty years later, in January 1990 Mr Hans Hoheisen donated his land to the Worldwide Fund for Nature, then known as the SA Nature Foundation, stipulating that it be included in the Kruger Park to be used and managed as part thereof.

WWF-SA later consolidated their acquisitions deep in the African bush, purchasing Ngala Lodge and the surrounding property known as Vlakgezicht and incorporating it with Mr Hoheisen's property.

NGALA PRIVATE GAME RESERVE

KRUGER NATIONAL PARK, NORTHERN PROVINCE

Two years later an agreement was entered into between the South African National Parks Trust and Conservation Corporation Africa granting the right to operate Ngala Game Lodge and to traverse Kempiana. Further negotiations with the National Parks Board gave rights to manage the Vlakgezicht property on which Ngala is situated. Both properties were proclaimed as part of Kruger National Park in March 1994. Accordingly Ngala became the only reserve to be statutorily incorporated into the world famous park.

Ngala's guests enjoy indulgent accommodation, cuisine and service, with décor – including fine antique furnishings – redolent of times long past. There are 20 luxurious cottages and the magnificent Safari Suite with private game viewing from its own expanse of deck overlooking the Mapone River. This is just one small vantage point over a total of 15 000 hectares of magnificent and unspoilt game country which boasts one of the highest concentrations of lion and breeding herds of elephant in southern Africa.

ABOVE *Lavish afternoon tea is served on the deck of the lodge before the evening game drive.*
OPPOSITE PAGE TOP *Mango and Peanut Shortbread (page 21).*

Sesame-chilli Breadsticks with Smoked Trout and Lavosh Flatbread with Avocado Dip, served with iced lemon tea.

LAVOSH FLATBREAD WITH AVOCADO DIP

50 g brown bread flour
175 g white bread flour
2 ml salt
10 g (15 ml) instant dry yeast
200 ml warm water (approximate amount)
AVOCADO DIP
1 large avocado
1 small red onion, finely chopped
1 clove garlic, peeled and crushed
2 ml Dijon mustard
salt, milled black pepper

AVOCADO DIP Peel, stone and roughly mash the avocado. Mix in the onion, garlic and mustard, and season with salt and pepper. Cover and chill.

LAVOSH Sift together the flours and salt in a bowl. Mix in the yeast. Add sufficient water to make a soft dough. Knead until smooth and elastic. Place in a lightly greased bowl, cover and set aside for about 1 hour to rise.
  Knead the dough again lightly. Divide into 8 pieces, and roll into balls. Place on a floured tray, allowing space for spreading. Cover with a cloth and set aside for about 30 minutes until doubled in size.
TO SERVE Roll out the dough as thinly as possible and dust with flour. Heat a griddle or large frying pan and cook the lavosh for about 30 seconds on each side. Serve warm with avocado dip. MAKES 8

SESAME-CHILLI BREADSTICKS WITH SMOKED TROUT

250 ml cake flour
5 ml sugar
2 ml salt
2 ml chilli powder
10 g (15 ml) instant dry yeast
30 ml vegetable oil
125 ml warm water (approximate amount)
30 ml milk
sesame seeds
SMOKED TROUT
8 thin slices smoked trout
lemon juice, milled black pepper

Set the oven at 180°C. Grease a baking sheet.
  Sift together the flour, sugar, salt and chilli powder in a bowl. Mix in the yeast. Mix together the oil and water and mix in to make a medium-soft dough. Roll into 8 thin sausages about 12 cm long. Place on the baking sheet, allowing space for spreading. Cover with a cloth and set aside for about 30 minutes until doubled in size.
  Brush the sticks with milk and sprinkle with sesame seeds. Bake for about 20 minutes until crisp and golden. Cool on a rack.
TO SERVE Dip the trout in lemon juice and season with pepper. Wrap around the top of the breadsticks and arrange on a tray or in a tall container to hold them upright.
SERVES 8

> **WINE** Avocado dip served with flatbread calls for a dry or off-dry chenin blanc or semillon. Offer Villiera Chenin Blanc or Steenberg Sémillon. An unwooded chardonnay would also work well. A good blanc fumé (wooded sauvignon blanc) such as the one made by Jordan meets the demands of the smoked trout, affording a refreshing pick-up to the smoky, woody flavour. As an alternative, serve a medium-bodied, wooded chardonnay such as Bouchard Finlayson Kaaimansgat Chardonnay.

KARILINAH'S BUSH SCONES

500 ml cake flour
1 ml salt
60 ml sugar
15 ml baking powder
125 g butter, cut into blocks
150 ml milk
2 eggs

Set the oven at 220°C. Sift together the flour, salt, sugar and baking powder. Rub in the butter until the mixture is finely crumbled. Beat together the milk and eggs and mix in to form a soft dough. Add a little extra milk if the dough is too stiff. Roll out lightly on a floured surface to thickness of 2 cm.

Cut out 7,5 cm rounds and place on a lightly greased baking sheet, allowing space for spreading. Bake for 10-15 minutes until golden. Cool on a rack. Serve with butter, marmalade and whipped cream.
MAKES ABOUT 12

APPLE AND DATE CRUNCH CAKE

2 Granny Smith apples
185 g pitted dried dates, chopped
1 ml bicarbonate of soda
250 ml boiling water
125 g soft unsalted butter
250 ml sugar
1 egg
375 ml cake flour
1 ml salt
TOPPING
50 g unsalted butter
125 ml brown sugar
125 ml desiccated coconut

Set the oven at 180°C. Grease and flour a 23 cm springform cake tin. Peel and core the apples and chop into small pieces. Mix in the dates, bicarb and boiling water. Cool. Cream together the butter and sugar. Beat in the egg. Sift in the flour and salt and fold in with the apple/date mixture. Pour into the

prepared pan and bake for 50 minutes.
TOPPING Combine the ingredients in a small saucepan and stir over low heat until the butter melts and the ingredients are well mixed. Spoon onto the cake. Bake for 10-15 minutes more until golden and bubbling. Cool in the tin for about 10 minutes, then lift onto a rack. Serve warm or cool with softly whipped cream if you wish. SERVES 12

MANGO AND PEANUT SHORTBREAD

500 ml self-raising flour
250 ml sugar
1 ml salt
250 g unsalted butter, cut into cubes
1 egg
60 ml cold water
250 ml raspberry jam
500 g chopped dried mango, rehydrated in light syrup, or stoned dried dates
250 ml raw peanuts
60 ml castor sugar

Set the oven at 150°C. Butter a baking dish measuring approximately 30 cm x 30 cm.

Sift together the flour, sugar and salt in a bowl. Rub in the butter until the mixture is finely crumbled. Mix together the egg and water and mix in to form a stiff dough. Form into a ball and cut in half. Press one half into the buttered baking dish. Spread jam onto the surface. Cover with mango or dates. Roll out the remaining dough to fit and cover the dates. Press peanuts into the pastry and sprinkle with castor sugar.

Bake for 1 hour. Cool in the tin. Cut into fingers. Store in an airtight container.
MAKES APPROXIMATELY 24

GOATS' CHEESE SOUFFLE WITH RED CURRANT AND APPLE PRESERVE

melted butter, black poppy seeds
40 g butter
40 g cake flour
250 ml hot milk
1 egg yolk
250 g goats' milk cheese, crumbled
8 egg whites
30 ml lemon juice
salt, white pepper
Red Currant and Apple Preserve
   (page 139)

Set the oven at 200°C. Brush eight small soufflé dishes with melted butter and chill in the fridge until set. Repeat the process. Sprinkle with poppy seeds. Chill.

Melt the butter in a medium saucepan. Remove from the heat and add the flour and hot milk. Cook, stirring constantly, for 1-2 minutes. Remove from the heat and add the egg yolk and two-thirds of the goats' cheese, stirring until well blended. Cool.

Whisk the egg white to soft peaks. Add the lemon juice, season with salt and pepper and whisk until stiff. Fold into the sauce. Quarter fill the soufflé dishes. Top with the remaining goats' cheese. Fill to three-quarters with the remaining soufflé mixture. Place on a baking sheet.
TO SERVE Bake for 15-20 minutes until well risen and golden brown. Place on plates, spoon on red currant and apple preserve and serve immediately. SERVES 8

> **WINE** Goats' cheese with berry sauce places specific demands on an accompanying wine. The best choice would be a New World sauvignon blanc such as the Brampton, Parks best-selling wine, and justly so. It is made on Simon Barlow's Rustenberg Estate at Stellenbosch. With the venison serve Neil Ellis Cabernet Sauvignon-Merlot to create a harmonious marriage of flavour. It's a wonderfully multi-tiered wine with a firm yet gentle aftertaste reflecting its high proportion of cabernet sauvignon and superbly balanced oak.

VENISON ON RED CABBAGE WITH BLACK CURRANT AND APPLE SAUCE

1,5 kg boneless venison loin,
   trimmed and cut into 8 portions
Red Wine Marinade (page 134)
vegetable oil, salt, milled black pepper
BLACK CURRANT AND APPLE SAUCE
125 g finely chopped onion
250 g peeled, diced apple
1 bay leaf, 1 sprig fresh thyme
butter
60 ml castor sugar
250 g black currants
30 ml Crème de Cassis liqueur
2 litres Venison Stock, or half Chicken,
   half Beef Stock (page 134)
TO SERVE
Corn Pancakes (page 144)
400 g peeled vegetables (carrots, turnip,
   beetroot), formed into tiny balls
Braised Red Cabbage (page 144)
Chateau Potatoes (page 142)

Place the venison in a flat dish, pour the marinade over and set aside for 1-2 hours.
BLACK CURRANT AND APPLE SAUCE Sweat the onion, apple, bay leaf and thyme in a little butter in a covered saucepan until translucent. Add the castor sugar and cook until caramelized. Add the black currants and liqueur and cook uncovered until almost dry.

Add the stock and boil uncovered until reduced by half. Sieve into a clean saucepan. Boil uncovered until thickened. Check and correct the flavour, adding more castor sugar if necessary, and salt and pepper.
TO SERVE Steam or boil the vegetables separately to retain the colour. Drain the venison, pat dry and fry in hot oil until cooked to the desired degree. Season with salt and pepper. Slice.

Place hot corn pancakes on warm plates. Top with red cabbage, venison steak and potatoes. Pour sauce around. Scatter with vegetables. SERVES 8

22 ◆ GOURMET HIDEAWAYS

PARKS

CONSTANTIA, CAPE WINELANDS

PARKS RESTAURANT OCCUPIES A CHARMING VICTORIAN VILLA, with a pretty formal garden, which was built for a Dr Sauer as his residence and surgery.

From 1906 the Retief brothers ran a forage and grain store from the house, feeding the many horses that passed by on this main route from Cape Town to the Constantia Valley, one of the oldest wine farming regions in the country with a fine reputation for producing world-famous wines. The region was the focus of society life at the colony, and attracted travellers from around the world to enjoy the renowned Cape hospitality and purchase wine by the cask, even though the journey took several hours on horseback.

Mr Paulse, a blacksmith, bought the property in 1938, and served the passing trade by shoeing horses and fixing carts until the smoke from his forge caused his business to be termed 'undesirable' in 1948. Thereafter Alfred Dudley ran his successful (and less polluting) electrical contracting business until 1972, when it became part of Zonnestraal farm.

Twenty years later the owners, Dale and Elizabeth Parker, decided that the house should be restored and once again serve people passing this historical corner, this time not to see to the needs of their transport, but the needs of their stomachs!

Restaurateurs Michael and Madeleine Olivier (right) take care of Parks Restaurant in fine style and in an atmosphere of conviviality and comfort. Parks was awarded the Blazon of the Châine des Rôtisseurs in October 1997 and was nominated a Top Ten Restaurant in the restaurant guide, Eat Out, in 1997 and 1999.

THE PLETTENBERG

PLETTENBERG BAY, GARDEN ROUTE

THE PLETTENBERG, AN EXCLUSIVE RELAIS & CHATEAUX HOTEL, is perched on a rocky headland high above one of the most beautiful bays in the world in the heart of the Garden Route.

The bay was discovered in 1630 by Portuguese explorers and named Bahia Formosa or "beautiful bay". It was also once known as "the bay of plenty." The "modern" name of Plettenberg Bay was bestowed by Joachim van Plettenberg, Governor of the Cape, who in 1778 erected a stone pillar to mark the possession of the bay by the Dutch East India Company. The original beacon is now in the SA Cultural History Museum in Cape Town, and a replica stands in its place.

Plettenberg Bay, like Hermanus, is a safe haven for whales which come inshore in the latter half of the year, providing an unforgettable spectacle for the awestruck humans who were once their deadliest enemies. Peaceful "Plett" was once a slaughterhouse for the ancestors of the right whales – so-called because they yielded more oil and bone. Thankfully, the Norwegian whaling station on Beacon Island closed in 1920, and the bay began its ascent to renown as a holiday destination.

ABOVE Wellington offers champagne and canapés at the pool overlooking never-ending sea and beachscapes.
BELOW A comprehensive selection of wine is stored in a walk-in air-conditioned cellar.

Among the earliest holidaymakers were the Thesen family of Knysna, who in 1898 built a beach house on a prime site overlooking the bay. Some years later this became a small and unpretentious family hotel, The Lookout. Liz McGrath, who also owns the world-renowned The Cellars-Hohenort (page 52) and The Marine Hotel (page 82) discovered it in a dilapidated and tumbledown state. She rebuilt it with consummate care, producing an intimate Cape Georgian hotel with two swimming pools, and 26 individually decorated rooms furnished with antiques and South African works of art. The Plettenberg opened in 1988. A nearby property was later acquired and transformed into the luxurious Blue Wing, bringing the rooms and suites to a total of 40. Mrs McGrath's South African hotels are known as The Collection.

The Plettenberg's superb cuisine, accompanied by fine Cape wines, naturally emphasises freshly-caught fish from the bay as well as the famed lamb from the Karoo, just two hours away over the Swartberg mountains.

Plettenberg Bay, loved for its safe sandy beaches, tranquil lagoons and mountain backdrops, enjoys a pleasant temperate climate, both in winter and summer, and is ideal for water sports. Rock fishing, deep-sea angling and diving may be arranged by the hotel staff, as can golf, bowls and tennis at the nearby country club. Visitors may also drive through some of the most spectacular scenery the Cape has to offer, including the forests and lakes of the Knysna district, and the Tzitzikamma National Park nearby.

SEAFOOD SOUP

8 large prawns, shells on
500 g filleted fish
350 g calamari
18 black mussels
2 onions, sliced Chinese-style
olive oil
6 garlic cloves, peeled and crushed
15 ml crushed green ginger
15 ml Garam Masala (page 136)
juice of 1 lemon
400 g ripe tomatoes, blanched, peeled, seeded and chopped
15 ml tomato paste
2 sprigs fresh rosemary
1 small bunch fresh coriander
400 g can coconut cream
2 litres Fish Stock (page 134)
salt, milled black pepper
Garlic Crostini (page 145)

Devein and shell the prawns; leave tail shells on. Skin the fish and cut into blocks. Slice the calamari into rings. Steam open the mussels in a saucepan of boiling water. Drain and remove one shell from each.

Fry the onion in olive oil in a large saucepan until translucent. Add the garlic, ginger, garam masala, lemon juice, tomato and tomato paste. Add the rosemary and most of the coriander (retain a few sprigs for garnishing). Stir in the coconut cream and fish stock. Season with salt and pepper. Cover and simmer for 20 minutes.
TO SERVE Add the prawns to the soup and simmer for 1 minute. Add the fish and simmer for 1 minute more. Add the calamari and mussels and simmer for 2-3 minutes until cooked.

Ladle the soup into warm bows. Garnish with coriander and serve with garlic crostini or assorted breads. SERVES 8

LOBSTER TEMPURA WITH JASMINE RICE AND STIR-FRIED FINE GREENS

8 rock lobster tails
vegetable oil
TEMPURA BATTER
250 ml tempura flour
200 ml iced water
15 ml chopped fresh coriander
milled black pepper
JASMINE RICE
500 ml basmati rice
finely grated zest of 1 lemon
2 garlic cloves, peeled and crushed
30 g (30 ml) butter
2 ml salt
400 g can coconut cream made up to 600 ml with water
TO SERVE
Stir-Fried Fine Greens (page 27)
Lemon Butter (page 140)

Par-cook the lobster tails in a large saucepan of boiling water for 2 minutes. (Start timing only when the liquid comes back to the boil.) Cool in a basin of cold water. Cut the tails in half lengthwise, leaving the tail fan on. Devein.
TEMPURA BATTER Sift the tempura flour into a bowl. Lightly mix in the iced water with a wooden spoon; don't overmix. Mix in the coriander and season with pepper. Add a little extra water if necessary to make a medium batter.
JASMINE RICE Fry the lemon zest and garlic in the butter in a medium saucepan. Stir in the rice and salt. Add the coconut cream, cover and cook over low heat for about 20 minutes until the rice is cooked and all the moisture has been absorbed.
TO SERVE Dip the lobster tails in tempura batter and fry in deep vegetable oil for 3-4 minutes until crisp and golden. Drain on kitchen paper and salt lightly.

Mould the jasmine rice on warm plates. Top with stir-fried fine greens and intertwined lobster tails. Drizzle with lemon butter. SERVES 4

CHOCOLATE AMARULA TRUFFLE WITH RASPBERRY COULIS AND APRICOT AND ALMOND ICE-CREAM

100 g dark chocolate, roughly chopped
100 g white chocolate, roughly chopped
30 ml water
30 ml Amarula liqueur
10 g (15 ml) gelatine
40 ml liquid glucose
400 ml cream
TO SERVE
Apricot and Almond Ice-Cream (page 148)
Crème Anglaise (page 146)
Raspberry Coulis (page 146)

Melt the chocolates in separate bowls over simmering water. Remove from the heat. Pour the water and liqueur into separate bowls. Sprinkle half the gelatine onto each. Warm in a basin of hot water, stirring to dissolve. Stir half the liquid glucose into each. Stir the liqueur mixture into the white chocolate, and the water mixture into the dark chocolate.

Whip the cream to soft peaks. Fold half into each chocolate mixture, first folding in one-third to lighten the mixture, then the remainder. Layer in eight 150 ml ramekins. Chill for 3-4 hours until set.
TO SERVE Unmould the truffles onto plates. Top each with a scoop of apricot and almond ice-cream. Pour crème anglaise and raspberry purée around. SERVES 8

STIR-FRIED FINE GREENS

4 courgettes, finely sliced into shreds
5 spinach leaves, shredded
150 g mangetout, finely sliced
1 bunch spring onions, finely sliced
250 ml fresh bean sprouts
vegetable oil
3 drops sesame oil
30 ml soy sauce
5 ml fish sauce

Stir-fry the vegetables in vegetable oil in a hot wok or frying pan for 2-3 minutes until limp. Stir in the sesame oil, soy sauce and fish sauce. Tip into a warm bowl and serve immediately. SERVES 4

> **WINE** Choose a fresh, elegant wine with creamy body for the seafood soup; a wonderful marriage would be a bottle-aged sauvignon blanc, preferable a 1997 vintage such as Steenberg Reserve or Vergelegen. The lobster requires something more full-bodied — a lightly wooded chardonnay or L'Avenir Chenin Blanc for example. The rich dessert calls for sweetness but also good acidity for the raspberry coulis, like Stellenzicht Weisser Riesling Noble Late Harvest.

THE PLETTENBERG ♦ 27

96 WINERY ROAD

HELDERBERG, CAPE WINELANDS

ABOVE *From left to right: head chef Natasha Harris, Ken Forrester, Martin Meinert and Allan Forrester.*

KEN FORRESTER'S COLOUR-BRIGHT, RUSTIC RESTAURANT ALONGSIDE HIS HISTORIC CAPE DUTCH FARM offers uninterrupted views of the Helderberg mountains. The mood is relaxed, whether on the terrace in summer or beside the fire in winter. Menus, enlivened with South African touches, have a sense of fun and adventure, with changes dictated by the seasons. Choice cuts of beef are properly aged; desserts are sumptuous; ripened cheeses from local farms are served with Ouma Bredell's home-made preserves.

The extensive, well chosen and informatively annotated winelist is amusingly parochial, highlighting the Helderbeg region before moving on to "the rest of the world", ie from local to Portugal. Ken Forrester and wine-maker Martin Meinert own 96 Winery Road with Ken's brother Allan.

Scholtzenhof, originally known as Zandberg and measuring 64 morgen, was granted to Frederick Boot by Governor Simon van der Stel in 1689, just ten years after Stellenbosch was founded. Boot later changed his name to Botha, and was the forefather of the illustrious family of presidents of the early Free State Republic and, more recently, the "old" South Africa. Boot established the first documented agricultural partnership in the Cape with Jan Cornelisz (Jan Bombam) and fathered no fewer than eight children – out of wedlock – which earned him and his mistress banishment to Mauritius for ten years.

He was no less productive on his farm: in 1692, 12 000 vines were planted at Zandberg and Boot began construction on a house the same year. It still stands today, proudly restored, one of the few examples of 17th century buildings left in the Cape, and home of the Forrester family.

For the last 100 years or so quality grapes from this historic farm have been delivered to De Helderberg Co-op. In 1994 Ken Forrester pressed a small quantity of Sauvignon Blanc grapes, and with the help and support of Mike Dobrovic (Mulderbosch), produced the first Scholtzenhof/Ken Forrester wine, Blanc Fumé 1994. In 1995 a partially wood fermented Chenin Blanc was added to the range. In 1996 a fine Sauvignon Blanc, a unique (in South Africa) blend of Grenache/Syrah rounded out a fine range of quality wines. Since 1998 these wines have all been overseen by Martin Meinert (who successfully launched Vergelegen's wines) and are made in his cellar at Devon Crest with his own premium Cabernet/Merlot and Cabernet.

SWEET POTATO AND TOMATO TARTE TATIN WITH CHILLI AND BASIL DRESSING

2 small sweet potatoes, unpeeled
olive oil, salt, milled black pepper, butter
30 ml caramel brown sugar
2 large, ripe tomatoes, cut into quarters
400 g puff pastry
salad leaves
CHILLI AND BASIL DRESSING
100 ml olive oil
30 ml red wine vinegar
½ small red or green chilli sliced, seeded and finely chopped
3-4 fresh basil leaves, shredded

Set the oven at 180°C. Scrub the sweet potatoes, cut into wedges and scatter on a baking sheet. Drizzle with olive oil, season with salt and pepper and bake for about 30 minutes until tender.

Smear a small frying pan with a metal handle with butter and sprinkle with caramel brown sugar. Heat on the stovetop until the sugar begins to caramelize. Remove from the heat.

Arrange sweet potato and tomato wedges in the pan and season with salt and pepper.

Increase the oven temperature to 200°C.

Roll out the pastry to fit the pan and press down lightly onto the vegetables. Bake for about 20 minutes until the pastry is crisp, puffed and golden.
TO SERVE Turn out the tart, slice and place on warm plates. Garnish with salad leaves. Whisk together the dressing ingredients and drizzle over. SERVES 4

> **WINE** A complex, full bodied wine is required to stand up to the chilli and basil dressing of the tarte tatin. Choose Ken Forrester Chenin Blanc, a dry wood-aged wine from 24 year-old vines. The flavourful onion dish needs a powerful wine such as Ken Forrester Grenache-Syrah – a succulent blend, wood-aged in small French barrels to enhance the spicy finish. It's a perfect choice, especially if served slightly chilled.

CARAMELIZED ONIONS WITH BILTONG AND PECORINO

60 ml extra virgin olive oil
350 g pickling onions
5 ml brown sugar
5 ml fresh thyme leaves
salt, milled black pepper
30 ml water
60 ml balsamic vinegar
50 g thinly sliced biltong
50 g pecorino cheese, shaved
Cheese Straws (page 145)

Heat the olive oil in a saucepan and stir in the onions. Cover and cook over medium heat for 5 minutes. Add the brown sugar, thyme, salt, pepper and water. Cook over a low heat, stirring occasionally until the liquid starts caramelizing. Add the balsamic vinegar, cover and simmer gently until the onions are soft (10 to 30 minutes, depending on size). Uncover and simmer until the sauce thickens.
TO SERVE Spoon onions onto a warm plate and top with biltong, shaved pecorino and cheese straws. SERVES 4

STRAWBERRIES STEEPED IN MERLOT AND BLACK PEPPER

500 g strawberries, hulled and halved
600 ml merlot, or similar red wine
½ vanilla pod, split in half lengthwise
10 ml sugar
milled black pepper
TO SERVE
Vanilla Ice-Cream (page 147)

Pile the strawberries into pretty glasses. Warm the wine with the vanilla pod, sugar and a little pepper. Check the flavour, and add a little extra sugar if necessary. Discard the vanilla pod. Pour over the strawberries and top with a scoop of ice-cream. SERVES 4

> **WINE** Sparkling wine is perfect with strawberries, especially Villiera Monro Brut Millennium Cuvée, which is dry but not lean, has fine toasty, vanilla aromas, and is sufficiently rounded to carry the unexpected piquancy of the black pepper.

BUSHMANS KLOOF WILDERNESS RESERVE

CEDERBERG, WESTERN CAPE

ABOVE Guests at Bushmans Kloof have the privilege of exploring one of the world's largest open air art galleries encompassing 125 rock art sites dating back some 10 000 years.
BELOW Each spring, after winter rains have soaked the veld, wild flowers bloom in an an array of glory.

Bushmans Kloof, a member of the prestigeous Paris-based Relais & Chateaux, occupies a large expanse of unspoiled wilderness on the ochre plains below the foothills of the sun-drenched Cederberg. This is the meeting place of three of the country's most ecologically interesting regions – the Swartland, the Great Karoo and the West Coast – and offers leisure and business travellers a fascinating destination.

The adventure begins on the road to Wupperthal and the Biedouw Valley, where the tar road ends beyond Clanwilliam. Over the dramatic Pakhuis Pass, beyond the grave of renowned South African writer Louis Leopoldt, the gravel track winds through giant clusters of boulders into a land which time has forgotten.

The ecological oasis of the reserve encompasses open plains, rugged ravines, a diversity of plant- and animal life and prehistoric rock formations. A unique surface and subterranean river system ensures an abundance of water manifested in multiple rivers, majestic waterfalls and cool, dark pools worn into prehistoric rock. Until the turn of the century this was the home of wandering tribes of San, hunter-gatherers who painted the celebration of their lives in tapestries of colour under overhanging rock shelters. Settler farmers arrived from the nearby Olifants River Valley in the late 1800s when the region was well-populated with the trees (widringtonia cedarbergensis) that gave the mountains their name. Although the cedars are now severely threatened, their beautiful pale wood lives on in aged doors and beams, in churches and farmhouses, wagon chests and small items of furniture handcrafted in days long gone.

In 1991 Bill and Penny McAdam bought 7 500 hectares of overgrazed and severely neglected land, merging several farms to create Bushmans Kloof with the original Boontjieskloof farm at its heart. Their son Mark rehabilitated the veld, implemented a long-term land management programme and reintroduced indigenous plants and game as well as rare and endangered species like the Cape mountain zebra, the Cape clawless otter and the Clanwilliam yellow fish.

Today the reserve is a conservation success story, home to more than 140 bird species, 755 plant species and 34 species of mammals. It was opened to the public in 1996 and has a private airstrip, luxurious accommodation in the Manor House and luxury rooms and suites arranged on the banks of the Boontjies River. Activities include sunset game drives, guided rock art walks, mountain and river hikes, abseiling, fly-fishing and mountain biking.

DUCK BOBOTIE

750 g filleted, skinless duck breasts
1 large onion, finely chopped
Ghee (page 135) or butter and vegetable oil
5 ml Roasted Masala (page 136) or 15 ml curry powder
10 ml turmeric
3 slices bread
375 ml milk
60 ml smooth apricot jam
125 ml seedless raisins
60 ml lemon juice
7 ml salt, milled black pepper
4-6 bay or lemon leaves
3 eggs, lightly beaten
TO SERVE
basmati rice
Peach Chutney (page 139)

Set the oven at 180°C. Butter a casserole. Mince or finely chop the duck breasts. Fry the onion in ghee or butter and oil in a medium saucepan until translucent. Stir in the masala or curry powder and turmeric. Add the duck and stir until lightly sealed.

Soak the bread in the milk. Drain well and crumble; reserve the milk. Add the bread to the duck with the jam, raisins and lemon juice. Season with salt and pepper. Fill the casserole and pat down smoothly. Roll up the bay or lemon leaves and press into the mixture. Cover and bake for 30 minutes.

Mix together the reserved milk and eggs, season with salt and pepper and pour onto the bobotie. Increase the oven heat to 200°C and bake for 15-20 minutes more until the custard is set and golden. Serve with basmati rice and peach chutney. SERVES 4

BLACK MUSSEL AND POTATO SALAD WITH ROASTED GARLIC-MUSTARD DRESSING

2 kg black mussels, well scrubbed
500 new potatoes
salt, milled black pepper
2 medium fennel bulbs and tops
mixed salad greens and herbs
2 red or yellow peppers, seeded and sliced
2 oranges, peeled and cut into segments
ROASTED GARLIC-MUSTARD DRESSING
purée from 2 heads Roasted Garlic (page 135)
20 ml lemon juice
15 ml honey
30 ml cream
10 ml Dijon mustard
100 ml vegetable oil

ROASTED GARLIC-MUSTARD DRESSING
Whisk together the ingredients. Season with salt and pepper.

Place the mussels in a saucepan. Cover and boil until they open. Discard any which remain shut. Remove the shells, leaving 16 on the half-shell for garnishing.

Boil the potatoes in their jackets. Peel and cut in half. Season with salt and pepper. Cut the fennel into julienne strips.
TO SERVE Arrange the salad greens, mussels, potatoes, fennel, peppers and orange onto a large serving platter. Sprinkle the dressing over. SERVES 8

WINE Mussels are great with a chardonnay or wooded sauvignon blanc. Offer Jordan Blanc Fumé, a wine with upfront fruit.

32 ◆ GOURMET HIDEAWAYS

LITTLE MALVA PUDDINGS WITH ROOIBOS CREME ANGLAISE

250 ml castor sugar
1 egg
30 g (30 ml) soft butter
30 ml smooth apricot jam
250 ml cake flour
5 ml bicarbonate of soda
1 ml salt
250 ml milk
10 ml white wine vinegar
10 ml vanilla essence
SAUCE
125 ml cream
50 g unsalted butter
60 ml sugar
30 ml hot water
TO SERVE
Rooibos Crème Anglaise (page 147)

Butter individual dariole moulds; place on a baking sheet. Set the oven at 180°C. Beat together the castor sugar, egg, butter and jam until pale and fluffy. Sift together the flour, bicarb and salt. Mix together the milk, vinegar and vanilla essence. Fold these into the egg mixture gently but thoroughly.

Spoon the mixture into the moulds, filling them to three-quarters. Cover loosely with lightly oiled foil and bake for about 20 minutes until a skewer comes out clean. SAUCE While the pudding is baking combine the sauce ingredients in a small saucepan and stir over gentle heat until the butter melts and the sugar has dissolved. Pour over the pudding as it comes out of the oven.
TO SERVE Turn warm malva puddings out onto plates and pour rooibos crème anglaise around. SERVES 6-8

VENISON STEAKS WITH CRANBERRY APRICOT CHUTNEY

1,5 kg boneless venison loin, trimmed
Red Wine Marinade (page 134)
2 litres Beef Stock (page 134)
30 g (30 ml) cold butter, cut into blocks
vegetable oil, salt, milled black pepper
TO SERVE
Potato Croquettes (page 142)
Cranberry Apricot Chutney (page 139)

Mix the marinade ingredients in a roasting pan. Add the venison, cover and marinate in a cool spot for 24 hours. Wipe the venison dry and cut into eight steaks.

Pour the marinade into a large saucepan, add the beef stock and boil uncovered until reduced by half. Strain into a clean saucepan and continue reducing until the sauce thickens. Just before serving, whisk in the butter bit by bit.
TO SERVE Fry the steaks in hot oil until cooked to the desired degree. Season with salt and pepper. Arrange steaks and potato croquettes on warm plates. Serve with cranberry apricot chutney and the reduced sauce. SERVES 8

> **WINE** Duck bobotie and venison are perfect with a medium-bodied red wine such as Vergenoegd Shiraz. From Bushmans Kloof's award-winning winelist designed by Wine Concepts, enjoy Beaumont Goutte d'Or, a natural sweet wine, with this dessert.

BUSHMANS KLOOF WILDERNESS RESERVE ◆ 33

LE QUARTIER FRANÇAIS

FRANSCHHOEK, CAPE WINELANDS

ABOVE *Susan Huxter, owner of Le Quartier Français, with general manager, Linda Coltart and chef Margot Janse.*

FRANSCHHOEK WAS ORIGINALLY NAMED OLIFANTSHOEK on account of the vast herds of elephants which lived here. The essence of this picturesque winelands village lies in its French heritage, the legacy of the courageous Huguenots who fled their homeland in the face of religious persecution and settled in a bountiful valley at the southern tip of the African continent. They established farms on land granted to them by Governor Simon Van der Stel in 1688 naming them for their families or faraway villages – names which endure to this day. They were also responsible for the name of the place in which they resided to become known as de Fransche Hoek and later, Franschhoek, when the town was founded between 1845 and 1860.

The French Huguenot heritage provides a strong old world tradition of wine making, while the intelligent application of new world technology maximises the outstanding terroir of the Franschhoek Valley to produce an array of world class wines.

The lovely old building in the main street of the town that houses Le Quartier Français was originally built as a private home on a plot portioned off from the farm Cabrière, owned by Pierre Jourdan, one of the first Huguenots to settle in the valley. The dwelling was built in the early

1900s, and alterations done in 1982 transformed the home into a restuarant. The verandah was removed and details such as the pilasters on either side of the front door were added. Much remains of the original building, including the sash windows and round ventilation openings, which adds enormous charm to the historic ambience.

Susan Huxter bought Le Quartier Français in 1989 and opened an auberge behind the restuarant in 1991, bringing full circle a marriage of luxurious accommodation, gourmet cuisine and award-winning wines, which attracts visitors from all over the world. The renowned main restaurant is a showcase of modern Cape cuisine – an eclectic blend of the Cape's sunny flavours given a Provençal twist by executive chef Margot Janse. The cuisine is further enhanced by teaming wines with specific dishes on the menu.

The world class auberge is an enchanted sanctuary where the old world meets the new. Loft suites are decorated with elegant hand-painted fabrics, deep down duvets and king-size beds. A honeymoon suite has its own private swimming pool and courtyard. Garden paths meander through herb and flower gardens, secluded courtyards, and onward to the swimming pool. There's also a library, lounge, patio restaurant, and courtyard for breakfast, coffee, tea, cocktails and light meals.

A special pleasure is to dine alfresco on the terrace by day or on fine summer nights, watching village life go by. In the evenings, cognac and cigars are offered in the convivial bar. In the words of a contented guest: "When the art of living replaces the illusion of tourism, you have arrived in Franschhoek, South Africa, and at Le Quartier Français."

Double Baked Blue Cheese Soufflé with Fried Watercress Gnocchi and Red Pepper Compôte.
Butternut Risotto Cakes with Roasted Vegetables, Smoked Mozarella and Sage Butter.

DOUBLE BAKED BLUE CHEESE SOUFFLE WITH FRIED WATERCRESS GNOCCHI AND RED PEPPER COMPOTE

500 ml milk
1 onion, peeled and roughly chopped
2 whole cloves
100 g butter
200 ml cake flour
250 g blue cheese, crumbled
6 egg yolks
salt, milled black pepper
8 egg whites
TO SERVE
Watercress Gnocchi (page 141)
Red Pepper Compôte (page 140)
1 Granny Smith apple, peeled, cored and finely diced

Set the oven at 160°C. Butter eight soufflé dishes or teacups. Bring the milk, onion and cloves to the boil in a medium saucepan. Set aside for 10-15 minutes to infuse.

Melt the butter in a medium saucepan. Remove from the heat and whisk in the flour and strained milk. Cook, whisking constantly, until thick. Stir in most of the blue cheese; retain about 125 ml. Mix in the egg yolks, and season with salt and pepper. Cool.

Beat the egg white with a pinch of salt until stiff but not dry. Gently fold into the cheese sauce. Fill the soufflé dishes almost to the brim. Bake in a bain marie for about 20 minutes until firm to the touch. Cool the soufflés in the water.
TO SERVE Set the oven at 200°C. Butter a baking sheet. Turn the soufflés onto the sheet. Sprinkle with the reserved blue cheese and bake for about 10 minutes until lightly browned. Place on plates with watercress gnocchi, red pepper compôte and diced apple. SERVES 8

WINE Offer Môreson Soleil du Matin Sauvignon Blanc. With its "Granny Smith" nose and passionfruit aftertaste, it gives a crisp finish to the flavours of the blue cheese and the sweetness of the compôte.

36 ◆ GOURMET HIDEAWAYS

LAMB BURGER ON FOCACCIA WITH CREAMED AVOCADO, MARINATED TOMATOES AND PICKLED CUCUMBER

800 g lamb mince
1 onion, finely chopped
olive oil
1 green or red chilli, seeded and finely chopped
7 ml ground coriander
7 ml ground cumin
15 ml Worcestershire sauce
15 ml ketjap manis (sweet soy sauce)
30 ml chutney
1 sprig fresh marjoram, finely chopped
1 sprig fresh thyme, finely chopped
5 ml salt, milled black pepper
TO SERVE
4 focaccia
salad leaves
Creamed Avocado (page 141)
Marinated Tomatoes (page 141)
Pickled Cucumber (page 141)

Fry the onion in olive oil in a medium saucepan until translucent. Add the chilli, coriander and cumin. Fry for 1 minute, then add the Worcestershire sauce, ketjap manis, chutney and herbs. Cool. Mix in the lamb mince. Season with salt and pepper. Shape into four patties.
TO SERVE Fry the patties in olive oil until cooked on both sides. Toast the focaccia. Place hot burgers inside and serve with salad, marinated tomatoes, pickled cucumber and creamed avocado. SERVES 4

> **WINE** Lamb burgers and Pinehurst Chardonnay are great partners. The yeasty-buttery wine balances the sharpness of the burger, while the citrus aftertaste cuts the rich flavours, matching all the important features. Môreson Soleil du Matin Brut Méthode Cap Classique is fun with the butternut risotto cakes. The butter and honey aftertaste compliments the nutty flavours of the brown butter and roast vegetables, while the freshness of the bubbles lifts the whole dish.

BUTTERNUT RISOTTO CAKES WITH ROASTED VEGETABLES, SMOKED MOZZARELLA AND SAGE BUTTER

1 butternut (about 600 g), peeled and pipped
olive oil, salt, milled black pepper
1 onion, finely chopped
250 ml arborio rice (risotto rice)
250 ml white wine
750 ml vegetable stock
4 slices smoked mozzarella
ROASTED VEGETABLES
1 aubergine, cut in strips lengthways (skin on)
2 medium courgettes, cut into ribbons
2 Roasted Red Peppers (page 141)
SAGE BUTTER
50 g butter
60 ml whole sage leaves
lemon juice

Set the oven at 200°C. Cut the butternut into small cubes and scatter on a baking sheet. Drizzle with olive oil, season with salt and pepper and roast uncovered for about 30 minutes until tender.
Fry the onion in olive oil in a medium saucepan until translucent. Stir in the arborio rice. Season with salt and pepper. Add the wine and boil uncovered until reduced by half. Add a little of the stock and stir until it has been absorbed. Continue in this way, adding the stock little by little. Mash half the butternut and mix into the risotto with the cubed butternut. Chill.
ROASTED VEGETABLES Heat the oven grill. Arrange the aubergine strips on an oven tray. Drizzle with olive oil, season with salt and pepper and grill for 10 minutes. Add the courgettes and peppers and grill for about 5 minutes until golden.
Shape the butternut risotto into twelve flattish cakes with floured hands. Dust with flour and fry in olive oil in a non-stick frying pan until golden on both sides.
SAGE BUTTER Melt the butter in a small saucepan, add the sage leaves and cook until the butter browns and the leaves are crisp. Flavour with lemon juice, salt and pepper.
TO SERVE Place risotto cakes on warm plates. Top with roasted vegetables and another risotto cake. Add a slice of smoked mozzarella and place under the grill to melt. Drizzle over a little sage butter. SERVES 6-8

LE QUARTIER FRANÇAIS ◆ 37

AUBERGINE RESTAURANT

GARDENS, CAPE TOWN

Stepping into the warm, welcoming interior of the Aubergine in a charming part of the city of Cape Town, one is struck by the contrasts of old and new, and friendly formality blended with continental charm.

The characterful old buildings were once the fashionable 19th century home of Sir John Wylde, first Chief Justice of the Cape. In those far-off days the estate, near the Dutch East India Company's gardens, extended over several hectares.

By virtue of his office, Wylde was one of the most prominent figures in the colony. For more than a quarter of a century he not only ruled the Cape's Supreme Court and Legislative Council, but also presided over its flamboyant social life. His elegant table, fine wines and scintillating company were renowned, especially in the years following his separation from his wife, earning him the title "Gentleman Wylde".

Now, as in days gone by, the Cape table offers a generous harvest from land and sea, accompanied by the finest wines. Directed by the young and dynamic Harald Bresselschmidt, (photographed opposite) Aubergine embraces and enhances this rich legacy. Harald combines a Michelin pedigree with continental flair to produce impeccable haute cuisine in a convivial, relaxed atmosphere. Pioneers of innovation, Harald and his team of chefs combine textures and flavours which excite and surprise even the most jaded palate.

Seating in the main dining room is arranged on handsome church pews. Salvaged from the old Sending Gestig Kerk (Mission Church) in Long Street, which is a museum today, they lend a rich, classic glow to the decor. While Harald is tending to their starters, guests may enjoy an apéritif in the lounge or on the pool terrace with its magnificent view of Table Mountain.

Aubergine Scallopine and Tomato Compôte with Pine Seed Vinaigrette.

Grilled Tuna in Lemongrass Spiced Vegetable Minestrone with Coriander Pesto.

38 ◆ GOURMET HIDEAWAYS

AUBERGINE SCALOPPINE AND TOMATO COMPOTE WITH PINE NUT VINAIGRETTE

2 aubergines, peeled and cut in 5 mm slices
olive oil
30 ml balsamic vinegar
4 garlic cloves, peeled and crushed
10 ml finely chopped fresh rosemary
salt, milled black pepper
6 plum tomatoes, blanched, skinned, quartered and seeded
2 shallots or spring onions, finely chopped
3-4 fresh basil leaves, shredded
6 leaves rice paper, each broken into 3 pieces
vegetable oil
40 g pine nuts, roasted in a dry pan
salad leaves, bronze basil
Pine Nut Vinaigrette (page 137)

Lay the aubergine slices in a flat dish. Whisk together 125 ml olive oil with the balsamic vinegar, half the garlic and rosemary. Season with salt and pepper. Pour over the aubergine and set aside to marinate for 1-2 hours. Fry the aubergine in olive oil until golden and tender. Drain.

Set the oven at 180°C. Combine the tomatoes, shallot or spring onion, remaining garlic, 45 ml olive oil and basil in a baking dish and season with salt and pepper. Bake uncovered for about 8 minutes until soft.

Deep fry the rice paper in hot vegetable oil until crisp. Drain well.
TO SERVE Arrange the salad, aubergines, tomatoes and rice paper on plates. Garnish with pine nuts and bronze basil. Drizzle over the vinaigrette. SERVES 6

> **WINE** The flavour-zapped aubergine scaloppine starter requires a robust, spicy wine as a partner. Fairview Viognier, light, bright, flinty and nicely oaked would be a good bet. Choose a more mellow wine for the tuna, preferably a chenin blanc or lightly wooded chardonnay, such as De Wetshof Bateleur Chardonnay.

GRILLED TUNA IN LEMON-GRASS-SPICED VEGETABLE MINESTRONE WITH CORIANDER PESTO

6 x 180 g thick slices tuna
salt, milled black pepper, olive oil
Coriander Pesto (page 138)
PAYSANNE
2 potatoes, peeled
1 small leek, finely sliced
1 small celeriac, finely sliced
100 g white cabbage, finely sliced
1 courgette, finely sliced
2 tomatoes, blanched, peeled, seeded and finely sliced
MINESTRONE
3 small onions, finely chopped
1 garlic clove, peeled and chopped
vegetable oil, butter
400 g can tomatoes, chopped (don't drain)
500 ml Fish Stock (page 134)
1 bay leaf
3 star anise
1 small piece lemongrass
snipped greens of 1 bunch spring onions

CARAMELIZED CHICORY
30 g (30 ml) butter
15 ml brown sugar
3 small heads chicory
balsamic vinegar

PAYSANNE Cut the potatoes into tiny blocks. Blanch in boiling water for 3 minutes. Drain. Mix with the remaining ingredients.
MINESTRONE Fry the onion and garlic in oil and butter in a medium saucepan until brown. Add the remaining ingredients and season with salt and pepper. Cover and simmer for about 20 minutes until tender.
CARAMELIZED CHICORY Melt the butter and brown sugar over gentle heat in a frying pan. Add the chicory and cook, turning regularly, until tender and caramelized. Remove from the heat and sprinkle with balsamic vinegar.
TO SERVE Add the paysanne to the minestrone and simmer for a few minutes until the vegetables are crisp-tender.

Season the fish with salt and pepper. Brush with olive oil and pesto. Sear in oil and butter for 2-3 minutes on each side. Spoon minestrone onto plates. Place fish on top. Garnish with pesto and chicory. SERVES 6

Predecessors of today's splendid Blue Train trace their origins to the 1890s, when advertisements offering direct-route journeys to the gold and diamond fields of South Africa offered: "England to Johannesburg in 19 days, the first seventeen across the ocean on board a Union or Castle line vessel to Cape Town, the remaining two on a train steaming through mountains and valleys and over South African veld to Kimberley and the Reef".

By the early 1920s the Cape Town to Johannesburg trains were called the Union Trains. Accommodation became even more luxurious and spacious with the introduction in 1928 of articulated coaches equipped with heating, hot and cold water, bunk lights and bells for summoning the coach attendant. In 1933, a new dining saloon called Protea was introduced on the Union Trains.

World War 11 interrupted the service until 1946, when new luxury all-steel, air-conditioned trains made in England were placed in service. They were finished in blue and grey and became popularly known as " those blue trains".

Steam gave way to electrification and diesel as the grand blue icon adapted to progress. More and more people booked on the Blue Train for the sheer pleasure of the experience rather than the business orientation of its earlier history. In 1956 the decision was taken to build a new Blue Train "Of a standard of luxury and quality of material and workmanship equal to the best in the world." Since then the Blue Trains have been upgraded twice, the second completed in 1972. In August 1997 the third incarnation of the Blue Train glided out of Cape Town station heralding a new era in the history of luxury train travel. At the 1998 World Travel awards in Miami, Florida, the Blue Train was voted the world's leading luxury train.

There are two Blue Trains, each 380 metres long, with 18 carriages and capable of travelling at 110 kilometres per hour. All compartments are air-conditioned, with telephones and television. In addition, luxury suites have CD players and video systems. A video channel allows guests to access short documentaries about the area through which the train is travelling, while a large screen in the Club Car provides a driver's view of the track ahead. One train has a conference car for 22 people, which when not in use, converts to an observation lounge with panoramic views of the journey.

Dining is a sumptuous affair, with seasonal menus incorporating the freshest ingredients. There are special menus for vegetarians, and kosher and halaal meals are provided on request. South African wines complement each course. High tea is served each afternoon in the Lounge Car, and guests relax in the Club Car over a post-prandial cognac and cigars.

THE BLUE TRAIN

CHICKEN BREASTS WITH MACADAMIA NUT STUFFING AND SPICED APRICOT SAUCE

4 chicken breasts; bone in, skin on
1 small onion, finely chopped
unsalted butter
4 rashers rindless streaky bacon, chopped
100 g salted macadamia nuts, finely chopped
230 g can water chestnuts, chopped
finely grated zest of 1 orange
salt, milled black pepper
TO SERVE
Spiced Apricot Sauce (recipe follows)
Wild Rice Pilaf (page 143)

Set the oven at 180°C. Fry the onion in butter in a frying pan until translucent. Add the bacon and fry for 2-3 minutes. Add the macadamia nuts, water chestnuts and orange zest and season with salt and pepper. Cool.

Lift the chicken skin and push stuffing underneath. Tuck the skin around again neatly. Place in a baking tray, season with salt and pepper and brush liberally with melted butter.

Bake uncovered for 25-30 minutes until cooked and golden. Grill for a few minutes if necessary to brown the skin.
TO SERVE Place chicken on warm plates and serve with spiced apricot sauce and wild rice pilaf. SERVES 4

SPICED APRICOT SAUCE

50 g dried apricots
375 ml Chicken Stock (page 134)
5 ml honey
1 small onion, finely chopped
unsalted butter
20 ml mango chutney
15 ml cumin seeds, roasted, ground and sifted
salt, milled black pepper

Combine the apricots, chicken stock and honey in a small saucepan, cover and simmer gently for about 15 minutes until soft.

Fry the onion in butter in small frying pan until translucent. Drain and place in a food processor with the apricots (and stock), chutney and cumin. Purée until smooth. Season with salt and pepper. Reheat. SERVES 4

TIMBALE OF SMOKED FISH WITH CUCUMBER ZEST

250 g smoked trout or salmon, cut into
    small pieces
50 g English cucumber, cut into fine strips
50 g radish, cut into fine strips
60 ml cream, whipped
100 ml plain yogurt
10 ml creamed horseradish
10 ml finely chopped fresh dill
salt, milled black pepper
50 ml salmon caviar
fresh dill sprigs to garnish

Place the smoked fish into a bowl. Set aside a few cucumber strips for garnish. Mix the remainder into the fish with the radish, whipped cream, yoghurt, horseradish and chopped dill. Season with salt and pepper.

Place a pastry cutter on each plate, and fill with fish mixture to shape into rounds. Remove the rings and decorate the timbales with reserved cucumber, salmon caviar and dill sprigs. SERVES 4

42 ◆ GOURMET HIDEAWAYS

SPRINGBOK STEAKS WITH CHILLI-ROASTED ONIONS

750 g boneless springbok loin
cracked black pepper, cracked Szechuan
 or white peppercorns, salt
4 small onions, peeled and quartered
8 spring onions, trimmed
8 shallots, peeled
1-2 red or green chillies, sliced and seeded
vegetable oil
castor sugar
¼ Chinese cabbage, shredded
400 ml Beef Jus (page 140)

Slice the springbok into medallions and flatten slightly with a mallet. Season with black and Szechuan or white pepper and a little salt.

Set the oven at 200°C. Scatter the onion quarters, spring onions, shallots and chilli in a roaster and toss in 125 ml vegetable oil. Roast uncovered for 15 minutes, stirring once or twice. Stir in 15 ml castor sugar. Reduce the oven temperature to 170°C and cook for about 20 minutes more until the onions are soft and starting to caramelize. Remove the onions from the pan and keep hot. Add the roasting juices to the beef jus and reheat.

Deep fry the Chinese cabbage in hot oil for about 2 minutes until golden brown. Drain on kitchen paper and sprinkle with 15 ml castor sugar and a little salt.
TO SERVE Fry the steaks in a little oil for about 30 seconds on each side. Spoon onions onto warm plates and place the steak on top. Drizzle jus around and onto the steaks and top with cabbage. SERVES 4

> **WINE** Balance the smoked fish timbale with Boschendal Chenin Blanc, a wonderfully rich and full-flavoured wine. Sylvanvale Dry Pinotage Rosé would be wonderful with the chicken breasts. It is bone dry yet with sufficient underlying fruit to complement the spiced apricots in the sauce. Choose a powerful wine with well-balanced oak for the venison, such as the highly acclaimed Linton Park Capell's Court Shiraz.

PEARS IN RED WINE WITH CINNAMON MOUSSE

4 pears, peeled and cored (leave stalks intact)
500 ml full-bodied red wine
1 cinnamon stick
200 ml sugar
CINNAMON MOUSSE
200 ml sugar
4 egg yolks
200 ml hot milk
5 ml ground cinnamon
20 ml gelatine
250 ml cream

CINNAMON MOUSSE Beat together the sugar and egg yolks until pale and thick. Mix in the hot milk and cinnamon. Pour into a medium saucepan and cook over low heat without boiling, stirring constantly, until the custard coats the spoon. Remove from the heat and stir in the gelatine. Cool to room temperature; do not allow it to set. Whip the cream to soft peaks and fold in.

Pour into four lightly oiled moulds, cover and refrigerate for at least 2 hours to set.

Bring the wine, cinnamon and sugar to the boil in a medium saucepan. Add the pears, cover and simmer for about 30 minutes until soft. Allow the pears to cool in the liquid. Drain and set aside. Boil the liquid uncovered until reduced and syrupy.
TO SERVE Slice the pears at a slant from the shoulder, keeping the fruit intact at the stalk. Fan onto plates and spoon reduced wine syrup around. Unmould a cinnamon mousse next to each pear. SERVES 4

> **WINE** Pears in red wine combine gentle fruit flavours with a fair amount of sweetness, and a fortified sweet wine along the lines of a liqueur muscat or German riesling would do the honours in fine style. Another good choice would be Pineau de Laborie, a splendid dessert wine in traditional Cognac style, very lightly oaked, fortified with pot-stilled brandy, and utterly luxurious.

THE BLUE TRAIN ◆ 43

CAPE MALAY RESTAURANT AT THE CELLARS-HOHENORT

CONSTANTIA, CAPE PENINSULA

FOR MORE THAN THREE CENTURIES, home-grown wines, fruit, vegetables and flowers have supplied the homes and hostelries of the Constantia valley, a tradition that endures to this day. The freshest seasonal ingredients and a fine selection of local wines are the keynotes of The Cellars-Hohenort Hotel, which has its roots in one of the earliest farms in the fertile Constantia valley: the 1693 Klaasenbosch estate.

In earlier times there was a thatched homestead and an array of outbuildings here. In 1906 Klaasenbosch's owner, Cape Town businessman Arnold W Spilhaus, demolished the old homestead as he considered it "not worth restoring". In its place he built a grand Edwardian-style gabled mansion as his family home. He named it Hohenort, meaning "high place" in old German. It was designed by architect Mr Seeliger, a contemporary of Sir Herbert Baker. Today The Hohenort is the home of the Cape Malay Restaurant, an establishment that pays tribute to one of the world's great cuisines – one which has made an immeasurable contribution to the Cape culinary heritage.

To bring the finest of Cape Malay cuisine to her table, The Cellars-Hohenort owner Liz McGrath teamed up with authoritative cook and author, Cass Abrahams. After extensive research, discussions, tastings and trials, the Cape Malay Restaurant was born, manifesting the wonderful synergy between two women who have passionate ideals about food and hospitality. The Cape Malay Restaurant is also one of the very few venues where tourists and Capetonians can enjoy authentic, traditional local fare, served in the spirit of the cooks who made it great.

Cass Abrahams, in the introduction to her book, The Culture and Cuisine of the Cape Malays, says "Food plays an important role in the Cape Malay community and is always central to their colourful religious and family feasts. There is an old Javanese tradition which says 'It is not sufficient that man should place food before his guests; he is bound to do more. He should render the meal palatable by kind words of treatment, to soothe him after his journey and to make his heart glad while he partakes of refreshment'".

SMOORSNOEK

Cape-Malay 'smothered fish' may be prepared with any smoked fish, although smoked snoek is traditionally used. It is delicious for breakfast, lunch and dinner, accompanied by chutney.

750 g smoked fish, boned, skinned and roughly flaked
2 onions, finely sliced
vegetable oil
3 potatoes, peeled and cut into small cubes
10 ml crushed garlic
5 ml crushed green ginger
2 red or green chillies, sliced and seeded
5 whole cloves
3 whole allspice
salt, milled black pepper

Lightly brown the onion in oil in a large frying pan. Add the potato cubes and fry until golden. Stir in the garlic, ginger, chilli, cloves and allspice and cook over gentler heat for a few minutes more.

Mix in the smoked fish, cover and steam over low heat until the potato is cooked and the fish is hot. Season with salt and pepper. SERVES 6

CAPE-MALAY CHICKEN CURRY

1 kg filleted, skinless chicken breasts
15 ml Roasted Masala (page 136)
125 ml cake flour
salt, milled black pepper
butter, vegetable oil
2 large onions, finely sliced
10 ml cumin seeds
10 ml fennel seeds
1 fresh or dried bay leaf
400 g can whole tomatoes, chopped (don't drain)
5 ml turmeric
5 ml crushed garlic
2 green chillies, finely chopped
250 ml plain yoghurt
5 ml Garam Masala (page 136)
½ bunch fresh coriander, chopped

Cut the chicken into large cubes. Mix together the masala and flour, and season with salt and pepper. Sprinkle over the chicken and toss to coat.

Heat butter and oil in a large saucepan and fry the chicken until lightly sealed. Remove from the pan and set aside. Fry the onion until translucent (add extra oil and butter if necessary). Stir in the cumin, fennel and bay leaf. Add the tomato, turmeric, garlic and chilli. Cook for a few minutes. Return the chicken to the pan and simmer for about 15 minutes until cooked. Add the yoghurt and heat through. Just before serving, sprinkle over the garam masala and chopped coriander. SERVES 6

> **WINE** Spicy smoorsnoek needs an off-dry wine such as Groot Constantia Weisser Riesling, while chicken curry prefers a fruity, complex wine which is not too heavy. Flagstone Pinot Noir BK5 will do perfectly.

CAPE MALAY RESTAURANT AT THE CELLARS-HOHENHORT ◆ 45

GAMETRACKERS
BOTSWANA

Botswana's landlocked surface is 6 000 square kilometres in extent, a region of vast spaces and many surprises. Two thirds of the country consists of Kalahari desert, and at its heart lies one of the world's great ecological wonders – a vast delta which gives life to a scorched land.

Gametrackers lodges and camps are strategically positioned in the most beautiful locations of the Okavango Delta, to give visitors an unforgettable safari experience. Guests enjoy all the natural wonders of three highly specialised eco-systems, against a background of unparalleled luxury in both desert and delta environments.

Savute Elephant Camp is in the north-east, inside the boundaries of the Chobe National Park; Khwai River Lodge, further south, is on the banks of the Khwai river bordering the Moremi Wildlife Reserve; Eagle Island Camp at Xaxaba lies west of Chief's Island, in the wetlands of the Okavango Delta. Visitors, therefore, may savour not only the awesome expanses of African savannah teeming with wildlife, but also the magic and mystery of the delta system with its floodplains, crystalline channels and myriad islands and waterways.

Gametrackers is part of Orient-Express Hotels African Collection, owners of the Mount Nelson in Cape Town (page 56), and The Westcliff in Johannesburg (page 70). Through ongoing investment and considerate management, which includes educational programmes and sensitive environment controls, the company has played an active role in helping the people of Botswana preserve their land.

Gametrackers' accommodation is not only superbly comfortable, but also appropriate to the environment. Local labour and indigenous materials have been used wherever possible. Starting in May, winter brings clear, sunny days and chilly nights. Through October, November and December, temperatures rise. December marks the coming of the first rains of the season which can carry through to April.

Hundreds of species of birds flock into the area and resident animals such as zebra and impala give birth to their young. A profusion of wild flowers bursts into bloom, together with a diverse and colourful array of newly-hatched moths and butterflies, while the trees and grasslands recover from the ravages of the dry winter months.

Visitors can enjoy a sundowner at the end of the day and witness spectacular sunsets over the lagoon. Game viewing includes safari walks and slow rides along the clear, quiet channels in traditional mekoros – dugout canoes used by the local river people for the last 1 000 years.

ABOVE *Elephants enjoying a drink at twilight near Khwai River Lodge.*
LEFT *Thatched lounge at Eagle Island Camp.*

Ostrich carpaccio with Pickled Ginger and Wasabi Oil (in front); Tandoori Chicken Salad.

TANDOORI CHICKEN SALAD

4 skinless filleted chicken breasts
500 ml plain yoghurt
60 ml tikka spice mix
salt, milled black pepper
1 onion, sliced
2 tomatoes, sliced
3 red or green chillies, finely sliced
1 piece green ginger, finely shredded
1 bunch fresh coriander, chopped
   (retain a few sprigs for garnish)
vegetable oil
2 red, yellow or green peppers, seeded
   and quartered
15 ml mint jelly
30 ml honey
mixed salad leaves and herbs
Vinaigrette (page 137)
½ English cucumber, shredded

Place the chicken breasts in a flat dish. Mix half the yoghurt with the tikka spice. Season with salt and pepper. Pour over the chicken and marinate for 1 hour.

Set the oven at 160°C. Fry the onion, tomato, chilli, ginger and chopped coriander in oil in a large frying pan. Season with salt and pepper. Drain the chicken and place on top. Bake uncovered for 15-20 minutes until cooked.

Grill the peppers in a ridged pan until tender and scorched. Mix together the mint jelly and honey into the remaining yoghurt. Season with salt and pepper.
TO SERVE Build salads on plates, or in bowls, alternating the salad leaves, chicken and peppers. Scatter cooked onion on top and drizzle with vinaigrette. Drizzle the minted yoghurt around the plate. Toss cucumber in vinaigrette and scatter on top as a garnish. SERVES 4

> **WINE** Offer chilled Meerlust Pinot Noir Reserve with the carpaccio, as it will complement the variety of flavours in the dish. A gewürztraminer such as Altydgedacht will balance the spice in both the chicken salad and spiced fish dishes. Sticky chocolate pudding is delicious with sparkling wine.

OSTRICH CARPACCIO WITH PICKLED GINGER AND WASABI OIL

250 g well-trimmed ostrich fillet
salt, milled black pepper
PICKLED GINGER
50 g green ginger, very finely sliced
30 ml mirin or sherry vinegar
WASABI OIL
20 ml wasabi powder
2 ml olive oil

Firm up the meat in the freezer (don't allow it to freeze). Slice very finely and arrange in overlapping circles on a plate. Seal with plastic wrap and chill.
PICKLED GINGER Place the ginger in a small bowl, pour over the mirin or vinegar, cover and chill.
WASABI OIL Mix together the wasabi powder and olive oil to form a paste. Add a little more olive oil if necessary.
TO SERVE Season the carpaccio with salt and pepper. Serve with pickled ginger and wasabi oil. SERVES 4

SPICED FISH ON PASTA WITH OLIVES AND TOMATO

Telapa fish, caught in Botswana rivers, are served to Gametrackers' guests, cooked in this method, prepared either over the coals or in a hot frying pan. Any fresh fish may be substituted.

6 filleted fish steaks, each about 200 g, skin on
melted butter
300 g tagliolini pasta
CAJUN SPICE MIXTURE
30 ml paprika
15 ml onion salt
15 ml garlic powder
10 ml milled black pepper
10 ml cayenne pepper
10 ml dried oregano
5 ml dried thyme
5 ml ground white pepper
TOMATO AND OLIVE SAUCE
2 onions, finely chopped
olive oil
15 ml crushed garlic
5-6 ripe tomatoes, blanched, seeded and chopped
wine vinegar, salt, milled black pepper, sugar
60 ml pitted black olives

CAJUN SPICE MIX Mix together the ingredients in a screw-topped bottle. Store in the fridge until required; it will remain fresh for up to 2 months.
TOMATO AND OLIVE SAUCE Fry the onion in olive oil in a medium saucepan until translucent. Add the garlic, then stir in the tomato. Cover and cook for about 10 minutes. Season with vinegar, salt, pepper and sugar. Stir in the olives and heat through.

Brush the fish with melted butter and sprinkle liberally with Cajun spice mixture, pressing it into the surface of the fish to coat fairly evenly.
TO BARBECUE Enclose the fish in a lightly oiled hinged grid. Cook over hot coals, flesh-side down, until dark and crusty. Flip the fish over and barbecue on the skin side until cooked through.

TO PANFRY Heat a heavy cast iron or non-stick frying pan and swish it with just a little oil (make sure the pan is very hot and keep it as dry as possible). Seal the flesh side of the fish. Turn the fish and reduce the heat to cook through more gently.

Cook the pasta in salted boiling water until done. Drain.
TO SERVE Pile pasta on warm plates. Place fish on top, and spoon the sauce around. SERVES 6

STICKY CHOCOLATE PUDDING

200 g butter, cut into blocks
200 g dark chocolate, roughly chopped
4 whole eggs, 4 egg yolks
250 ml sugar
125 ml cake flour
Crème Anglaise (page 146)
Almond Praline (page 147)
CHOCOLATE SAUCE
125 ml milk
125 ml sugar
125 ml cocoa powder, sifted
100 g dark chocolate, roughly chopped

Set the oven at 180°C. Grease eight dariole moulds. Melt together the butter and chocolate in a bowl over simmering water. Whisk together the eggs, yolks and sugar until thick and pale. Slowly mix in the chocolate mixture. Sift in the flour and stir in. Pour into the moulds and bake for 15-20 minutes, just until the surface is crusty; the centres will still be runny.
CHOCOLATE SAUCE Bring the milk, sugar and cocoa to the boil in a medium saucepan. Remove from the heat and add the chocolate. Stir until melted.
TO SERVE Turn out the puddings onto plates and serve with warm chocolate sauce, crème anglaise and almond praline. SERVES 8

GAMETRACKERS ◆ 49

OLD JOE'S KAIA

SCHOEMANSKLOOF, MPUMALANGA

ABOVE *Rob and Christine van der Velde in a corner of the dining room hung with family photographs.*

THE SPIRIT OF OLD JOE'S KAIA EVOKES MEMORIES OF HALF-FORGOTTEN HISTORY, some happy, some sad. In its dying days the Anglo-Boer War swept across the escarpment, gateway to the Lowveld. Homesteads were razed, men flocked to join General Louis Botha, while the British forces took most of the women and children away to concentration camps at Barberton.

The kloof takes its name from Oom Kleinpiet Schoeman who came here well before the war. He exchanged a team of oxen for a vast tract of land alongside the Crocodile River. When the hostilities had ended Charlie Parsons built a country store near the side of the dirt road that linked Machadodorp and Nelspruit. This store is the core of Old Joe's Kaia. In the 1950s Mrs Boers built a few rondavels for a primitive rest camp, a casual stop-over that remains a nostalgic memory for those who travelled to and from Lourenço Marques (now Maputo) before Mozambique's independence from Portugal in 1975. "Old Joe" himself – a slab of rock painted in a caricature of a human figure – stands on the roadside a few kilometres from the entrance of the 'Kaia'. Some say it was a marker placed there by road builders. Others insist that in the 1940s Major Graham, a master at Hilton College, took a group of his pupils to paint it in college colours. They named it for the likeness to another of their schoolmasters. Whichever version is correct, Old Joe is regularly repainted by whoever feels the urge.

"Kaia" means home in Swazi, which aptly describes the warm, homely inn that Rob and Christine van der Velde and their co-General Managers Colin Vincent and Lee Bradbury have created. The van der Velde's bought the inn in 1989 and added log cabins to the original rondavels and kaia rooms, and revamped all the rooms in country-comfort style. In 1993 the historic main building was razed in a devastating fire, which destroyed many priceless family heirlooms. The lodge was rebuilt and redecorated, and despite the loss, is now more beautiful than ever.

The management team and staff are dedicated to ensuring that each pampered guest has a memorable stay, one that will long be remembered for good food, good company and personal service warmly wrapped in the wonderful ambience of Old Joe's Kaia.

Wipe the oxtail well. Toss in flour seasoned with salt and pepper. Seal in oil and butter in a large saucepan. Add the onion, garlic, beef stock, oregano, rosemary, ginger, bay leaves, red wine and half the celery. Mix together the tomato purée, sugar, vinegar and lemon juice and add to the saucepan. Cover and simmer gently for 2-3 hours until the meat is tender. 30 minutes before serving, add the remaining celery.

Serve with nutty rice and baby beans with tomatoes and feta. SERVES 8

WINE Serve easy-drinking Forrester Petit Chenin with the pasta, it's a perfect foil for avocado and lively enough to cope with the bacon. Shiraz and oxtail are great mates. Choose Stellenzicht Syrah, a big wine for a flavour-filled dish.

SPARKLING MANGO

8 small or 6 large stringless mangoes, peeled, pipped and sliced
15-30 ml castor sugar
750 ml chilled sparkling wine

Purée the mango and castor sugar. Pour into eight champagne flutes to fill up to three-quarters and chill well.
TO SERVE Place the glasses in front of your guests and top up with chilled sparkling wine. SERVES 8

ANGEL HAIR PASTA WITH AVOCADO AND BACON

2 avocados, peeled and pipped
10 ml Roasted Garlic purée (page 135)
60 ml loosely packed fresh basil leaves
lemon juice
salt, milled black pepper
8 rashers rindless back bacon, chopped
vegetable oil, butter
250 g angel hair pasta
TO SERVE
grated or shaved parmesan cheese

Purée the avocado, garlic and basil. Flavour with lemon juice. Season with salt and pepper. Cover and chill. Fry the bacon until crisp in oil. Drain on kitchen paper.
TO SERVE Cook the pasta in a large saucepan of salted boiling water, to which you have added a knob of butter. Drain, and pile onto four warm plates. Top with avocado purée, bacon and parmesan.
SERVES 6-8

OLD JOE'S OXTAIL

2 kg oxtail pieces, trimmed of fat
60 ml cake flour
salt, milled black pepper
olive oil, butter
3 onions, sliced
4 garlic cloves, peeled and crushed
500 ml Beef Stock (page 134)
15 ml chopped fresh oregano, or 5 ml dried oregano
15 ml chopped fresh rosemary, or 5 ml dried rosemary
2 ml crushed green ginger, or 1 ml ground ginger
4 bay leaves
500 ml dry red wine
400 g can tomato purée
30 ml brown sugar
125 ml white wine vinegar
15 ml lemon juice
1 bunch celery, leaves included, chopped
TO SERVE
Baby Beans with Tomatoes and Feta (page 144)

OLD JOE'S KAIA ◆ 51

THE CELLARS-HOHENHORT

CONSTANTIA, CAPE PENINSULA

ABOVE *Crème Brûlée Espresso with Seed Biscuits, vanilla ice-cream and Butterscotch sauce (Page 55).*
BELOW *French provincial style is Liz McGrath's passion, and happy evidence of it is in every nook and cranny of The Cellars-Hohenort. The garden is an exuberance of plumbago, abelia, catmint and iceberg roses. In fact, it was in these gardens that Mr Fisher, a former owner of The Cellars hybridised the rose Chris Barnard named after the famous heart surgeon.*

THE CELLARS-HOHENORT, ONE OF THE GREAT HOTELS OF SOUTH AFRICA, and part of Liz McGraths group of hotels known as The Collection, is an integral part of the Cape's legacy of gracious living and fine hospitality, with a history dating back to the late 17th century.

The earliest buildings on the present estate were already standing in 1693, just 41 years after Jan van Riebeeck, the first commander of the Cape had landed. Occupying a fine, wooded knoll on the eastern slopes of Table Mountain, the "opstal" (homestead and outbuildings) were known as Klaasenbosch. The house, built in Cape Dutch style, was the home of Hendrik ten Damme, chief surgeon of the Dutch East India Company. The farmstead comprised several buildings – a wine cellar, a water mill for milling grain, vineyards, stables and a wagon shed.

During the 1700s Klaasenbosch, with neighbouring Alphen and Groot Constantia, became part of the flourishing farming and wine producing area of the lush Constantia valley. In 1906, after many changes in ownership, Cape Town businessman, Arnold W Spilhaus, bought Klaasenbosch and demolished the old thatched homestead. In its place he built a grand Edwardian-style gabled mansion as his family home and named it Hohenort, meaning "high place" in old German. It was designed by architect Mr Seeliger, a contemporary of Sir Herbert Baker. Spilhaus died in 1947 at the grand old age of 101. After his death the property was subdivided and sold with the old cellars and grain mill being converted first into a private residence and later, a country guesthouse known as The Cellars.

In 1991, master-hotelier Liz McGrath bought The Cellars, which she restored, enlarged and refurbished, taking great care to protect the origins of the elegant, time-worn buildings. Original ceiling beams were restored, an oregon pine staircase was crafted from old roofing timbers, a restaurant was built around a huge oak tree as old as the cellar and the old dining-room became a cosy living room. Liz consolidated her venture two years later by buying Hohenort next door, and restored it with the same consummate care. Finally the two properties with four hectares of meticulously landscaped gardens, were united once again. The gardens feature roses, herbaceous borders, herbs, indigenous flora, as well as a unique knot garden.

Emphasis throughout the restoration process was on preserving and underlining the beauty of the surroundings and the impressive history of the estate. Today Liz's consummate touch is evident in every detail from the remarkable gardens to the fine antique furnishings and individual decoration of each suite – including the presidential Madiba Suite.

Novelli at The Cellars, the Cellars' signature restaurant, has been another very special project masterminded by Liz McGrath and Jean Christophe Novelli the internationally acclaimed Michelin-starred chef. The restaurant offers a distinctive, refined and elaborate gourmet menu combining the best of French cuisine with top quality local produce, freshly caught fish and superb fruits and vegetables.

ROASTED SPRINGBOK FILLET, SWEET POTATO TATIN AND PICKLED BEETROOT

750 g springbok fillets, trimmed
peeled cloves from 2 heads garlic
12 shallots or spring onions
50 g butter, cut into small blocks
olive oil
400 ml Venison Jus (Page 140)
SWEET POTATO TATIN
1 large sweet potato
4 rounds puff pastry, each 8 cm in diameter
50 g butter
45 ml sugar
PICKLED BEETROOT
5 beetroot, peeled and grated
50 ml balsamic vinegar
50 ml port
125 ml sugar

Set the oven at 250°C. Scatter the garlic and shallots or spring onions in a baking dish. Dot with butter and roast uncovered for about 15 minutes until soft.
SWEET POTATO TATIN Cut four rounds of sweet potato about 2 cm thick. Cover completely with pastry, leaving the bottom clear of pastry. (They may be chilled in the fridge for up to 2 hours.)
  Set the oven at 220°C. Melt the butter in a small roaster, add the sugar and stir over gentle heat until well caramelized. Add the sweet potato parcels pastry side up and bake for about 20 minutes until the potato is soft and the pastry is golden.
PICKLED BEETROOT Stir-fry the beetroot in olive oil for about 5 minutes. Add the balsamic vinegar and port and boil uncovered until reduced by half. Stir in the sugar until completely dissolved. Reduce, stirring constantly, until the sauce is syrupy.
TO SERVE Panfry the springbok fillets in hot olive oil for about 5 minutes until done to the desired degree, turning frequently. Allow to rest for 5 minutes
  Spoon beetroot onto warm plates. Top with sweet potato tatin and steak. Place garlic and shallots or spring onions around and pour jus over. SERVES 4

TERRINE OF TOMATOES, RED PEPPER AND BASIL WITH SULTANA AND CAPER DRESSING

20 large plum tomatoes, blanched, peeled, seeded and cut in half
12 Roasted Red Peppers (page 141), sliced
150 ml olive oil
50 ml balsamic vinegar
salt, milled black pepper
100 g fresh basil leaves
SULTANA AND CAPER DRESSING
50 g bleached sultanas
100 g capers
100 ml water
30 ml finely chopped fresh herbs (parsley, thyme, basil)
1 ripe tomato, cut into small cubes

SULTANA AND CAPER DRESSING Plump the sultanas and half the capers in the water for 2-3 hours. Tip into a food processor or blender and whiz until finely puréed. Mix in the chopped herbs, tomato and remaining capers. Season with salt and pepper.

Place the tomatoes in a flat dish with the peppers. Pour over the olive oil and balsamic vinegar, mix in and season with salt and pepper. Set aside to marinate for about 30 minutes. Drain well.

Line a small loaf tin with plastic wrap, allowing plenty of overhang. Layer in the marinated tomato, pepper and basil leaves (set some aside for garnishing). Fold over the plastic wrap to cover, weigh down and chill for 24 hours.
TO SERVE Turn out and unwrap the terrine. Cut into slices, place on plates and spoon the dressing around. Garnish with baby basil leaves. SERVES 8-10

WINE The terrine demands a wine with good acidity and fruit. Serve Neil Ellis Groenekloof Sauvignon Blanc. The springbok needs complexity and fruit in its matching wine; offer Zandvliet Kalkveld Shiraz. The multi-faceted dessert requires balanced acidity and sweetness. De Wetshof Edeloes Noble Late Harvest will do the honours perfectly.

CREME BRULEE ESPRESSO WITH SEED BISCUITS, VANILLA ICE-CREAM AND BUTTERSCOTCH SAUCE

375 ml cream
125 ml espresso coffee
1 vanilla pod, split in half lengthwise
8 egg yolks
100 g castor sugar
SEED BISCUITS
50 g butter
50 g castor sugar
50 g poppy seeds
50 g sesame seeds
15 ml honey
50 ml cake flour, sifted
BUTTERSCOTCH SAUCE
250 ml sugar
100 g butter
125 ml cream
60 ml milk
TO SERVE
Vanilla Ice-Cream (page 147)

Set the oven at 150°C. Lightly grease six dariole moulds. Bring the cream, coffee and vanilla pod to the boil in a medium saucepan. Cover and set aside for about 15 minutes for the flavours to infuse.

Beat together the egg yolks and castor sugar until thick and pale. Strain in the hot cream mixture. Cool. Pour into the moulds and bake in a bain-marie for about 40 minutes until slightly set. Chill.
SEED BISCUITS Grease a baking sheet. Melt the butter in a medium saucepan. Stir in the castor sugar, seeds and honey and heat gently, stirring, until the sugar has dissolved. Remove from the heat and add the sifted flour. Chill until set. Roll into eight balls. Roll out, place on the baking sheet and bake for 8-10 minutes until golden. Lift onto a cooling rack.
BUTTERSCOTCH SAUCE Combine the sugar and butter in a medium, deep saucepan. Heat, stirring constantly, until the sugar dissolves. Increase the heat and boil uncovered until the mixture caramelizes to a pale golden brown. Remove from the heat and stir in the cream and milk. Boil for 1-2 minutes. Pour into a jug and cool.
TO SERVE Unmould the crème brûlée onto plates. Place biscuits on top. Place a scoop of ice-cream on the biscuit. Pour butterscotch sauce around. SERVES 6

Terrine of Tomatoes, Red Pepper and Basil with Sultana and Caper Dressing.

THE CELLARS-HOHENHORT ◆ 55

THE MOUNT NELSON HOTEL

GARDENS, CAPE TOWN

ABOVE *Corporate Executive Chef, Garth Stroebel who has won a string of prestigious awards, including the Pinnacle Chef Award, and is at the fore-front of development of an exciting new cuisine in South Africa.*

THE LUXURIOUS MOUNT NELSON, NAMED IN MEMORY OF ADMIRAL LORD NELSON, is one of the great hotels of the world, and has been synonymous with Cape hospitality for over a century. In 1741 Baron Pieter van Rheede van Oudtshoorn, a Dutch midshipman on his way to the East, fame and fortune, arrived in Table Bay. He decided to stay, and was rewarded with a generous land grant across the way from the gardens of the Dutch East India Company. It is on the remainder of this historic site that the Mount Nelson was built, opening its doors on March 1 1899.

The great hotels of Britain and the Continent played an important role in its design, decoration, and the style and standard of accommodation, as the owners, the directors of the Castle Line, would not permit themselves to be outdone by anything superior in London, the capital of the world.

It was a time when leisure and business travel was commonplace among the upwardly and outwardly mobile classes of the northern hemisphere. They sailed into Table Bay on steamships of the Union and Castle Lines, anxious to escape the northern winter in favour of the sunnier southern tip of Africa. The vessels were crammed not only with holidaymakers but also entrepreneurs and fortune-seekers.

In the century of its existence, the Mount Nelson has hosted many members of the world's royalty as well as countless rich and famous, continuing the tradition established by South Africa's first 'innkeeper', Jan van Riebeeck, who welcomed visitors to the 'Tavern of the Seas' three hundred years ago.

The hotel is the flagship of Orient-Express Hotels' African Collection, whose legendary standards are consistent throughout its exclusive collection of properties worldwide. It is set in glorious parklike gardens at the foot of Table Mountain – the very heart of old Cape Town.

Travellers enjoy the highest standards of hospitality, luxury, exclusivity and tradition – prerequisites which have ensured that the Mount Nelson is ranked with New York's Waldorf-Astoria, Hong Kong's Peninsula, and the Hotel de Crillon in Paris. The hotel is perfectly located for walks down oak-lined Government Avenue into the city, or excursions to the V&A Waterfront, the Cape winelands, beaches, the National Botanic Garden at Kirstenbosch and nature reserves, coastal resorts and charming fishing villages along the eastern and western seaboards of the peninsula.

SPICY CHICKPEA BATTERED PRAWNS WITH LIME AND CORIANDER VINAIGRETTE

16 large prawns, shelled and deveined
salt, milled black pepper
cake flour, vegetable oil
mixed salad greens
4 Chargrilled Limes (page 135)
BATTER
60 ml Hummus (page 139)
10 ml paprika
10 ml ground cumin
100 ml cake flour, sifted
100 ml soda water
LIME AND CORIANDER VINAIGRETTE
125 ml peanut oil
finely grated zest and juice from
   2 Chargrilled Limes (page 135)
1 red pepper, finely diced
small bunch fresh coriander leaves, chopped

BATTER Mix together the ingredients and season with salt and pepper.
VINAIGRETTE Mix together the ingredients and season with salt and pepper.
TO SERVE Season the prawns with salt and pepper. Dip into flour then in batter and deep fry in hot vegetable oil.
   Toss salad leaves with vinaigrette and place on plates. Arrange prawns on top and garnish with chargrilled limes. SERVES 4

CAPE-MALAY SPICED FISH WITH COCONUT AND LEMONGRASS BROTH

1 kg skinless, filleted fish cut into
   6 portions
Cape-Malay Spice Mix (page 136)
5 ml crushed green ginger
250 g finely sliced vegetables
   (leeks, cucumber, green beans,
   red and yellow pepper)
4 small bok choy, quartered
Ghee (page 135), salt, milled black pepper
BROTH
400 g can coconut cream
250 g lemongrass (3-4 stalks), trimmed
   and finely chopped
250 ml Chicken Stock (page 134)
50 ml milk

BROTH Combine all the ingredients in a medium saucepan and simmer uncovered for about 25 minutes until slightly thickened. Purée in a blender or food processor. Sieve into a clean saucepan. Reheat and season with salt.
TO SERVE Season the fish with Cape-Malay spice mix. Fry the ginger, sliced vegetables and bok choy in ghee in a large frying pan until limp. Season with salt and pepper.
   Fry the fish in ghee in a large frying pan until golden and cooked through. Place fish and vegetables in warm bowls and pour broth around. SERVES 6

> **WINE** Spicy foods enjoy riesling wines; Boschendal Riesling with the prawns would be delicious. Serve De Trafford Chenin Blanc with the Cape-Malay spiced fish.

TUNA BRIX WITH HARISSA MAYONNAISE

Brix are snacks similar to Cape-Malay samoosas, and also make an interesting summer lunch dish. Uncooked brix and harissa mayonnaise may be chilled for up to 8 hours.

300 g poached, steamed or canned tuna, drained and flaked
1 red onion, finely chopped
olive oil
1 garlic clove, peeled and crushed
30 ml chopped fresh parsley
1 egg, lightly beaten
salt, milled black pepper, lemon juice
12 24 cm x 12 cm sheets spring roll pastry
30 g (30 ml) butter, melted
Harissa Mayonnaise (page 138)

Fry the onion in olive oil in a medium frying pan until translucent. Add the garlic and parsley. Cool. Stir in the flaked tuna and beaten egg. Season with salt, pepper and lemon juice.
 Brush the pastry with melted butter. Add the tuna mixture and roll into neat cylinders. TO SERVE Shallow fry the tuna brix in hot olive oil. Drain on kitchen paper. Cut in half, place on plates with harissa mayonnaise. SERVES 6

Grilled Pineapple with Buttered Mint Glaze.

Ostrich Fillet with Pesto and Beetroot and Spinach Salad (left); Tuna Brix with Harissa Mayonnaise.

OSTRICH FILLET WITH PESTO AND BEETROOT AND SPINACH SALAD

1,5 kg ostrich fillet, trimmed
375 ml ketjap manis (sweet soy sauce)
200 ml red wine vinegar
2 dried chillies
6 garlic cloves, peeled and crushed
Mixed Herb Pesto (page 138)
BEETROOT AND SPINACH SALAD
150 g baby spinach leaves, well washed
2 medium raw beetroot, peeled and cut into fine slivers
Mustard Seed Vinaigrette (page 137)

Place the ostrich fillet in a dish. Whizz together the ketjap manis, wine vinegar, chillies and garlic in a blender. Pour over the ostrich, cover and set aside to marinate for 24 hours, turning frequently.
BEETROOT AND SPINACH SALAD Toss the spinach and beetroot in a bowl. (Tear the leaves into pieces if you wish.) Pour the mustard seed vinaigrette over the salad, toss well and set aside to wilt slightly.
TO SERVE Pat the meat dry and cut into medallions. Brush lightly with olive oil. Grill for 2 minutes on each side in a hot pan. Place salad on warm plates. Top with ostrich and dollop with pesto. SERVES 6

GRILLED PINEAPPLE WITH BUTTERED MINT GLAZE

2 small pineapples cut into wedges
250 ml sugar
250 g butter
30 ml vodka
60 ml chopped fresh mint
TO SERVE
Cinnamon Ice-Cream (page 147)

Skin the pineapples if you wish and place on a baking sheet. Heat the oven grill.
 Combine the sugar, butter and vodka in a small saucepan and heat gently, whisking until the sugar dissolves. Add the mint.
TO SERVE Brush the pineapple with glaze and grill until soft and golden. Serve hot with cinnamon ice-cream. Offer the glaze separately as a sauce. SERVES 8

> **WINE** Serve Haute Cabrière Chardonnay-Pinot Noir with the tuna brix; the pinot noir will give body and balance to the gentle heat of the harissa. Pinotage, such as Backsberg Pinotage, would meet the sharpness of the mustard seeds in the ostrich main course. Offset the acidity of the pineapple dessert with well-chilled Petit Pierre Ratafia.

THE PRUE LEITH COLLEGE OF FOOD & WINE

CENTURION, PRETORIA

THE PRUE LEITH COLLEGE OF FOOD & WINE WAS FOUNDED IN CENTURION, between Pretoria and Johannesburg, in 1996. The college is housed in the imposing buildings and grounds of the Lyttleton Manor House, a fine Colonial style building with an historic water tower which still stands today. Other relics are an old buttress wall and the farmhouse – one of the oldest still remaining in the area – which were built by Italian prisoners of war.

These elegant buildings provide a fitting home for the academic quarters of the college and its on-site restaurant, The Odd Plate, run by the students as part of their training. As testimony to its excellence, the restaurant has been awarded the blazon of the Paris-based Confrèrie de la Chaîne des Rôtisseurs.

The spacious grounds are large enough for sizeable functions, and the college has an on-site boma for dining alfresco under the stars around a roaring fire. As in days gone by, garden parties are often held out of doors under marquees.

Before establishing the college its trustees approached Prue Leith OBE with a request to stand as patron. Through this endorsement, the college gains an association which ensures ongoing standards of the highest order. This includes access to the latest trends and techniques, an international rating, assurance that standards are maintained, and the benefits to students of personal interaction with a culinary figure of world renown.

This has been a first for Prue Leith – the only time that she has given her name to a project outside of the United Kingdom. Her huge contribution has gone beyond the bounds of the agreement with her. She has shown an intense interest in college affairs and is regularly in touch with the trustees. Her annual visits are the highlight of the year.

Within a remarkably short time, the college bearing the Prue Leith insignia has established itself as one of the leading institutions of its kind in the country.

ABOVE *The Odd Plate, elegant ochre-walled training restaurant of the college. A sideboard displays a unique collection of plates gathered from all over the world by patron Prue Leith OBE. On weekends African fusion food is prepared on open fires and served in the lapa.*

CAPE COUNTRY HOUSES ARE THE STATELY HOMES OF SOUTH AFRICA, set characteristically against majestic mountains in oceans of vineyards. Roofs are thatched, walls are whitewashed, gables are etched against an azure sky. Designed in the Cape Dutch architectural style, country houses are to be found in the winelands of Paarl, Stellenbosch, Franschhoek and Constantia.

Roggeland is a classic example of a Cape Dutch country house; perfectly proportioned, warmly welcoming, and built to last. The farm takes its name from *rogsecale africanum*, the wild rye growing in the foothills of the Drakenstein mountains which form a dramatic backdrop to the marvelously maintained, time-worn buildings. Fascinating architectural details include an old kitchen hearth, the *vethok* (pen) in which chickens and pigs were fattened, and a curved staircase which goats climbed to reach the attic where they spent the night in days gone by. The farm, the oldest in the valley, is known as a *ringmuur plaas* (ring-walled farm) due to its surrounding whitewashed wall, which kept wild animals at bay.

Roggeland is set beneath the majestic Drakenstein Mountains in the Dal Josaphat valley. This valley was the cradle of Afrikaans, a South African language closely linked to Dutch. Arnold Pannevis, an influential teacher who spent time at Roggeland translating the Bible into Afrikaans, gives his name to one of the eleven individually decorated guest bedrooms.

The first owner of Roggeland was a German, Peter Buek, who was granted the land by Willem Adriaan van Der Stel in 1693. At that time he and the owner of Nederburg were the only non-French settlers in the area. They were allocated their land in an effort to encourage the integration of different cultures. Beuk called the farm Dal Josaphat (the Valley of Temptation), the name that in time came to refer to the entire district. His house, still intact, is a quaint whitewashed cottage overlooking the vegetable and herb garden.

ROGGELAND COUNTRY HOUSE

PAARL, CAPE WINELANDS

The Du Toit family, of French Huguenot descent, bought the farm in 1779 and built the main H-shaped farmhouse. It is a flawless example of Cape Dutch architectural style, and features a rare diamond-panelled yellowwood and stinkwood front door, and a four-leaf diamond-panelled *port visite* separating the entrance hall from the lounge.

Today Roggeland is run by a family in an atmosphere of warm, friendly and refined hospitality. Lee-ann, Jacqui, Gordon and Marie Minkley welcome visitors to spend a little quality time in the age-old homestead, and to enjoy the tranquil setting from the side of the pool, or while walking, golfing, fishing, mountain-biking or horse riding nearby.

Menus are inspired by the regional produce of Paarl valley and vegetables and fresh herbs grown in Roggeland's own gardens.

TOP *The Minkley family on the lawns of the Manor House: Jacqui, Marie, Gordon and Lee-ann.*
ABOVE *Roggeland's elegant dining room which has views over the herb and vegetable garden.*

Roast Duck with Oriental Sauce (left); Caramelized Onion and Tomato Tarte Tatin.

ROAST DUCK WITH ORIENTAL SAUCE

1 pekin duck, well cleaned
honey
ORIENTAL SAUCE
200 ml honey
200 ml white wine vinegar
80 ml sesame oil
5 ml prepared English mustard
2 ml each ground ginger, ground coriander, ground five spice, curry powder, ground cardamom
5 ml each caraway seeds, fennel seeds, whole cloves
500 ml Beef Jus (page 140)
15 ml cornflour
30 ml water
TO SERVE
Couscous with Roasted Vegetables (page 143)

Set the oven at 150°C. Place the duck on a rack in a roaster and roast uncovered for 2½-3 hours until cooked. Cool.
ORIENTAL SAUCE Combine the honey, vinegar, sesame oil, mustard, spices, seeds and beef jus in a saucepan and simmer for 5 minutes. Mix together the cornflour and water and add to the pan. Simmer, stirring, until the sauce is thickened and clear.
TO SERVE Set the oven at 200°C. Cut the duck into quarters and remove most of the bones, leaving leg and wing bones in. Place on a baking tray and brush with honey. Roast for about 15 minutes until crisp and hot. Serve with oriental sauce and couscous with roasted vegetables. SERVES 4

WINE Ken Forrester Chenin Blanc would do wonders for the tomato tart, which requires a flamboyant wine to meet the demand. Serve Welmoed Shiraz with the duck; it has sufficient spiciness and berry flavours to balance the sweet and spicy sauce. Sparkling wine is great with the chocolate mousse cake, as it offsets the richness and enhances the flavours of the fruit garnish. Twee Jongegezellen Rose Brut will do the honours in style; its promise of sweetness on the nose is nicely balanced by the dryness in the flavour.

CARAMELIZED ONION AND TOMATO TARTE TATIN

3 onions, finely sliced
30 g (30 ml) butter
20 ml brown sugar
4 spinach leaves, well washed
olive oil
500 g cherry tomatoes
salt, milled black pepper
400 g puff pastry
TO SERVE
mixed salad leaves
Basil Pesto (page 138)

Fry the onion in the butter in a frying pan until golden. Stir in the brown sugar and cook gently until caramelized. Cut out and discard the thick spinach stalks. Blanch the leaves briefly in boiling water and drain well.

Set the oven at 200°C. Brush six straight-sided 10 cm tartlet pans with olive oil. Pack in the tomatoes. Spoon caramelized onion on top. Place spinach on the onion. Season with salt and pepper.

Unroll the pastry on a floured surface and roll out. Cut out six 12 cm circles. Place on top of the pans to form lids. Bake for about 15 minutes until crisp and golden.
TO SERVE Turn out the tarts on plates, with pastry underneath. Garnish with salad leaves and basil pesto. SERVES 6

CREAM CHEESE SOUFFLE

melted butter, castor sugar
3 eggs, separated
45 ml icing sugar
250 g cream cheese
finely grated zest of 1 lemon
80 ml icing sugar
15 ml cornflour
sifted icing sugar to garnish

Brush eight small soufflé dishes with melted butter and dust with castor sugar. Set the oven at 180°C.

Beat together the egg yolks with the first measure of icing sugar until well blended. Mix in the cream cheese and lemon zest. Beat the egg white to soft peaks. Gradually beat in the second measure of icing sugar and cornflour until stiff and glossy. Fill the prepared soufflé dishes.
TO SERVE Bake the soufflés for 12-15 minutes until well risen and golden. Place the dishes on plates, dust with sifted icing sugar and serve immediately. SERVES 8

CHOCOLATE MOUSSE CAKE

4 eggs, separated
125 ml castor sugar
60 ml cocoa powder
fresh fruit and chocolate shavings to garnish
CHOCOLATE MOUSSE
100 g dark chocolate, roughly chopped
150 g soft unsalted butter
150 ml cocoa powder
250 ml cream
60 ml icing sugar
4 eggs yolks
125 ml castor sugar

Set the oven at 200°C. Grease and flour a 20 cm x 30 cm baking sheet. Line a 170 mm x 70 mm bread tin with greaseproof paper.

Mix together the egg yolks, castor sugar and sifted cocoa. Do not overmix. Whisk the egg white until stiff and glossy. Fold gently into the yolk mixture. Spread into the baking sheet and bake for 8-10 minutes until firm to the touch. Cool in the baking sheet. Cover with a cloth.
CHOCOLATE MOUSSE Melt together the chocolate, butter and sifted cocoa in a bowl over simmering water. Cool. Beat together the cream and icing sugar to ribbon stage (when the beater is lifted it leaves a ribbon trail on the surface). Whisk together the egg yolks and castor sugar until pale and thick. Fold in the melted chocolate-butter mixture. Fold in the cream. Fill a piping bag fitted with a large star nozzle.

Cut the cake into three pieces to fit the bread tin. Place one piece in the tin. Pipe on a layer of mousse. Top with another piece of cake, more mousse, then the remaining cake. Cover with foil and chill overnight or freeze for 3-4 hours.
TO SERVE Turn the cake out and cut into thin slices. Garnish with fruit and chocolate shavings. SERVES 8

ROGGELAND COUNTRY HOUSE ◆ 63

CARRIGANS COUNTRY ESTATE
HAZYVIEW, MPUMALANGA

CARRIGANS, WHICH IN GAELIC MEANS 'OF THE ROCK', was the name of Anthony Berlein's grandmother's home in County Monaghan in Ireland. A fitting name if there is to be a little corner of the Emerald Isle in the Mpumalanga Lowveld. For here, overlooking the distant mountains of the Drakensberg, stands a granite massif. This site, according to folklore, was the meeting place of tribal elders and warriors, who gathered to ponder the spirits and the stars that cast their light upon the earliest beginnings of man in Africa. If this Archaean granite outcrop could tell its story we would know something of the dawn of our planet.

Looking across the ancient valleys below, where less than a hundred years ago lion and elephant roamed freely through the riverine forests and rolling grass-covered hills, the dimensions of time and space allow the visitor a moment to consider his passing insignificance and, like the warrior spirits of long ago, ponder the journey that awaits us all to our Maker beyond the stars.

Reminiscent of the early gold mining days, Carrigans is set in luxuriant indigenous gardens. Five Victorian-style cottages comprise two bedrooms en-suite, spacious sitting rooms with open fireplaces, dining rooms and deep, cool verandas. Inspired by the work of Clarence Bicknell, the French botanist and eccentric who lived in the South of France in the late 19th century, Claire and Tess, daughters of the owners, have painted the interiors creating a floral fantasy, reflecting the romance of a bygone era.

Alma and Anthony Berlein extend a warm welcome to all those who pass this way and offer a unique form of hospitality. Simon Sithole attends the Berlein's dinner table as he has done since 1964, preparing gourmet meals served with the pomp and ceremony of colonial days. Over the years Simon's skill has grown as has his repertoire of delicious recipes. It is expertise based on an inherent understanding of cooking methods and a respect for good ingredients.

ABOVE *Simon Sithole in the grand dining room of the manor house.*

SMOKED TROUT SALAD WITH PAPINO AND CHILLI SALSA

mixed salad leaves, sliced cucumber
1 orange, peeled and cut into segments
1 small papino peeled, seeded and sliced
   (retain seeds for the dressing)
1 small red onion or 4 spring onions, sliced
4 smoked trout fillets
100 g roasted cashew nuts
PAPINO AND CHILLI SALSA
45 ml raspberry vinegar
10 ml honey
2 ml Dijon mustard
salt
125 ml walnut oil
2-3 green chillies, sliced and seeded
45 ml papino seeds

PAPINO AND CHILLI SALSA Blend the vinegar, honey, mustard and salt in a blender or food processor. Add the oil in a thin stream. Add the chilli and papino seeds and blend until coarsely ground. TO SERVE Arrange salad leaves and cucumber on a platter. Mix the orange segments, papino and onion with most of the salsa. Arrange on the salad. Place trout fillets on top. Scatter with cashew nuts and pour over the remaining salsa. SERVES 4

QUAIL WITH FENNEL, MUSHROOM AND MACADAMIA STUFFING AND PORT SAUCE

4 quail, partially boned (leg and
   wing bones in)
butter, salt, milled black pepper
Fennel, Mushroom and Macadamia
   Stuffing (page 137)
8 rashers rindless streaky bacon
500 ml Chicken Stock (page 134)
TO SERVE
Red Bean and Mangetout Tartlets (page 145)

Set the oven at 180°C. Brush four pieces of greaseproof paper with butter, each large enough to wrap a quail. Stuff the quails with the stuffing. Close with cocktail sticks and brush liberally with melted butter. Wrap each bird in two rashers of bacon, then in buttered greaseproof paper. Place in roaster and roast for 30 minutes. Open the parcels and brown the birds for about 10 minutes. Remove from the paper and keep warm.

Add the reserved port from the stuffing to the pan juices and boil uncovered until reduced by half. Add the chicken stock and reduce until thickened. Check and adjust the flavour and whisk in a knob of butter. TO SERVE Place the quail on warm plates and pour over a little sauce. Serve with red bean and mangetout tartlets. SERVES 4

WINE Smoked fish demands an elegantly oaked wine to do it justice, and to tone down the hint of chilli in the dressing. Select Klein Constantia Chardonnay. Quail enjoys New World pinot noir, such as Bouchard Finlayson Pinot Noir Galpin Peak which is made in the cool coastal area of Hermanus.

CHOCMINT ICE-CREAM

150 g dark chocolate, roughly chopped
250 ml finely packed fresh mint leaves
60 ml sugar
500 ml cream
4 eggs, separated
2 drops peppermint essential oil
30-45 ml Crème de Menthe liqueur

Melt the chocolate in a bowl over simmering water. Cool slightly. Finely chop the mint leaves with half the sugar. Whip the cream fairly stiffly. Fold in the chopped mint.

Beat together the egg yolks, peppermint oil, liqueur and remaining sugar. Fold in the cream and mint. Beat the egg white until fairly stiff but not dry. Fold in. Drizzle in the melted chocolate and drag through to give a marbled effect. Pour into a mould and freeze for about 6 hours until firm. TO SERVE Turn the ice-cream out onto a chilled platter. Slice and serve with almond biscuits or biscotti. SERVES 4

CARRIGANS COUNTRY ESTATE ♦ 65

FANCOURT HOTEL AND COUNTRY CLUB ESTATE

GEORGE, GARDEN ROUTE

FANCOURT NESTLES IN THE SHADOW OF THE OUTENIQUA MOUNTAINS on the scenic Garden Route. Its history takes us back to the early 1800s, when Cape Colonial Secretary Sir John Montagu commissioned Australian engineer Henry Fancourt White to build a road linking the coastal towns of George and Knysna with the Karoo. The Montagu Pass opened in 1848.

Ten years later Henry, his wife and baby son Ernest Montagu White, built a home, today's Manor House, and established a farm at Blanco. After his parents' death, Ernest upgraded the homestead with local forest woods (yellowwood, stinkwood and blackwood) and named it Fancourt in memory of his father. Tragedy struck on 10 April 1916. As was customary, he collected wild forest mushrooms for dinner. Ernest and five members of his family died from mushroom poisoning. For several years the homestead stood abandoned in its overgrown gardens, and to this day locals believe the Manor House is haunted by the unfortunate family.

From 1918 to 1925, Mr Rubin John Greer, his wife and four daughters resided happily at Fancourt, ghosts notwithstanding. Dances were held in the dining room (now the Montagu Room),

ABOVE Fancourt's Manor House was built by Ernest Montagu White in 1858.
BELOW Mrs Sabine Plattner, owner of Fancourt.

which rang with the sounds of revelry. The band included a violinist, a concertina player and a banjo player, all of whom needed a little liquid refreshment to keep the ghosts away. Fancourt entered a troubled financial period between the world wars and again stood forlorn and empty until 1960 when the renowned brain surgeon, Dr A Krynauw, restored the home, added a wing (now the Country Kitchen) and created the splendid parklands. Entrepreneur and property developer, Mr A Pieterse subsequently converted the Manor House into a Country Inn, and commissioned Gary Player to establish the 'finest golf course in South Africa'.

In 1994 the estate was acquired by Dr Hasso and Mrs Sabine Plattner who initiated a development project to place Fancourt among the best luxury destination resorts in the world.

The estate boasts two internationally rated golf courses and a golf school, and entered the millennium with a third links-style course. There is a health and beauty pavilion, a world class gym and extensive sporting facilities such as tennis, bowls, squash and swimming.

Investors in Fancourt real estate have access to one of South Africa's most exclusive addresses while business visitors enjoy state-of-the-art conference facilities. Four restaurants provide a cosmopolitan choice of menus. Luxurious Oaklands, a valet-serviced English country house, and Glentana Beach House on a dramatic cliffside perch are available to special guests.

Fancourt is the 1999 holder of The Africa/Middle East Golf Resort of the Year award presented by hertz International Golf Travel.

SPICED SEMOLINA WEDGES WITH ORIENTAL VEGETABLES

500 ml milk
30 g (30 ml) butter
250 ml semolina
2 egg yolks
1 ml ground coriander
small bunch chives, finely snipped
salt, milled black pepper
fresh coriander leaves to garnish
ORIENTAL VEGETABLES
200 g vegetables (patty pans, mangetout, baby corn, baby carrots, courgettes)
200 ml teriyaki sauce
15 ml sesame seeds
20 ml lemon juice
2-3 garlic cloves, peeled and crushed
butter

Bring the milk and butter to the boil in a medium saucepan. Stir in the semolina, cover and cook over very low heat for 3 minutes. Remove from the heat. Stir in the egg yolks, ground coriander and chives. Season with salt and pepper. Tip into a baking tray to cool, then cut into wedges.
VEGETABLES Cut the vegetables into shapes and place in a bowl. Stir in half the teriyaki sauce and all the sesame seeds, lemon juice and garlic. Cover and marinate for about 2 hours.
TO SERVE Warm the semolina wedges in the oven at 180°C for 6-8 minutes. Drain the vegetables (retain the marinade) and fry in butter. Pour in the marinade and heat. Place the semolina wedges on warm plates with the vegetables. Garnish with fresh coriander. SERVES 4

WINE Light-bodied wines like chenin blanc and weisser riesling are delicious with the semolina dumplings; choose Hartenberg Weisser Riesling or Hazendal Chenin Blanc. Ostrich calls for a good red wine, such as full-bodied merlot, shiraz or cabernet sauvignon. For something different, offer Backsberg Malbec.

OSTRICH CARPACCIO WITH PEACH CHUTNEY AND AVOCADO PARFAIT

250 g well-trimmed ostrich fillet
olive oil
60 ml finely chopped fresh herbs
Peach Chutney (page 139)
AVOCADO PARFAIT
1 avocado
salt, milled black pepper
5 ml lemon juice
45 ml Mayonnaise (page 138)
30 ml sour cream
10 g (15 ml) gelatine
60 ml hot water

Roll the ostrich fillet in olive oil and herbs. Roll tightly in plastic wrap and place in the freezer for 1½-2 hours until firm. (Fillet of beef or venison may be used if preferred.)
AVOCADO PARFAIT Peel and stone the avocado. Scoop the pulp into a bowl, mash and season with salt, pepper and lemon juice. Stir in the mayonnaise and sour cream. Dissolve the gelatine in the hot water and stir into the parfait. Chill for 1½-2 hours until set.
TO SERVE Slice the ostrich finely and arrange on plates. Garnish with peach chutney and avocado parfait. Garnish if you wish with salad. SERVES 4

PLAITED SALMON TROUT WITH TWO SAUCES AND RIBBON VEGETABLES

2 x 500 g whole salmon trout, skinned and filleted
PARSLEY CREAM SAUCE
250 ml Béchamel Sauce (page 140)
100 ml cream
15 ml chopped fresh parsley
30 g (30 ml) butter
salt, milled black pepper
ORANGE BUTTER SAUCE
250 ml orange juice
100 ml cream
100 g cold butter, cut into blocks
RIBBON VEGETABLES
1 large carrot
1 medium courgette
1 medium leek

Remove the fish bones with a pair of tweezers. Cut each fillet in three pieces lengthwise to within 1cm of the top and plait neatly. Season with salt and pepper.
PARSLEY CREAM SAUCE Prepare the béchamel sauce in a medium saucepan. Add the cream and parsley. Beat in the butter. Season with salt and pepper.
ORANGE BUTTER Bring the orange juice to the boil in a medium saucepan and boil uncovered until reduced by one-third. Add the cream and reduce to thicken slightly. Remove from the stove and beat in the butter. Season with salt and pepper. Strain into a warm jug.
RIBBON VEGETABLES Slice the carrot, courgette and leek lengthwise into ribbons with a vegetable peeler. Blanch in salted boiling water for 2 minutes. Drain well.
TO SERVE Panfry the plaited fish in a little butter and oil. Fry the vegetables in a little butter to heat through. Arrange on warm plates, top with fish and spoon the sauces alongside. SERVES 4

> **WINE** Serve salmon trout with a medium-bodied unwooded sauvignon blanc, such as the one from Backsberg. With the bread and butter pudding Delheim Edelspatz Noble Late Harvest is a pleasing partner.

BREAD AND BUTTER PUDDING WITH VAN DER HUM

1 litre full cream milk
1 vanilla pod, split in half lengthwise
6 eggs
200 ml castor sugar
150 ml Van der Hum liqueur
300 g sliced white bread, brioche or croissant
125 ml butter, melted
100 g sultanas
grated nutmeg
TO SERVE
Brandied Figs (page 147)

Set the oven at 180°C. Bring the milk to the boil in a medium saucepan with the vanilla pod. Set aside to infuse until cooled to room temperature. Whisk together the eggs and castor sugar. Gradually strain in the milk, whisking gently to avoid frothing. Add the Van der Hum.

Cut the bread into triangles, brush with melted butter and arrange in a pie dish or individual dishes. Sprinkle sultanas between the slices. Pour in half the custard and set aside for about 10 minutes to soak in. Add the remaining custard and sprinkle nutmeg on the surface. Bake in a bain-marie for about 50 minutes until set, and the bread is crisp. Serve with brandied figs. SERVES 8

FANCOURT HOTEL AND COUNTRY CLUB ESTATE ◆ 69

HONEY-LEMON CHICKEN WITH SWEETCORN PANCAKES

6 chicken breasts (bone in; skin on)
100 ml honey
50 ml lemon juice
50 ml olive oil
Chicken Stock (page 134)
grated lemon zest to garnish
SWEETCORN PANCAKES
300 ml cake flour
100 ml milk
2 eggs
30 g (30 ml) butter, melted
salt
400 g can whole kernel corn
butter, vegetable oil

Place the chicken in a flat dish. Whisk together the honey, lemon juice and olive oil. Pour over the chicken and set aside to marinate for about 10 minutes.
SWEETCORN PANCAKES Sift the flour into a bowl. Stir in the milk. Whisk in the eggs, melted butter and salt. Add the corn.

Heat a non-stick frying pan and add a little butter and oil. Fry spoonfuls of the pancake mixture until crisp and golden on both sides and cooked through. Drain well and keep warm. Continue cooking fritters until all the batter has been used up.

Drain the chicken and pat dry. Pour the marinade into a saucepan, add the stock and boil uncovered until reduced to a syrup.
TO SERVE Set the oven at 200°C. Sear the chicken until golden on both sides in oil in a frying pan. Place in a roaster and roast uncovered for 15 minutes until cooked. Place sweetcorn pancakes on warm plates. Place chicken on top and drizzle sauce around. Garnish with lemon zest and serve with vegetables. SERVES 6

> **WINE** In general, many styles of white wine – the grander the dish, the finer the wine – suit both chicken and fish. The full flavours of both these dishes, though, would be best served by wooded wines, either a buttery Backsberg Chardonnay or Cloete Sauvignon Blanc.

FISH WITH SCALLOPED POTATOES AND LIME AND TOMATO CONFIT

6 x 180 g portions filleted fish, trimmed
600 g new potatoes
butter
chopped fresh parsley
350 g cherry tomatoes, cut in half
olive oil
50 ml white wine
45 ml lime juice
400 ml tomato juice
salt, milled black pepper, sugar

Parboil the potatoes until nearly cooked. Slice into scallops approximately 5 mm thick. Fry in butter until crisp and golden and sprinkle with parsley.

Fry the tomatoes in olive oil in a frying pan for 1-2 minutes. Add the wine and boil uncovered until reduced by half. Add the lime juice, tomato juice, a little olive oil and chopped parsley and reduce to thicken. Season with salt, pepper and sugar.
TO SERVE Panfry the fish skin down in olive oil for about 3 minutes. Turn and cook for 1-2 minutes more until firm to the touch. Arrange potatoes on the plates. Place fish on top, skin up. Spoon tomato and lime confit around. SERVES 6

LEMON TART

Rich Shortcrust Pastry (page 145) baked blind
grated zest and juice of 4 washed lemons
9 eggs
450 ml castor sugar
300 ml thick cream
Crème Anglaise (page 146) and berries

Set the oven at 150°C. Beat together the lemon zest, juice, eggs and castor sugar. Mix in the cream. Pour into the pastry shell and bake for 40 minutes. Cool. Serve with crème anglaise and berries. SERVES 8

THE WESTCLIFF

JOHANNESBURG, GAUTENG

THE FIRST MENTION OF WHAT WOULD BECOME THE EXCLUSIVE SUBURB OF WESTCLIFF is in the minutes of a meeting of directors of the Braamfontein Company held on 2nd September 1901. The land, offered for sale for 200 pounds an acre, was situated north of Johannesburg on a spectacular ridge, far from the hurly-burly of the busy mining and commercial town below.

The history of Westcliff is inextricably linked with that of architect Sir Herbert Baker. The area was formally proclaimed a suburb the next year, 1902, fortuitously coinciding with Sir Herbert's arrival from the Cape. It was his work in Westcliff and neighbouring Parktown during the decade before he left for India, that laid the foundations for a vernacular architecture in this country – the first original contribution since the old days of the Cape Dutch style.

Today, The Westcliff stands as a hotel of distinction among the enduring legacies of Sir Herbert Baker's style – the gracious homes on large estates developed a century ago. As a reflection of the wealth and status of their owners, land was levelled for croquet lawns and soil brought in by the ton to plant the cork trees and oaks, palms and jacarandas tangled with bougainvillea which still shade the suburb's quiet streets. The original homes were mainly in the English Picturesque tradition or Kent Hall House category, with innovations such as deeply recessed verandas to combat the heat of the African sun. They fitted most comfortably into their environment. In turn, The Westcliff's architects have created a Mediterranean hillside "village" set in formal landscaped gardens laid out around fountains and charming cobbled pathways that follow the contours of the slope.

The all-encompassing views sweep from the Zoological Gardens complete with strolling elephant below, to the distant Magaliesberg mountains 50 kilometres away. At night, the lights of the great metropolis are an awe-inspiring spectacle. The Westcliff is part of the Orient-Express Hotels African Collection which includes the award-winning Mount Nelson Hotel (page 56) in Cape Town and the luxury safari operation Gametrackers (page 46) in Botswana. The Mount Nelson opened in March 1899, The Westcliff in March 1998. Shortly after opening, The Westcliff joined the exclusive Leading Hotels of the World organization. All that separates these famous siblings is 99 years of history, but there is little doubt The Westcliff will follow in the celebrated footsteps of The Mount Nelson.

ABOVE *Not unlike the fortified villages of medieval days, guests of the westcliff enjoy absolute security and seclusion provided by the elevated position.*

GLENSHIEL COUNTRY LODGE

MAGOEBASKLOOF, NORTHERN PROVINCE

ABOVE *Chocolate Avocado Mousse with Lemon Coulis served in a chocolate casing with chocolate leaves.*

IN HIS BOOK, AFRICAN COLONY, John Buchan wrote of his journey over Pietersburg towards the Wolkberg foothills as "An endless path as if laid out by a landscape gardener with broad dales set with coppices and little wood covered hills". This is the same tranquil view, towards the northern Drakensberg, seen from Glenshiel's gracious dining room.

The lodge is near the historic village of Haenertsburg which boomed during the gold rush, then faded into near-oblivion. In more recent times the area has developed into a tranquil eco-tourist destination, within easy reach of the Kruger Park. Close by is the Modjadji Forest, home of the famous Modjadji cycad, one of the biggest known cycad species in the world. The area was proclaimed a national monument in 1936 and is protected by successive generations of the mysterious Modjadji, the Rain Queen, hereditary ruler of the Balobedu district. Also within easy reach are the spectacular Debegeni Falls in a luxuriant woodlands setting.

The original owner of Glenshiel was John Swinburne, who took up farming after the Anglo-Boer War. He named his farm after a lonely glen in Scotland on the road to Skye via Kyle of Lochalsch. His friends, famous writers Sir Henry Rider Haggard and John Buchan, used to stay in the old wattle and daub farmhouse. Both were captivated by the magic of the Mistlands and both drew their inspiration from campfire tales heard while travelling near Sekhukhuneland in the Lydenburg area.

The subsequent owner, Charles Kingsley Lathan, sold Glenshiel in 1953 to Peer Carst, grandfather of some of the present shareholders, the Iuel family, who converted Glenshiel into an idyllic retreat of colonial charm and blue blooded service. Magnificently established gardens and lush vegetation give fifteen spacious suites privacy and a sense of calm. Fine antiques and family heirlooms abound.

Each day ends with the romantic glow of candlelight, the gleam of silver and, in proper deference to fine gourmet cuisine for which Glenshiel is famous, an atmosphere which invites pampered guests to relax.

SWEET POTATO, CORIANDER AND BUTTERMILK SOUP

2 onions, finely chopped
butter
1 kg sweet potato, peeled and roughly chopped
750 ml Chicken Stock (Page 134)
500 ml buttermilk
5 ml grated nutmeg
salt, milled black pepper
60 ml chopped fresh coriander

Fry the onion in butter in a large saucepan until translucent. Add the sweet potato and fry until golden. Add the stock, cover and simmer for about 30 minutes until the vegetables are soft. Purée the soup in a blender or food processor and strain into a clean saucepan. Add the buttermilk and season with nutmeg, salt and pepper. Heat and stir in the coriander just before serving.
SERVES 8

WINE The natural sweetness of sweet potatoes in the soup calls for an off-dry, flavourful white wine such as Klein Constantia Rhine Riesling. Ostrich goes well with full-bodied merlot or shiraz, but especially with a cabernet sauvignon such as those made by Brampton, Fleur du Cap or Delheim. Eikendal Special Late Harvest is perfect with the creamy chocolate and avocado mousse.

OSTRICH MEDALLIONS WITH DIJON MUSTARD CRUST AND CAPE VELVET SAUCE

4 x 180 g ostrich fillet steaks, trimmed
butter, vegetable oil
salt, milled black pepper
400 g can apricots, drained and fanned
DIJON MUSTARD CRUST
250 ml toasted crumbs
60 ml chopped fresh oregano
15 ml chopped fresh sage
60 ml Dijon mustard
2 garlic cloves, peeled and crushed
CAPE VELVET SAUCE
1 onion, finely chopped
500 ml Beef Stock (page 134)
60 ml Cape Velvet liqueur

Set the oven at 180°C. Mix the crust ingredients together in a bowl, season with salt and pepper and chill in the fridge for about 20 minutes. Fry the steaks on both sides in butter and oil until sealed. Season with salt and pepper. Place on a baking tray and top with the crust mixture.
CAPE VELVET SAUCE Fry the onion in butter in a medium saucepan until translucent. Add beef stock and boil uncovered until reduced and thickened. Just before serving, add the liqueur. Season with salt and pepper.

TO SERVE Set the oven at 180°C. Bake the steaks for 10-15 minutes until cooked to the desired degree. Lift steaks onto warm plates, garnish with apricots and serve with the hot sauce and vegetables.
SERVES 4

CHOCOLATE AVOCADO MOUSSE

200 g white chocolate, roughly chopped
50 g butter, cut into blocks
30 ml Crème de Cassis liqueur
3 eggs, separated
30 ml castor sugar
1 large, ripe avocado
125 ml cream

Melt the chocolate, butter and liqueur in a bowl over simmering water, stirring until smooth. Cool. Beat together the egg yolks and castor sugar until thick and pale. Beat into the chocolate mixture. Peel, stone and mash the avocado and fold in. Whip the cream stiffly and fold in. Beat the egg whites until stiff but not dry and fold in. Fill small cups and chill for at least 6 hours until set. Alternatively serve in a chocolate casing with Lemon Coulis (page 146) and Chocolate Leaves (page 146). SERVES 6

GLENSHIEL COUNTRY LODGE

WINE Two of Hazendal's wines go well with the chicken: their beautifully balanced Hazendal Chardonnay, whose butter-and-honey flavour and long, crisp finish would meet the demands of the fruity sauce, and Hazendal Cabernet Sauvignon-Shiraz, the blend that won the 1999 Diners Club Winemaker of the Year award for winemaker Ronell Wiid. Blinis and caviare call for something refreshing, sparkling and luxurious, such as Hazendal's sensuous White Nights, a stylish Méthode Cap Classique made specially for the estate's tercentenary and the millennium. The wine evokes the rare phenomenon of the Northern Lights – luminous bands that bathe the ancient Russian city of St Petersburg in a mystical silvery glow.

ROAST BABY CHICKENS WITH MANGO-CORIANDER SAUCE

6 baby chickens, washed and dried
salt, milled black pepper, paprika
60 ml olive oil
30 ml lemon juice
30 ml crushed garlic
fresh rosemary sprigs
MANGO-CORIANDER SAUCE
5-6 spring onions, sliced
50 g celery, chopped
50 g butter
10 ml curry powder
30 ml cake flour
500 ml cream
2 ripe mangoes peeled stoned and chopped, or 425 g can mangoes, drained and chopped
small bunch fresh coriander, chopped
small bunch fresh chives, chopped
100 g cashew nuts, chopped and roasted
TO SERVE
Roasted Vegetables (page 144)

Set the oven at 180°C. Season the chickens inside and out with salt, pepper and paprika. Place in a roaster. Mix together the olive oil, lemon juice and garlic and brush onto the skin. Sprinkle rosemary sprigs around. Roast for about 50 minutes until the chickens are golden, and thigh juices run clear when pierced with a skewer.
MANGO-CORIANDER SAUCE Fry the spring onion and celery in the butter in a medium saucepan until golden. Stir in the curry powder and flour. Add the cream and mango, and season with salt and pepper. Cover and simmer for about 10 minutes. Add the coriander, chives and cashew nuts and heat through.
TO SERVE Place chickens on warm plates, and serve with mango-coriander sauce and roasted vegetables. SERVES 6

RUSSIAN BLINIS WITH SMOKED SALMON

250 ml cake flour, sifted
1 ml salt
1 egg
200 ml milk
vegetable oil
TO SERVE
mixed salad leaves
250 g sliced smoked salmon
250 ml sour cream
salmon caviar
1 small onion, very finely chopped
3 hard-boiled eggs, finely chopped

Sift the flour and salt into a bowl. Add the eggs and milk and mix to form a smooth batter. Set aside for 30 minutes.

Fry tablespoonfuls of batter in oil in a large non-stick frying pan over medium heat for about 30 seconds on each side until golden and cooked. Lift blinis onto a cooling rack in a very low oven, piling them on top of each other to keep moist. Add more oil to the pan when necessary.
TO SERVE Arrange blinis and salad leaves on plates. Top with smoked salmon, sour cream and caviare, and garnish the plates with onion and egg. SERVES 6

74 ♦ GOURMET HIDEAWAYS

HAZENDAL ESTATE

STELLENBOSCH, CAPE WINELANDS

OLD OAKS DAPPLE THE 18TH CENTURY HOUSE with sunlit textures falling onto the walls, layered with many years of limewash. This play of light and shade on time-softened whiteness, so typical of Cape Dutch buildings, is nowhere more lovely than at Hazendal. The estate is a national monument and one of the few remaining outstanding examples of early Cape Dutch architecture at the Cape.

The first road from Cape Town to Wellington ran along the farm boundary, and the vlei which once lay in its present-day paddocks was a public outspan where Simon van der Stel and other luminaries broke their journeys for refreshment. The original gate posts and the kraal where oxen were outspanned still form part of the werf or farmyard.

In 1699 Hazendal was granted by Governor Willem Adriaan van der Stel to German-born Christoffel Hazewinkel (Haasenwinkel, meaning 'hare's corner'), a messenger of the court. In 1762 it was bought by the Van As family who built the house that still stands. Izaak Bosman bought Hazendal in 1831, forefather to five generations of Bosmans who lived and farmed there until the mid-1990s.

In 1994 Russian-born Dr Mark Voloshin, chairman of the international Marvol Group, became the proud new owner. He has restored the estate to its former grandeur, paying particular attention to the preservation of its cultural heritage and continuing the spirit and tradition of its wine making. A new cellar has been added, and vineyards have been upgraded.

Hazendal now offers some of the most varied and beguiling attractions of any Cape wine farm. These include winetasting and sales, meals at the Hermitage Restaurant at Hazendal, picnics in summer, conference, function and corporate entertainment facilities. Visitors may also view the Marvol Museum of Russian Art and Culture, a brilliant and colourful exhibition of 20th century Russian paintings, icons (traditional objects of the Russian Orthodox Church), objects of decorative art and contemporary Faberge Easter eggs, and The Faberge Showroom, which displays jewellery, crystal, porcelain and eye frames.

Reinvestment in natural and human resources has ensured that this splendid estate stands among the handful of great houses representing our earliest architectural heritage, and that it will endure for the benefit of future generations.

ABOVE *Dr Mark Voloshin at the entrance to Hazendal Manor House, which flaunts one of the most delicately frivolous gables in the Cape.*

EMILY'S BISTRO

WOODSTOCK, CAPE PENINSULA

EMILY'S OPENED ITS DOORS IN THE TRAFFIC-MAD ROODEBLOEM ROAD in Woodstock during 1992, a suburb singled out by a top local magazine as being one of Cape Town's trendy 'hot spots'.

The restaurant started off as a little bistro housed in a 19th century double storey building adjacent to a vibrant area known as District Six which was demolished by the previous government. As does the architecture of the entire street, the quaint building in which Emily's is housed eloquently captures the spirit of a colourful community that once lived, loved, danced, sang and died here. This was the erstwhile address of the local Post Office, and the King Edward letterbox in the wall beside the entrance is still in use.

Since opening, Emily's has evolved into one of the country's finest eateries. From a starting point of Afro-Euro-centric, the food philosophy now makes the strongest single statement for South African food in the country. Each plate becomes a canvas of the very best available ingredients with flavours from all over the continent. On the home front there is "boere-nouvelle": Soweto-surprises, Zulu-zest, Tswana touches, Xhosa-putu, Sotho exotica and mysterious Malay and Indian spices. Patron Peter Veldsman and Chef de Cuisine Johan Odendaal do not neglect their British, French, Italian, Greek, Portuguese and Dutch heritage either, and traditional dishes from Morocco, Sudan, Tunisia, Egypt, Ethiopia, Nigeria, Zaire, Ghana, Ivory Coast, Sierra Leone, Cameroon, Kenya, Mozambique, Mauritius, Angola and Namibia are skillfully recreated. Occasionally a recipe is not altered; sometimes it merely forms a foundation to build a recreation on.

Emily's efforts have found favour with food journalists and restaurant critics, both at home – where Emily's is frequently honoured in Top 10 ratings – and abroad. The New York Times singled the restaurant out as one of the very best in South Africa.

Emily's is also the home of the Culinary Art Institute of Africa (CAIA) where students are trained to enter the hospitality industry. There is a one-year Bed and Breakfast training programme, and professional training over a three-year period culminating in an Associate Diploma, passport to employment anywhere in the world. After two years students may divert to a Catering Certificate course. CAIA graduates differ from those of other South African training establishments, as they are equipped to take responsibility and enter the profession on a high level. Graduates have found employment all over the world, including Botswana, Scotland, Singapore and England. Many, though, choose to remain in South Africa!

ABOVE *Patron Peter Veldsman (seated centre) with Chef de Cuisine Johann Odendaal and students of the Culinary Art Institute of Africa (CAIA).*
RIGHT *Emily's is housed in zany, colour-bright interleading rooms of a time-tattered double storey building. Eclectic decor and bold artworks offset the stylized presentation of hightly original dishes.*

TOP Baked Beetroot with Harissa and Mustard Foam. BOTTOM Pienangvleis.

BAKED BEETROOT WITH HARISSA AND MUSTARD FOAM

24 small beetroot, leaves trimmed
salt, milled black pepper
200 ml Court Bouillon (page 134)
50 ml balsamic vinegar
2 ml Harissa Paste (page 136)
3 egg yolks
30 ml sugar
30 ml prepared English mustard
15 ml finely grated orange zest
TO SERVE
50 large spring onions, lightly poached
50 ml horseradish cream
Potato and Pistachio Wafers (page 142)

Set the oven at 120°C. Wash the beetroot and place in a baking dish. Cover snugly with foil and bake for about 90 minutes until tender. Peel and slice 20 beetroot. Arrange in a flat dish and season very, very lightly with salt and pepper. Cover with plastic wrap and refrigerate.

Purée the remaining four beetroot with the court bouillon in a liquidizer or food processor. Pour into a medium saucepan. Add the balsamic vinegar and harissa paste, cover and simmer gently. Meanwhile place the egg yolks, sugar, mustard and orange zest in a double boiler over simmering water and whisk until hot and thickened. Whisk in the beetroot sauce little by little to form a sabayon. Remove from the heat. Season with a little salt.
TO SERVE Arrange beetroot on warm plates. Dribble with sabayon and horseradish cream. Serve with potato and pistachio wafers. SERVES 10

WINE The pink blush and fine bubbles of Pierre Jourdan Cuvée Belle Rose Cap Classique will be delicious with the beetroot, as the wine has just enough dryness and body to withstand the horseradish.

Peter Veldsman's personal wine choice for the pienangvleis is Groot Constantia Weisser Riesling. Other matches include Spice Route Chenin Blanc (which has big fruit), and Simonsig Gewürztraminer (the perfect spice match),

PIENANGVLEIS

2,5 kg mutton chops, trimmed of fat and wiped clean
vegetable oil, salt, milled black pepper
12 large garlic cloves, peeled and crushed
250 ml hot Veal Stock (page 134)
PIENANG CURRY
2 large onions, finely chopped
50 mm piece green ginger, peeled and finely chopped
6 garlic cloves, peeled and finely chopped
2-3 red or green chillies, seeded and finely chopped
100 ml Sri Lankan Spice Mixture (page 136)
10 ml turmeric
75 ml Tamarind Water (page 136)
TO SERVE
Yellow Rice with Raisins (page 143)
chutney and sambals of your choice

Bring water to the boil in a large saucepan and blanch the meat. Drain, scrape off all the bone dust and pat dry with kitchen paper.

Heat oil in a large saucepan and fry the chops a few at a time until brown. Drain each batch on kitchen paper. Season with salt and pepper. Return the meat and garlic to the saucepan. Add the hot veal stock, cover and simmer for 2-2½ hours until the meat is tender. Cool, then refrigerate until chilled. Remove all the fat that has congealed on the meat. Jug the meat (shred finely with a fork) and discard the bones. Reserve the stock.
PIENANG CURRY Fry the onion in oil in a large saucepan until translucent. Stir in the ginger, garlic and chilli and stir-fry for 2-3 minutes. Stir in the spice mixture and turmeric and cook for another 2 minutes. Moisten with tamarind water. Spoon the shredded meat into the curry mixture with a fork. Add the reserved stock. Simmer uncovered over low heat until fairly dry.
TO SERVE Mould pienangvleis on warm plates and serve with yellow rice with raisins and chutney and sambals of your choice. SERVES 6

WINE JELLY

750 ml dry white wine
1 whole clove
1 cinnamon stick
1 small piece star anise
5 cardamom seeds, lightly crushed
125 ml sugar
20 g (30 ml) gelatine
75 ml muscadel or sherry
about 50 grapes skinned, halved and pipped
TO SERVE
Lemon and Green Peppercorn Ice-Cream (page 148)
Van der Hum Sauce (page 146)
tiny balls of fresh fruit to garnish

Combine the wine, clove, cinnamon, star anise and cardamom in a medium saucepan, cover and heat to below boiling point. Set aside for about 30 minutes for the flavours to infuse.

Remove the spices from the wine, add the sugar and stir until dissolved. Return to the heat and boil for 3 minutes. Remove from the heat. Meanwhile sprinkle the gelatine onto the muscadel or sherry in a small bowl. Allow to sponge, then microwave at full power for 30-40 seconds until clear. Stir the gelatine into the warm wine. Place in a basin of iced water until the jelly just starts to set and thicken.

Lightly spray six dariole moulds with oil. Spoon in a layer of jelly and refrigerate until set. Arrange grape halves on top and cover with another layer of jelly. Use more grapes and jelly until the moulds are full. Cover and refrigerate until set.
TO SERVE Quickly dip the moulds into hot water and unmould the wine jelly onto cold plates. Place a scoop of ice-cream alongside and garnish with Van der Hum sauce, vine curls and fruit. SERVES 6

WINE The nuance of lemon in Neethlingshof Weisser Riesling Noble Late Harvest will bring the flavours of the wine jelly together.

EMILY'S BISTRO ◆ 79

ROSENHOF COUNTRY LODGE

OUDTSHOORN, LITTLE KAROO

ABOVE *Poppy Seed Orange Cakes with Liqueur Oranges, served with a glass of chilled Boplaas Cape White Port from the nearby Little Karoo town of Calitzdorp.*

The placid plains of the Little (Klein) Karoo are cradled in rugged mountain ranges – the Swartberg to the north, and the Langeberg and Outeniquas to the south – which form a natural buffer between the interior and the coastal terrace. The Cango Valley, with its pretty "Ostrich Capital" of Oudtshoorn, is a slim valley between the two mountain ranges.

The only gateway to the high, wide spaces of the interior and the Great Karoo, is through awesome mountain kloofs with long-forgotten names like Attaqua, Platte, Cradock and Caledon, passages so daunting that it wasn't until Friday 28th January 1689, that the first whites journeyed through. The party was led by Ensign Isaac Schrijver. His brief: to find the mysterious Inqua Hottentots, the most powerful of all the Hottentot tribes, who called this valley home. And in the hills lived hardy San (Bushmen). Now long gone, their sojourn here is perpetuated by their paintings which adorn the intricate network of the Swartberg caves. Today visitors from all over the world come to travel the poorts and passes of the Swartberg – the Swartberg Pass, Meiringspoort and Seweweekspoort – and to wonder at their magnificence.

Rosenhof is situated at the outskirts of Oudtshoorn on the main road to the Cango Caves, one of the great wonders of the world, discovered by man in prehistoric times. These are considered to be among the finest examples of dripstone caves in the world, with endless mysterious caverns and chambers lined with aeons-old stalagmites and stalactites displaying the wonder and beauty of the interior of the earth.

Rosenhof, in an elegant Victorian house with original yellowwood beams and ceilings, has spectacular views of the Swartberg mountains, and is named for its lovely garden filled with roses and herbs. Owners Nic and Ferda Barrow have meticulously restored the property. There are several lovely sitting rooms decorated with antiques and rich fabrics, and walls hung with works by well-known South African artists such as Gregoire Boonzaaier, Bettie-Cilliers Barnard, Jan Vermeiren, Claerhout and Ampberger.

Nic is an avid wine collector who maintains a fine cellar for the enjoyment of guests, and Ferda cooks traditional country cuisine with a gourmet touch. On sunny days tea is served in the gazebo, and conference facilities are available in the old wagon-house.

OSTRICH STEAKS WITH COUNTRY MUSHROOM DUXELLE, GINGER CRISPS AND PORT JUS

800 g ostrich fillet steak, trimmed
125 ml port
vegetable oil, butter
salt, milled black pepper
COUNTRY MUSHROOM DUXELLE
1 onion, finely sliced
olive oil
250 g mushrooms, sliced (mix oyster, button and black mushrooms)
GINGER CRISPS
50 g green ginger
TO SERVE
Port Jus (page 140)

Cut the ostrich into twelve thick steaks. Place in a dish, pour over the port and set aside for about an hour.
COUNTRY MUSHROOM DUXELLE Fry the onion in olive oil in a frying pan until golden. Add the mushrooms and fry until golden and soft. Season with salt and pepper.
GINGER CRISPS Peel the ginger and shave thinly, using a vegetable peeler. Deep fry in hot vegetable oil until golden brown. Drain on kitchen paper.
TO SERVE Heat oil and butter in a large frying pan and fry the steaks for approximately 2 minutes on each side until well browned and cooked to the desired degree. Season lightly with salt and pepper. Pour hot port jus on warm plates. Place steaks on top and mushroom duxelle on the steak. Top with another steak and garnish with ginger crisps. SERVES 6

> **WINE** When preparing Rosenhof's recipes, it's fun to serve them with locally-made Little Karoo wines. With the ostrich steak sip Die Krans Cabernet Sauvignon, a partnership which will bring out the best in both the softly-fleshed palate of the wine, and the ostrich, which enjoys a full-bodied wine. Enjoy slightly chilled Boplaas Cape White Port as a refreshing adjunct to the citrussy dessert. Both wines are from nearby Calitzdorp.

POPPY SEED ORANGE CAKES WITH LIQUEUR ORANGES

45 ml poppy seeds
100 ml milk
100 g soft butter
125 ml castor sugar
2 eggs
250 ml self-raising flour
5 ml vanilla essence
ORANGE SYRUP
60 ml orange juice
30 ml castor sugar
10 ml finely grated orange zest
LIQUEUR ORANGES
2 oranges, peeled and sliced
125 ml sugar
125 ml water
15 ml orange liqueur

Set the oven at 180°C. Grease six 200 ml metal dariole moulds. Stir the poppy seeds into the milk and set aside for 1 hour. Cream together the butter and castor sugar. Mix in the eggs one by one. Sift in the flour and fold in with the milk and poppy seed mixture, and the vanilla essence. Spoon the mixture into the moulds, filling each about two-thirds full. Place the moulds on a baking sheet and bake for 20-25 minutes until a skewer comes out clean. As soon as they come out of the oven, pour over the hot syrup.
ORANGE SYRUP Stir the orange juice, castor sugar and orange zest together in a small saucepan until the sugar dissolves. Bring to the boil.
LIQUEUR ORANGES Place the orange slices in a bowl. Combine the sugar, water and liqueur in a medium saucepan and heat, stirring, until the sugar dissolves. Boil for a few minutes until thickened to a light syrup. Pour over the oranges. Cool.
TO SERVE Arrange orange slices on plates. Pour a little liqueur syrup over. Turn out cakes on top. SERVES 6

THE MARINE

HERMANUS, OVERBERG

ABOVE *Liz McGrath is internationally acclaimed for meticulous restoration of her South African hotels called The Collection, The Marine, The Plettenberg (page 24) and The Cellars-Hohenhort (page 52)*
ABOVE RIGHT *Berry Soufflé with Passionfruit Coulis (page 85).*

THE MARINE, SITUATED ON THE CLIFFTOPS ABOVE WALKER BAY in one of the most spectacular locations in Africa, has a colourful and romantic history. A landmark in Hermanus, its distinguished Edwardian silhouette is an icon to generations of holiday-goers who have seen the sleepy seaside village grow up into a sophisticated resort. Today The Marine appropriately ranks with the finest resort hotels in the world.

The history of modern Hermanus starts with a 19th century shepherd, Hermanus Pieters, who brought his flock of sheep into the valley in search of better grazing. He discovered a fresh water spring, which became known as Hermanuspietersfontein. Soon other shepherds followed his lead. They fed on the fish caught off the rocks of Walker Bay and news of the rich hauls spread quickly.

Although Cape Town was still several days' trek by ox wagon over the Hottentots Holland Mountains, the fishermen were undeterred and the settlement grew rapidly. Soon, the place was bulging at the seams and locals began taking in guests. One such was Walter McFarlane who accommodated visitors in his cottage in Main Street – expanding within ten years to become the Victoria Hotel. At the same time General Smut's brother-in-law, Dr Joshua Hoffman, built a sanatorium which led to Hermanus' fabled 'champagne air' achieving international recognition as a cure-all. At the turn of the century the sanatorium became the Windsor Hotel.

Walter McFarlane then built the modest 21-roomed Marine Hotel in 1902. It offered comfortable accommodation but had no electricity or running water in the bedrooms. It did, however, sport two flush toilets on each floor! There have been many changes in ownership since then, each reflecting the mood and fashion of the time. In the early days the flamboyant Lord Craven, a remittance man, made his headquarters here and threw deliciously decadent parties for his many guests. Other early visitors to the hotel included travellers on the steamships of the Union and Castle Lines who escaped to the Cape during the chilly European winter months.

The 1920s were golden years as the Marine played host to the rich and famous, including Princess Alice in 1923. They danced the decade away in the hotel ballroom, to the beat of the Cape's most fashionable big bands of the day.

After years of post-war euphoria, fashions in travel and holidays changed. The impact was sorely felt at the Marine, and the hotel began a sorry decline which ended only in the early 80s when David Rawdon, a hotelier of great style and elegance, came to the rescue. After four years of painstaking renovation, the doors re-opened triumphantly in December 1985.

Thirteen years later, Rawdon was looking for a new custodian to launch the grand old lady into the new millennium. Liz McGrath, internationally acclaimed for her restoration of The Cellars-Hohenort and The Plettenberg became the new owner in March 1998. Eight months later in October that year, the new General Manager Oliver Cooke, opened a now five-star Marine. And in January 2000 the hotel was accepted as a member of Relais & Chateaux.

PARFAIT OF CHICKEN AND DUCK LIVERS WITH GRAPE CHUTNEY AND ROOIBOS JELLY WITH TOASTED BRIOCHE

500 g chicken livers
250 g duck livers
milk, melted butter
1 garlic clove, peeled
2 ml grated nutmeg
5 ml salt, milled white pepper
3 eggs
750 ml cream
45 ml brandy
45 ml Beef Stock (page 134)
TO SERVE
Grape Chutney (page 139)
Rooibos Jelly (recipe follows)
24 peeled grapes
sliced, toasted Brioche (page 145)

Soak the chicken and duck livers in milk for 24 hours. Set the oven at 160°C. Butter a 30 x 8 x 8 cm terrine dish with a lid, or a small loaf tin. Line with greaseproof paper. Brush the paper with melted butter.

Drain the livers (discard the milk) and whizz smoothly in a food processor with the garlic. Season with nutmeg, salt and pepper. Blend in the eggs. Add the cream, brandy and beef stock and purée until smooth. Check the seasoning and adjust if necessary. Push the mixture through a fine sieve into a jug. Pour into the prepared mould and cover with the lid or well oiled foil. Bake in a bain-marie for about 1½ hours until firm to the touch and a skewer comes out clean. If it's not quite done, cook for about 10 minutes more. Remove from the water bath and cool. Chill for 2-3 hours.

Dip the mould into hot water and turn the parfait out onto a board. Remove the paper. (The parfait may be wrapped in plastic and refrigerated for up to 3 days.) TO SERVE Slice the parfait and place on plates. Garnish with grape chutney, rooibos jelly, a dash of olive oil and grapes. Offer with toasted brioche. SERVES 16

WINE The delicate creamy texture of the parfait demands an off-dry wine such as Paul Cluver Gewürztraminer, which has a fruity, spicy taste. Lamb requires an aged merlot, such as Buitenverwachting Buitenkeur.

ROOIBOS JELLY

1 small onion, finely chopped
½ stalk celery, roughly chopped
vegetable oil
30 ml rooibos leaves
375 ml grape juice
375 ml white wine
250 g white grapes, peeled
10 g (15 ml) gelatine

Fry the onion and celery in a little oil in a medium saucepan until translucent. Add the rooibos leaves, grape juice, white wine and grapes. Cover and simmer for 1 hour. Strain through a muslin cloth and hang overnight over a saucepan to drain. Heat the liquid to just below boiling point. Remove from the stove, sprinkle the gelatine onto the surface and stir in until dissolved. Strain into a bowl, cool then chill for 4-5 hours until set. MAKES ABOUT 600 ml

ROAST RACK OF LAMB WITH RAGOUT OF MUSHROOMS, LIVER AND KIDNEYS

8 racks of lamb, each weighing about 350 g (select three- or four-boned racks of lamb)
salt, milled black pepper, olive oil
crushed fresh garlic, fresh rosemary sprigs
RAGOUT OF MUSHROOMS, LIVER AND KIDNEYS
100 g calf's liver, trimmed and cubed
100 g sheep's kidneys, cleaned, trimmed and cut into quarters
butter
500 g mushrooms (mix oyster and wild mushrooms)
TO SERVE
Garlic Creamed Potato (page 141)
Confit of Baby Onions (page 144)
500 ml Port Jus (page 140)
Garlic Confit (page 135)

Trim the lamb bones so they stand about 3 cm clear of the meat. Season with salt and pepper. Brown all over in olive oil in a frying pan. Place in a roaster. Flavour with crushed garlic and tuck rosemary sprigs between the chops.
RAGOUT OF MUSHROOMS, LIVER AND KIDNEYS Fry the liver and kidneys in butter in a frying pan until lightly sealed. Add the mushrooms and season with salt and pepper. Fry for about 5 minutes until tender. Moisten the mixture with a spoonful of red wine jus.
TO SERVE Set the oven at 190°C. Roast the lamb for about 20-25 minutes until cooked to the desired degree.

Shape garlic creamed potato on warm plates. Carve the lamb into chops and arrange on top. Spoon the ragoût and onions alongside. Sauce with red wine jus. Garnish with garlic confit. SERVES 8

BERRY SOUFFLE WITH PASSIONFRUIT COULIS

200 g strawberries or raspberries
50 g butter, melted
castor sugar
5 ml lemon juice
100 ml sugar
50 ml cornflour
80 ml water
8 egg whites
4 eggshell halves
vegetable oil
PASSIONFRUIT COULIS
250 ml orange juice
200 ml icing sugar
10 passionfruit (granadillas)

PASSIONFRUIT COULIS Mix the orange juice and icing sugar in a small saucepan. Heat, stirring until the sugar melts. Cut the passionfruit in half, scoop out the pulp and add to the coulis. Cool.

Brush four teacups with butter. Chill until set. Brush once more with butter and sprinkle with castor sugar. Keep chilled.

Purée the berries. Pour into a medium saucepan. Add the lemon juice and half the sugar. Boil, stirring, until the sugar dissolves. Mix the cornflour into the water. Whisk slowly into the boiling liquid until it becomes thick and clear. Cover and cool.

Whisk the egg white to soft peaks. Add the remaining sugar and whisk until stiff and glossy. Whisk one third of the meringue into the purée. Fold the rest in gently. Fill a piping bag fitted with a large nozzle. Fill the prepared cups. Lightly oil the eggshells and bury them in the soufflés.
TO SERVE Set the oven at 190°C. Bake the soufflés for 12-15 minutes until well risen and golden. Remove the eggshells. Place the cups onto plates. Fill the hollow with passionfruit coulis. Serve, if you wish, with fresh berries. SERVES 4

WINE Match the berries in the soufflé with the raspberry flavour of Pierre Jourdan Cuvée Belle Rose, a deliciously sparkling Méthode Cap Classique.

SHANGANA CULTURAL VILLAGE

HAZYVIEW, MPUMALANGA

The traditional villages of Shangana are nestled in the shade of great ancient African Chestnut trees (called umbhaba trees in the Shangaan language) in a tranquil reserve of forest and grassland. This area, between the Kruger Park and the scenic mountains of Mpumalanga, is the ancestral home of the Shangaan people.

The Shangaan draw their name from Soshangana, a Zulu chief sent by King Shaka to conquer the Tsongas. But Soshangana encountered a peace-loving and prosperous nation and merged with them instead. Dishes prepared by the Shangaan people are distinguished by their use of hot, spicy peppers, introduced centuries ago by Arab traders who plied their wares along the east coast of Africa.

Today the Shangaan culture is not well known, but the people of Shangana have decided it is time to show their pride, rich traditions and dignified society. And so, guests are invited to share their way of life by visiting the villages where they live.

Local craftspeople work and trade at the central market village, and here visitors are led by guides to different kraals. In one, a family may be tending cattle, grinding maize or making traditional beer. In another, the Sangoma or traditional healer is making muti (medicine) from wild herbs (pictured below). Famed for their hospitality, Shangaans welcome the chance to share a midday meal with visitors to their homes.

As the sun is setting, guests may hear the sound of distant drums and the blowing of kudu horns. This signals the evening festival in the kraal of the chief, a dramatic village lit by flame torches and bonfires, where choirs and dancers gather to tell the story of the Shangaan people (left). The wives of the Chief prepare a wide range of traditional foods, served from great iron pots, and invite guests to share a feast that lasts long after the stars have risen in the African sky.

SPICY PEANUT CHICKEN

1 chicken, trimmed and portioned
1 onion, finely chopped
butter, salt, milled black pepper
30 ml chopped fresh herbs (parsley, thyme, oregano), or 5 ml dried mixed herbs
2 ml paprika
2 ml cayenne pepper
4 tomatoes blanched, skinned and chopped
30 ml tomato paste
5 ml crushed garlic
250 ml Chicken Stock (page 134)
100 g crushed peanuts
2 bay leaves
TO SERVE
Pap (page 143)
Spinach with Peanuts (page 143)
Glazed Sweet Potatoes (page 142)

Fry the onion in butter in a large saucepan until golden. Add chicken and fry until lightly sealed on all sides. Season with salt, pepper, herbs, paprika and cayenne pepper. Add the tomato, tomato paste, garlic, chicken stock, peanuts and bay leaves. Cover and simmer gently for about 50 minutes until the chicken is cooked. Serve with the suggested accompaniments. SERVES 8

COAL-ROASTED CORN

4-5 fresh green mealies or sweetcorn
melted butter, salt

Strip the corn of leaves and silk. Brush generously with melted butter and roast on a grid over medium-hot coals for 15-20 minutes until tender and brown. Serve with extra butter and salt. SERVES 4

> **WINE** Oaked chardonnay will do justice to the complex nuances of the chicken, with its richness of nuts and gentle hint of spice. Thelema Chardonnay is an impressive choice. Offer Monis' highly acclaimed Tawny Port with the after-dinner peanut snacks.

MAIZE AND CHEESE BREAD

500 g wholewheat flour
300 ml warm milk
10 g (1 sachet) instant dry yeast
10 ml salt
15 ml brown sugar
150 g packet brown onion soup powder
50 g soft butter
410 g can cream-style sweetcorn
100 g grated cheddar cheese

Place the flour in a large bowl. Mix the milk, yeast, salt, brown sugar, soup powder and butter. Mix into the flour with the sweetcorn and cheese to form a soft dough (add a little extra milk if necessary).

Mould into two loaf shapes and place on greased baking sheets. Cover and set aside in a warm spot to rise until doubled in bulk. Meanwhile set the oven at 180°C. Bake the loaves for about 50 minutes until they sound hollow when tapped. Cool on a wire rack. MAKES 2 LOAVES

TRADITIONAL SWEET PEANUT SNACKS

These traditional sweet treats are usually prepared by stamping the ingredients together to form a stiff paste. If preferred, whizz them in a food processor.

200 g raw, unsalted peanuts
150 g butter
250 ml maize meal or polenta
2 ml salt
125 ml sugar

Fry the nuts in a dry frying pan until golden. Remove from the pan and cool. Add half the butter to the pan and fry the maize meal or polenta until golden. Stamp the peanuts until they are a pasty consistency. Add the remaining butter, salt and sugar, stamping and kneading until well mixed and stiff. Press into a greased dish, flatten well and chill until firm. Slice into small squares, and serve as sweet snacks. SERVES 8-10

SAVOY CABBAGE

HERITAGE SQUARE, CAPE TOWN

ABOVE *The typically Victorian facade of the building makes an impressive entrance to Savoy Cabbage above which Brendhan Dickerson has created an appropriate mini-sculpture.*
BELOW *Caroline Bagley and Janet Telian (left), whose cooking reflects both past and contemporary trends. Spontaneity is the key, and her food is accessible to both the serious foodie and the more casual diner.*

IN WHAT OTHER URBAN BLOCK WILL YOU FIND A LUXURY HOTEL, restaurants, and a specialist wine shop (in what was the kitchen of a modest Georgian house) all clustered around a peaceful, sun-dappled courtyard shaded by the oldest fruit-bearing vine in the Cape? This is also the address of Savoy Cabbage Restaurant and Champagne Bar.

Heritage Square is a unique project that involved the restoration by the Cape Town Heritage Trust of the largest surviving group of derelict eighteenth century buildings in Cape Town. Solid Dutch architecture co-exists with elegant Georgian and Victorian features.

In 1998 Janet Telian, patron chef of Savoy Cabbage, and her partner Caroline Bagley from London were scouting for premises. When they saw the undeveloped section of Heritage Square they knew this was the perfect place. The restaurant opened in August the same year.

Savoy Cabbage is located on the side of the square at 101 Hout Street, originally thought to have been built in 1902 on the site of a demolished town house. However, removal of plaster has revealed that the original structure had not been destroyed but extensively renovated.

Leon Saven's interior design incorporates both a nostalgic sense of Cape history and international contemporary elements. A bricked-in ancient archway, exposed brickwork and original ceilings have been retained, cleverly combined with glass and metal to create an atmosphere of unique elegance. Whimsical cabbage chandeliers were designed by Stephanie Fassler Ross and paintings are by Fred Schimmel. Depending on where you are seated, your perspective changes. If dining upstairs or seated at the champagne bar you look down on the impressive length of the Buitengracht Room or at the bustling entrance. When sitting downstairs, you watch staff and guests going up and down the glass-balustraded staircase.

Although Janet may be seen working with her team in the open kitchen, she prefers the mysteries of her pots to being out front. Her natural heritage is American-Armenian, which is not immediately obvious as an influence on her cooking, unlike her love of classic European cuisine which she augments with a healthy dollop of South African cooking. She is inspired by the simplicity of fresh ingredients. And, although she loves the intensity of garlic and chilli, Janet also relates to gentle tastes and does not believe in spicing up dishes which are not meant to be overseasoned. Menus change frequently, according to market dictates and Janet's creative whim.

The acclaimed Harridans and Pomegranate, both in Johannesburg, first introduced diners to her unpretentious yet elegant cuisine. Savoy Cabbage is her third restaurant, and one that has captured the attention of South Africa's food critics, who have placed it in all the top restaurant listings in the country. More importantly, Savoy Cabbage consistently pleases culinary cognoscenti from all over the world.

BLACK MUSSELS WITH SMOORVIS-FILLED CABBAGE ROSES IN GINGER BROTH

'Smothered Fish' is a traditional South African recipe. Snoek is most often used, though any smoked fish may be used.

6 large cabbage leaves, washed
100 g butter, melted
SMOORVIS
1 onion, chopped
2 green chillies, seeded and finely chopped
vegetable oil
2 potatoes (about 250 g), peeled and cut in 1 cm dice
300 g filleted, skinless smoked fish, roughly flaked
salt, milled black pepper
MUSSELS
36-42 black mussels
250 ml white wine
1 sprig fresh thyme
1 stalk celery, chopped
1 onion, roughly chopped
GINGER BROTH
10 ml crushed green ginger
1 ripe tomato, blanched, peeled, seeded and diced
6 spring onions, sliced
50 ml cream (optional)
sprigs from 1 bunch fresh coriander

Cut out centre ribs of the cabbage leaves. Blanch in salted boiling water for 3-4 minutes until tender. Drain well.

Set the oven at 200°C. Grease a baking sheet.
SMOORVIS Fry the onion and chilli in vegetable oil in a frying pan until translucent. Add the potato and fry until golden and cooked. Gently stir in the smoked fish and season with salt and pepper.

Divide the smoorvis between the cabbage leaves and wrap to resemble a rose. Place on the baking sheet and brush with melted butter. Roast uncovered for 5-7 minutes until the edges are crisp and brown.
MUSSELS Scrub the mussels well. Combine the wine, thyme, celery and onion in a medium saucepan and bring to the boil. Add the mussels, cover and boil until they open. Drain and cool. Retain the stock.
GINGER BROTH Strain the stock into a clean saucepan. Add the ginger broth ingredients and mussels and heat through.
TO SERVE Place cabbage roses in warm bowls. Arrange mussels around and ladle the broth over. SERVES 6-8

WINE Mussels are well matched by sauvignon blanc, a wine which also suits the flavour of cabbage and the smokiness of smoked fish. Springfield Sauvignon Blanc Special Cuvée is a good choice. An alternative wine would be a well-made chenin blanc.

POACHED FENNEL AND STRAWBERRIES IN VANILLA SYRUP

200 ml sugar
400 ml water
1 vanilla pod, split in half lengthwise
2 fennel bulbs, trimmed and cut into quarters, or 6 heads baby fennel, trimmed
18 large, ripe strawberries

Combine the sugar, water and vanilla pod in a wide saucepan. Cover, and simmer for 5 minutes. Add the fennel, cover and poach for about 10 minutes until tender. Drain the syrup into a medium saucepan and boil uncovered until it thickens.
TO SERVE Arrange fennel and strawberries in bowls, pour sauce over. Serve, if you wish, with Fennel and Honey Ice-Cream, page 147. SERVES 6

WINE Meerendal Natural Sweet is delicious with this dessert, as it effectively enhances the gentle vanilla and fruit flavours.

ROAST SPICED LOIN OF LAMB WITH APRICOTS AND ROOIBOS

1,5 kg loin of lamb, boned, trimmed and ready to roll (about 1 kg prepared weight)
125 ml water
125 ml red wine
1 rooibos tea bag
50 g dried or sun-dried apricots
fresh basil leaves, honey
SPICE MIXTURE
5 ml ground coriander
2 ml ground cardamom
2 ml chilli flakes (or more to taste)
2 ml dried ginger
2 ml ground cinnamon
10 ml sea salt
2 garlic cloves, peeled and crushed
RED WINE SAUCE
250 ml Beef Stock (page 134)
1 small onion, chopped
30 g (30 ml) butter
salt, milled black pepper

Lay the meat on a board. Mix together the spice mixture and spread on the inside surface. Cover and set aside in a cool spot for a couple of hours.

Bring the water, red wine and rooibos to the boil in a small saucepan and simmer for about 3 minutes. Strain over the apricots in a bowl and set aside for 30 minutes.

Set the oven at 180°C. Line the lamb with basil leaves. Remove the apricots from the tea mixture (retain for the sauce) and lay on the basil. Roll up and tie with string. Place in a greased roaster and roast uncovered for 25-30 minutes. Check for doneness; roast awhile longer if you prefer your lamb more well done.
RED WINE SAUCE Bring the stock, reserved tea mixture and onion to the boil in a medium saucepan, cover and simmer for about 15 minutes until the onion is soft. Simmer uncovered for a few minutes to thicken slightly. Whisk in the butter. Season with salt and pepper.
TO SERVE Slice the lamb and place on warm plates. Drizzle over a little honey and season with salt and pepper. Offer the sauce separately. SERVES 4

WINE Cordoba Merlot would be a happy match with the lamb, which always enjoys being partnered with a medium bodied red.

SAVOY CABBAGE ◆ 91

SELATI LODGE AT SABI SABI

SABI SAND, MPUMALANGA

SABI SABI PRIVATE GAME RESERVE IS A MAGICAL HAVEN where the peace of the African bushveld rules. As a concession to history, the old steam train era has been recreated in décor rich with railway memorabilia and antiques. An old wagon has been used as a Land Rover 'landing' platform. The farm was never electrified, and it has been kept that way. Nights are lit by flickering oil lamps and lanterns; hot water is provided by gas geysers.

Selati Lodge is smaller and more luxurious than Sabi Sabi's other two camps, accommodating only 16 guests in eight thatched suites, including the Lourenço Marques, Honeymoon and Ivory Presidential Suite. Interiors are sumptuously furnished with antiques, and the walls hung with valuable old documents. Well-travelled trunks, leather suitcases, hat boxes and other accessories of the early days in Africa contribute to an authentically colonial environment.

The lodge was named to commemorate the once-rich and colourful history of the now derelict Selati railway line, commissioned by Paul Kruger while he was President of the Transvaal Republic. The line was laid in the nineteenth century, through what is now Sabi Sabi, providing access to the busy port of Delagoa Bay. Controversy shrouded the construction of the line between 1892 and 1912. The builders, Baron Eugene Oppenheim and his brother Robert, were more intent on making money from selling shares than completing the work. It was later found that 40 kilometres of unnecessary bends and loops in the railway line had been built.

The lounge and bar at Selati Lodge open onto a sheltered leisure and dining deck overlooking open savannah. A nearby waterhole, kept filled by an old windmill, ensures a regular cast of animals who come to drink at sunset. It is a magical spot, providing guests with ringside seats in the theatre of the wild.

Selati's innovative African fusion cuisine may be enjoyed in several different settings, all with spectacular views to the vast plains beyond. The farmhouse kitchen has as its focal point a long oak table laden with brass and copper utensils shining in the warm glow of lamps and candles. Guests may have breakfast and lunch on the cool, shaded timber decks, while dinner is served in an intimate outdoor boma, under a canopy of stars.

EAST AFRICAN BREAKFAST KUKU WITH TOMATO CHUTNEY

250 g rindless back bacon, sliced
vegetable oil
125 g button mushrooms, sliced
2 red or yellow peppers, seeded and sliced
125 g courgettes, trimmed and grated
12 eggs
80 ml cream
10 ml wholegrain mustard
5 ml lemon juice
30 ml chopped fresh oregano
salt, milled black pepper, cayenne pepper

Set the oven at 180°C. Fry the bacon until crisp in oil in a 30 cm frying pan with a metal handle. Add the mushrooms and cook until soft. Stir in the pepper strips and courgettes and cook for about 1 minute more until most of the liquid has cooked away. Remove from the heat.

Beat together the eggs, cream, mustard, lemon juice and oregano and season with salt, pepper and cayenne pepper. Pour into the pan. Bake for about 15 minutes until set and golden. Slice like a tart and serve with tomato chutney. SERVES 6–8

TOMATO CHUTNEY

2 kg ripe tomatoes blanched, peeled and chopped
finely grated zest of 2 lemons
750 g brown sugar
8 whole cloves
1 cinnamon stick
2 bay leaves
500 ml dry red wine

Combine all the ingredients in a large, deep saucepan and bring to the boil, stirring until the sugar dissolves. Simmer uncovered for about 1½ hours until the mixture has thickened to the consistency of jam. Stir occasionally. Pour into hot, sterilised jars and store in the fridge. Serve hot or cool.
MAKES 1 LITRE

CHILLI BEANS

420 g can baked beans in tomato sauce
410 g can butter beans, drained
410 g can red kidney beans, drained
1 large onion, finely chopped
vegetable oil
3 garlic cloves, peeled and finely chopped
3 red chillies, seeded and chopped
15 ml tomato paste
15 ml balsamic vinegar
5 ml ground cumin
10 ml brown sugar
salt, milled black pepper
30 ml chopped fresh basil
30 ml chopped fresh coriander

Fry the onion in oil in a medium saucepan until golden. Add the garlic and chilli and fry for 30 seconds. Add the beans, tomato paste, balsamic vinegar, cumin and brown sugar, and season with salt and pepper. Heat through. Just before serving, stir in the chopped herbs. SERVES 8

WINE Sparkling wine is the perfect choice for an outdoor breakfast. Choose Twee Jonge Gezellen Krone Borealis Brut, a distinguished Méthode Cap Classique wine, which is produced in the Tulbagh valley. Serve it well chilled, or add sliced nectarines, peaches or strawberries for a change of pace.

BOSCHENDAL

GROOT DRAKENSTEIN, CAPE WINELANDS

LESS THAN AN HOUR'S DRIVE FROM CAPE TOWN, surrounded by the magnificent scenery of the Groot Drakenstein valley, you will find Boschendal, probably the finest complex of eighteenth century farm buildings, each a masterpiece of Cape Dutch architecture, still to be found in the Cape.

The Boschendal farm was granted by Governor Simon van der Stel in 1685 to two French Huguenot émigrés, Lanoy and Le Long, who sought sanctuary at the Cape after the revocation of the Edict of Nantes. In 1715 the property was bought by Abraham de Villiers, and remained in his family's possession until 1884. Soon after, it was bought by Cecil John Rhodes to become one of the Rhodes Fruit Farms. Today the property is owned by Anglo American Farms.

The Manor House was completed in 1812 by Paul de Villiers for his bride, Anna Susanna Louw. Between 1974 and 1976 it was restored, authentic in every detail, right down to the dados – wall paintings rediscovered under many layers of paint. The house is furnished as the home of a prosperous rural family, reflecting the transitional period from Dutch to English influences at the end of the eighteenth century. Among its treasures is one of the world's most important collections of Ming porcelain, named kraak porselein, because the Dutch first saw it in the hold of a captured Portuguese carrack.

Elegantly housed in the old wine cellar of the De Villiers' homestead is the Boschendal Restaurant, which serves a sumptuous buffet reflecting French-Huguenot influence on Cape cooking. From November to April Le Pique-Nique offers picnic lunches on the lawns under soaring stone pines. Le Café serves light lunches and teas under spreading oaks outside or inside the old slave quarters of the Homestead. In the original coach house is the Waenhuiswinkel, a gift shop where visitors may select keepsakes from a range of wine, pottery, handcrafts and preserves.

Across the great lawn from the Winery, on the farm Le Rhone, stands the beautifully restored Taphuis, perhaps the oldest building on the property, where visitors can taste and buy a full range of noble Boschendal wines.

SMOKED SNOEK PATE

This traditional Cape-Malay-inspired pâté is included in the picnic baskets at Le Pique-Nique. Snoek is preferred, though any fish may be substituted.

300 g smoked snoek, skinned, filleted and flaked
100 g soft butter
30 ml cream
15 ml lemon juice
10 ml horseradish sauce
salt, milled black pepper

Blend together the snoek and butter in a food processor. Add the cream, lemon juice and horseradish sauce, and season with salt and pepper. Purée until smooth. Scoop into a bowl and chill well before serving with brown bread. SERVES 8

CURRIED BUTTERNUT SOUP

A flavourful soup served in Boschendal Restaurant. Pumpkin may be used instead of butternut. Adjust the amount of curry to suit your taste.

1 kg butternut, skinned and pipped
2 onions, finely chopped
80 g butter
15 ml curry powder
1,5 litres Chicken Stock (page 134)
2 Granny Smith apples, peeled, cored and chopped
250 ml apple juice
salt, milled black pepper

Cut the butternut into 3 cm cubes. Fry the onion in the butter in a large saucepan until translucent. Stir in the curry powder, then add the chicken stock, apple and butternut. Cover and simmer for about 30 minutes until tender. Strain (reserve the stock) and purée in a food processor. Pour back into the saucepan, add the reserved stock and apple juice. Reheat, and season with salt and pepper. SERVES 8-10

VENISON PIE

A favourite winter dish in the Boschendal Restaurant. The cooking time of venison varies, depending on the cut; take this into account when preparing the pie.

1 kg boneless stewing venison, trimmed
vegetable oil, salt, milled black pepper
200 g rindless streaky bacon, chopped
1 onion, finely chopped
1 garlic clove, peeled and crushed
45 ml cake flour
60 ml red wine
500 ml Chicken Stock (page 134)
30 ml red currant jelly
400 g puff pastry
TO SERVE
Glazed Sweet Potatoes (page 142)

Cut the venison into cubes. Lightly brown in batches in hot oil in a medium saucepan. Remove from the pan and season with salt and pepper. Add the bacon to the pan and fry until fairly crisp. Add the onion and garlic, and a little more oil if necessary, and fry until translucent. Stir in the flour then add the wine, chicken stock and red currant jelly.

Return the meat to the pan, cover and simmer gently for 1½-2 hours until tender. Remove the meat from the saucepan and discard any fat. Simmer the gravy uncovered until reduced and thickened. Check and correct the seasoning, pour over the meat and transfer to a pie dish. Cool. TO SERVE Set the oven at 180°C. Unroll the pastry, roll out to fit the pie and cover. Decorate with left-over pastry. Bake for about 30 minutes until crisp, golden and piping hot. SERVES 6

BOBOTIE

1 kg minced beef
3 onions, finely chopped
50 g butter
15 ml curry powder
5 ml turmeric
300 ml milk
4 eggs
3 slices white bread cut into small cubes
30 g dried apricots, chopped
1 Granny Smith apple, peeled, cored
   and finely chopped
50 ml chutney
50 g seedless raisins
30 ml smooth apricot jam
45 ml lemon juice
1 garlic clove, peeled and crushed
salt, milled black pepper, lemon leaves

Set the oven at 160°C. Fry the onion in the butter in a medium saucepan until translucent. Stir in the curry powder and turmeric. Add the mince and stir until lightly sealed. Remove from the heat.

Measure 60 ml of the milk into a medium bowl. Mix in 1 egg and the bread. Add the apricots, apple, chutney, raisins, jam, lemon juice and garlic, and season with salt and pepper. Mix into the meat. Fill a buttered ovenproof dish and press down. Lay lemon leaves on the surface. Seal with foil and bake for 1 hour.

Increase the oven temperature to 200°C. Mix together the remaining milk and eggs, and season with salt. Pour over the bobotie and bake uncovered for 20 minutes until set and lightly browned. Serve with rice and chutney. SERVES 6-8

WINE Smoked fish pâté requires lightly oaked wine; choose Boschendal Chardonnay. The delicate spiciness of the butternut soup requires a medium dry white wine such as Boschendal Chenin Blanc. The spicy-fruitiness of bobotie enjoys a medium sweet wine such as Boschendal Le Bouquet. Venison pie is complemented either by Boschendal Lanoy or Boschendal Merlot. Boschendal Vin d'Or, a crisp, lively sparkling wine is perfect with the rich cheesecake.

MILLE-FEUILLE CHEESECAKE

300 ml milk
6 egg yolks
250 ml icing sugar
5 ml vanilla essence
10 g (15 ml) gelatine
500 g cream cheese
375 ml cream
2 x 400 g rolls puff pastry
30 ml smooth apricot jam

Grease a 24 cm springform cake tin. Scald the milk in a medium saucepan. Beat together the egg yolks and sifted icing sugar until well blended. Mix in the warm milk, then strain back into the saucepan. Stir over low heat until the custard thickens.

Remove from the heat and stir in the vanilla essence. Sprinkle the gelatine onto the surface and stir in until dissolved. Cool to room temperature. Mix in the cream cheese. Whip 250 ml of the cream to soft peaks and fold in. Pour into the prepared cake tin and chill for 3-4 hours.

Set the oven at 180°C. Unroll the pastry and roll out slightly. Cut into 24 cm rounds. Place on baking sheets and bake for about 20 minutes until crisp and golden.
TO SERVE Place a pastry round on a plate and spread with apricot jam. Carefully turn out the cheesecake on top. Whip the remaining cream stiffly. Cut the remaining pastry into eight wedges and place on top, with points facing the centre. Support thicker ends with whipped cream. SERVES 16

CLOCKWISE FROM LEFT *Yellow Rice with Raisins (page 143); Bobotie, Mille-Feuille Cheesecake; Curried Butternut Soup; Smoked Snoek Pâté.*

A DRIVEWAY LINED WITH ANCIENT TURPENTINE AND JACARANDA TREES LEADS TO CYBELE, one of the most glamorous and romantic getaways in Mpumalanga. Cybele is the perfect springboard from which to explore nearby game parks and natural wonders such as God's Window, Bourke's Luck Potholes, Blyde River Canyon and the historical town of Pilgrim's Rest.

CYBELE FOREST LODGE

WHITE RIVER, MPUMALANGA

ABOVE *Executive Chef Wayne Walkinshaw with Sous Chefs Beauty Makou and Gertie Mathebula present Hazelnut Meringues with Berries and Cream (page 99).*

The property dates back to 1889, when the Kruger National Park, now one of the world's prime tourist destinations, was in the early stages of its development. The original farmstead was built as a hunting lodge on 300 acres of African paradise surrounded by timber plantations nudging the boundaries of the park.

Previous owners farmed coffee and macadamia nuts on the land. In the late 1970s barns and tractor sheds were converted into casual rooms for overnight guests in need of a tranquil getaway far from the bright city lights of Gauteng. Barbara and Rupert Jeffries visited in 1978, fell for it, and bought Cybele the following year – even though there was no electricity and no facilities such as a swimming pool. In the ensuing years they have developed Cybele to its present level of luxury, accommodating no more than 30 privileged guests from all corners of the globe.

The upgrading (including the building of no less than seven swimming pools, including private pools for every suite) has made Cybele a hotel of world repute. It was the first property in southern Africa to be granted membership of the exclusive Relais & Chateaux group, and it has been included in top international listings such as British Airways' Top 37 Favourite Hotels in the World and UK Tatler Magazine's 50 Most Outstanding Hotels in the World. Cybele has also been named South Africa's Top Country Hotel.

In terms of luxury, Cybele has come far, but the underlying spirit of relaxation, privacy, service and good food remains unaltered.

TOMATO AND OLIVE TARTE TATIN WITH FETA AND BASIL PESTO

8 tomatoes, blanched and skinned
12 black olives, stoned and quartered
salt, milled black pepper
2 onions, finely sliced
butter, vegetable oil
15 ml brown sugar
30 ml balsamic vinegar
400 g puff pastry
TO SERVE
Basil Pesto (page 138)
2 wheels feta cheese, cut into cubes
18 large fresh basil leaves to garnish

Cut the tomatoes into quarters and gently squeeze out the pips. Arrange in six small baking dishes with the olives. Season with salt and pepper and press down firmly. Fry the onion in a little butter and oil in a frying pan until translucent. Stir in the brown sugar and balsamic vinegar, and cook until caramelized. Top each tart with onion. Cool.
TO SERVE Set the oven at 200°C. Unroll the pastry and cut into circles slightly larger than the baking dishes. Place on the tarts. Bake for about 20 minutes until crisp and golden. Turn out onto plates with the pastry underneath and garnish with basil pesto and feta. Deep fry the basil leaves in vegetable oil and use as garnish. SERVES 6

SEARED BEEF FILLET WITH PARMESAN AND ROCKET

700 g fillet steak, trimmed
crushed black pepper, olive oil
1 large onion, thickly sliced
60 g rocket leaves
100 g shaved parmesan cheese
45 ml chopped fresh parsley
30 ml balsamic vinegar
30 ml olive oil

Slice the steak on the diagonal into twelve steaks about 1 cm thick. Season well with crushed pepper. Fry the onion rings until charred in olive oil in a frying pan. Remove from the pan and keep warm.

Toss together the rocket, parmesan, parsley, balsamic vinegar and olive oil.
TO SERVE Sear the steaks over high heat in olive oil, allowing about 30 seconds on each side. Place on warm plates. Top with rocket mixture, another steak and more rocket. Garnish with onion. SERVES 6

HAZELNUT MERINGUES WITH BERRIES AND CREAM

4 egg whites
300 g sugar
200 g hazelnuts, chopped and roasted
60 ml cake flour
TO SERVE
250 ml cream
berries, fresh mint sprigs, icing sugar

Set the oven at 170°C. Beat the egg white to soft peaks. Add the sugar little by little and continue beating until the mixture is stiff and glossy. Mix together the hazelnuts and flour and fold in.

Line two baking sheets with foil and spray with oil. Make eight flattish rounds from the meringue mixture. Allow space for spreading. Bake for about 25 minutes until crisp and pale golden. Cool.
TO SERVE Place meringues on plates. Garnish with whipped cream, berries, mint and sifted icing sugar. SERVES 8

> **WINE** The boldness of the tomato tart needs a wine with equal oomph, such as La Motte Blanc Fumé. Serve the highly acclaimed Klein Constantia Cabernet Sauvignon by winemaker Ross Gower with the fillet. Eikendal Special Late Harvest is delicious with meringues.

CYBELE FOREST LODGE

SPIER

STELLENBOSCH, CAPE WINELANDS

Historic Spier combines the charm of the world-renowned Cape wine route with the tempting flavours of traditional foods against a backdrop of warm South African hospitality. Several venues dotted about the estate serve food and wine, catering for a variety of pockets and preferences. The Jonkershuis offers a widely varied Cape-Dutch buffet. The Taphuis and Riverside Pub serves pub grub in a relaxed indoor-outdoor setting. Café Spier, backed by the majestic Helderberg mountains and overlooking rolling lawns, serves teas and lunches, and is a picturesque function venue.

Picnics around a duck-dotted lake are popular during the Cape's balmy summer months. Die Opstal can be hired for banquets, weddings and board meetings. A wide range of vegetables which are grown on the farm under the Spier Development Trust initiative may be purchased from the Farm Stall, along with a selection of other local delicacies. An extensive range of wines is available for tasting and for sale in the Wine Centre.

ABOVE *The Spier Manor House contains an important collection of old masters, rare antiques and porcelain.*
BELOW *Ralph Cupido, head chef of the Jonkershuis restaurant with a platter of koeksisters.*

The Dutch name Spier refers to a marsh of reeds or bullrushes and dates back to 1692, when Governor Simon van der Stel granted the land on the banks of the Eerste River to Arnout (or Aarnout) Jansz. The "first river" was so called because it was the first to be encountered by pioneering settlers who crossed it in 1679, leaving the security of the Cape colony in search of new farmlands.

Jansz, a German soldier in the service of the Dutch East India Company, planted the first 200 vines, but it wasn't until 1712 that a substantial quantity of wine was produced by the next owner, Hans Heinrich Hattingh, who recorded 7 leagures from his 12 000 vines in addition to a fine crop of wheat. After Hattingh's death the farm was managed by his widow and her new husband, Willem Riebeeck. In 1736 it was sold to Johannes Groenewald, a horse-breeder, whose son took over in 1748 and again increased the production of wine. In 1765 the farm was bought by Albertus Mijburgh, who constructed additional buildings, including the wine cellar, believed to be the oldest in the country, as well as the most prominent of the twenty-one gables.

In 1781 the farm was bought by Andries Christoffel van der Byl, in whose family it remained for 150 years. It is likely that he restored and added to the beautiful homestead on the site of the original farmhouse. Subsequent owners have included a Mr Cartwright, Mr C T Rhodes, a Mr Keppel and Mr Neil Joubert.

In late 1993 Spier was bought by businessman and former member of Parliament, Dick Enthoven. Charmed by the character of the area, he envisaged the concept of a simple yet elegant cultural village which would encapsulate the enchantment and vibrancy of the winelands. Dick Enthoven has taken on the role of custodian of a special heritage rather than simply enjoying the fruits of land ownership. He sees the rebirth of Spier estate as a means to celebrate the joy of South Africa's transition by breaking down barriers between people through wine, laughter, music, food and art.

FISH FRIKKADELS WITH CHILLI TARTARE SAUCE

500 g filleted, skinless white fish
2 slices stale white bread
1 onion, very finely chopped
1 firm, ripe tomato, finely chopped
60 ml chopped fresh parsley
5 ml crushed garlic
1 egg
5 ml salt
2 ml grated nutmeg
2 ml white pepper
CHILLI TARTARE SAUCE
500 ml Mayonnaise (page 138)
4 small gherkins, drained and chopped
2 hard-boiled eggs, finely chopped
½ red or green chilli, seeded and finely chopped
10 ml lemon juice

CHILLI TARTARE SAUCE Mix all the ingredients together in a bowl. Cover and chill for up to 3 days.

Finely chop the fish and place in a bowl. Soak the bread in water for 5 minutes. Squeeze out all moisture. Mix the bread into the fish with the onion, tomato, parsley, garlic, egg, salt, nutmeg, and pepper. Shape into patties. Shallow fry in medium-hot vegetable oil for about 5 minutes on each side, until golden brown. Serve hot with chilli tartare sauce. SERVES 4

> **WINE** The crisp freshness of Four Spears Sauvignon Blanc will cut through the richness of the fish frikkadels, while Bayview Pinotage with the mutton breyani will make for an authentic Cape eating and drinking experience.

MUTTON BREYANI

1,5 kg lean, boneless mutton or lamb
10 ml crushed green ginger
10 ml crushed garlic
salt
250 ml brown lentils
500 g long grain rice or basmati rice
vegetable oil
6 potatoes, peeled and cut into large cubes
3 large onions, finely sliced
a generous pinch of saffron
50 g butter
6 hard-boiled eggs
MARINADE
250 ml buttermilk
1 large, ripe tomato, finely chopped
3 cinnamon sticks
5 cardamom pods
2 green chillis, seeded and sliced
2 ml turmeric
5 whole cloves
30 ml breyani masala
TO SERVE
Date Salad (page 103)

Place the meat in a bowl and rub in the ginger, garlic and 5 ml salt. Mix together the marinade ingredients, pour over the meat and mix in thoroughly. Cover and set aside in a cool spot for about 3 hours.

Measure the lentils in a small saucepan. Add cold water to cover generously, cover and simmer for 5 minutes. Set aside for 1 hour. Drain, rinse and salt lightly.

Rinse and drain the rice. Heat a little oil in a medium saucepan. Stir in the rice. Add 125 ml hot water and 10 ml salt, cover and cook over very low heat for 5 minutes. Remove from the heat.

Heat more oil in a large, deep cast iron pot with a well-fitting lid and fry the potatoes for about 4 minutes until golden, stirring frequently. Remove from the pot and set aside. Add the onion (and more oil if necessary) and braise for 7-8 minutes, stirring occasionally, until well browned. Remove half the onions from the pot and set aside. Add the meat and marinade to the pot, cover and simmer very gently for 30 minutes. Stir occasionally. Remove the meat from the pot.

Set the oven at 160°C. Place the potatoes in the cast iron pot then half the rice. Arrange the meat on the rice. Sprinkle lentils on the meat, then the remaining rice. Top with the reserved onions. Sprinkle saffron on top, dot with butter and pour over 500 ml hot water. Close the pot, sealing the lid with foil if necessary. Bake in the oven for about 60 minutes until the meat is cooked. Do not open the pot while cooking.
TO SERVE Top the breyani with halved boiled eggs and serve from the pot with date salad. SERVES 10

DATE SALAD

250 g fresh or semi-dried dates
1 onion, finely sliced
salt
2 ml crushed dried red chillies
10 ml sugar
150 ml red wine vinegar

Stone the dates and cut into quarters. Tip into a serving bowl. Sprinkle the onion with salt in a bowl. Pour over plenty of boiling water. Drain well. Add to the dates with the crushed chilli. Stir the sugar and vinegar in a small saucepan over medium heat until the sugar dissolves. Bring to the boil, and pour over the salad.
SERVES 10

ABOVE *Mutton Breyani with Date Salad and sambals.*

BOEBER

There are many recipes for this Cape Malay milk drink, often served as a warm pudding, as it is here. It is always served after sunset on the 15th day of Ramadan to celebrate the middle of the fast.

80 ml sago
200 ml water
125 g butter
250 ml vermicelli
6-8 cardamom pods, lightly crushed
2 cinnamon sticks
125 ml sultanas
1,5 litres full cream milk
125 ml sugar, or to taste
100 ml sweetened condensed milk
15 ml rosewater or 10 ml vanilla essence
50 g blanched almonds (optional)

Soak the sago in the water for 30 minutes. Melt the butter in a medium, deep saucepan. Add the vermicelli and toss with a fork until lightly browned. Add the cardamom, cinnamon and sultanas, then pour in the milk and sugar and bring to the boil. Drain the sago, stir in and simmer uncovered for about 15 minutes until transparent. Stir occasionally. Mix in the condensed milk, rosewater or vanilla essence and almonds and simmer for 5-6 minutes more. Serve hot. SERVES 8-10

WINE Most desserts call for something sweet – although this is a matter of personal preference. The botrytis in Four Spears Noble Late Harvest is a fantastic companion to a rich, creamy boeber.

SPIER ◆ 103

MARINIERE OF SEAFOOD

500 g black mussels
150 g filleted red fish, skin on
150 g filleted white fish, skin on
2 small rock lobsters
8 medium oysters
½ onion, finely chopped
½ stalk celery, finely chopped
1 garlic clove, peeled and quartered
150 g cold butter, cut into small blocks
500 ml dry white wine
1 sprig fresh thyme

Scrub the mussels. Cut each fish fillet into four. Cut the lobsters in half lengthwise and devein. Rinse and open the oysters.

Sweat the onion, celery and garlic in 50 g of the butter in a large covered saucepan. Add the white wine and thyme and simmer for 1-2 minutes. Add the mussels, cover and cook for 2-3 minutes until they open. Strain the stock into a large, clean saucepan.

Gently pull out and discard the mussel beards and arrange mussels in four warm soup bowls. Cover and keep warm.

Add the lobsters to the stock and poach for 3 minutes. Add the fish and poach for about 1 minute until the lobsters and fish are cooked. Add the lobsters, fish and oysters to the bowls, pour over a little of the stock, cover and keep warm.

Measure 400 ml of the stock into a medium saucepan, and whisk in the remaining butter bit by bit. Ladle the sauce over the seafood. SERVES 4

WINE Select an unwooded chardonnay such as Bouchard Finlayson Sans Barrique for seafood. The dessert calls for a wine with spark, which will balance both the fruit and the creamy rice. Offer Graham Beck Brut Blanc de Blancs, or De Trafford Wines' signature white wine, Vin de Paille.

PAN-ROASTED FRUIT KEBABS WITH VANILLA RICE

VANILLA RICE
50 g arborio rice (risotto rice)
60 ml sugar
1 vanilla pod, split in half lengthwise
1 litre full cream milk
250 ml cream
Vanilla Sugar Syrup (page 137)
FRUIT KEBABS
40-50 pieces fresh fruit (pineapple, kiwi fruit, strawberries, grapes, nectarines)
unsalted butter
60 ml Grand Marnier liqueur

VANILLA RICE In a medium saucepan combine the arborio rice, sugar and vanilla pod. Stir in 100 ml of the milk. Cook, stirring, until all the milk has been absorbed. Continue in this way, adding the milk little by little. Add the cream and stir until the rice is tender. Discard the vanilla pod. Pour the pudding into a bowl, cover the surface with plastic wrap to prevent a skin from forming, and chill.
KEBABS Thread the fruit onto skewers.
TO SERVE Spoon vanilla rice onto plates. Pan-roast the fruit kebabs in butter in a frying pan until lightly coloured. Pour over the Grand Marnier and flame. Place the kebabs on the rice. Add the vanilla sugar syrup to the frying pan and bring to the boil. Pour the sauce over the kebabs. SERVES 4

AU JARDIN AT THE VINEYARD

NEWLANDS, CAPE TOWN

Two hundred years ago, the legendary Cape hostess Lady Anne Barnard described the thatched house on the banks of the Liesbeeck River as "our country cottage." As wife of the Secretary to the Governor of the Cape, she had bought the land in 1798 and built a rural retreat far from the formality of the Castle and Government House. Today the Vineyard Hotel stands in its stead, offering, as it did Lady Anne, a tranquil escape from the pressures of the outside world.

More important personages were to follow; the first was Elphinstone Holloway, builder of the Franschhoek pass. Then came John Marshall, president of the Lombard Bank, and Lieutenant General Meade, after whose father Clanwilliam was named. In 1832 the Honourable John Elliot rented the property for a year as a base for his peninsula painting trips with Sir Charles Doyly. Rudyard Kipling stayed there, some say, and TS Elliot certainly dined there.

The Petousis family now owns the meticulously restored Cape Georgian-style 160-roomed hotel situated in three hectares of lush parklands. Attached to the hotel is the independently-run Au Jardin Restaurant, home of great cuisine. Here French Chef-Patron Christophe Dehosse (right) approaches his art with an unerring creativity and style, seamlessly merging classic French cuisine with fine Cape ingredients. Like the hotel, Au Jardin retains the dignity of the gracious old Cape country house it once was. The views, of lavish gardens against the imposing buttresses of Table Mountain, are still as spectacular as those gazed upon by Lady Anne.

PHINDA PRIVATE GAME RESERVE

MAPUTALAND, KWAZULU-NATAL

FOUR INTIMATE, SECLUDED GAME LODGES AWAIT THE WORLD-WEARY TRAVELLER in the heart of Maputaland, a transition zone between the tropics and sub-tropics in South Africa's picturesque KwaZulu-Natal region.

This game-rich area, where the mystery of wild Africa first began, was originally settled by the Temba-Tonga tribe. In the mid-1850s an influx of white hunters arrived and decimated vast herds of game, especially elephant and hippo, for their ivory, and large antelope for trophies. The remaining herds were placed under the protective care of the Mkuzi Game Reserve, proclaimed in 1912. Tragically, rinderpest, tsetse fly and extensive insecticide spraying wiped out much of the remaining game as well as insect, bird life and flora.

In 1990 a group of conservationists acquired a large tract of land between the Mkuzi Game Reserve and Sodwana State Forest Reserve, and founded Phinda Resource Reserve. Systematic restocking of the land has resulted in a private game reserve of unequalled diversity and richness.

Phinda Private Game Reserve is owned and managed by CCAfrica, and offers luxurious accommodation, personalized service, superb cuisine and memorable wildlife experiences.

RIGHT Breakfast served soon after sunrise on a tranquil cruise on the Mzinene River.
BELOW Pawpaw Daquiri (page 108) served with skewers of fresh fruit.

The lodges have been sensitively constructed to suit the location and natural surroundings. On top of the world, with lofty views of the faraway coastal plains of St Lucia beyond the mystical Ubombo mountains, is Phinda Mountain Lodge. Chiselled from rock and indigenous tambouti forest, Phinda Rock Lodge commands beautiful vistas of the Lebombo valley with Leopard Rock as a distant focal point. Emerging from the environment in the form of rough sandstone walls and ochre-packed roofs, the six individually designed suites appear to have been crafted from the very rock itself. En-suite bathrooms, private outdoor showers and plunge pools are tucked away in the forest or suspended from the cliff's edge.

Phinda Forest and Phinda Vlei Lodges nestle in the dappled shade of a rare sand forest. The glass-encapsulated suites of Forest Lodge are set on stilts above the forest floor, reflecting the textures of the surrounding wilderness, and drawing you into the magic world of the indigenous fauna and flora. Vlei Lodge has a sophisticated African theme, with glassed suites built on timber frames. Each suite has a private leisure deck with its own plunge pool, affording the ultimate luxury in this wildlife haven.

The Phinda lodges span seven specialised eco-systems ranging from sand forest to ilala palm veld. This abundance and diversity enables a wide variety of adventure activities for guests – game viewing in open vehicles, guided bush walks beneath the cool forest canopy, canoeing or riverboat cruising on the Mzinene River which winds through the reserve, and evening sundowner cruises to enjoy the spectacular birdlife.

Trips to the Maputaland coastline can be arranged for scuba diving, snorkelling and big game fishing, bringing Phinda's magic full circle. No one will ever leave Phinda without lingering memories of this thriving wilderness wonderland.

SAUSAGE STACKS WITH CORN AND CHEESE CAKES

12 pieces thin boerewors or beef sausage
Ghee (page 135) or vegetable oil
CORN AND CHEESE CAKES
1 litre Chicken Stock (Page 134)
50 g butter
300 ml maize meal or polenta
340 g can whole kernel corn, drained
150 g (375 ml) grated mild cheddar cheese
4 large spring onions, finely sliced
2 ml Tabasco pepper sauce
salt, milled black pepper
3 eggs, lightly beaten

CORN AND CHEESE CAKES Bring the chicken stock to a boil in a large saucepan with 15 ml of the butter. Add the maize meal or polenta and stir quickly to mix. Cover and cook undisturbed over very low heat for 15 minutes. Remove from the heat and stir in the remaining butter, corn, cheese, spring onion and Tabasco. Season with salt and pepper. Mix in the eggs.

Heat a little ghee or oil in a frying pan and drop in spoonfuls of the corn mixture. Fry until golden on each side. Keep warm. TO SERVE Fry the sausage in ghee or oil in a frying pan. Stack with corn and cheese cakes. SERVES 6

MANGO AND CHILLI RELISH

1 ripe mango peeled, pipped and sliced into matchsticks
2 red chillies, sliced, seeded and finely chopped
1 red onion, finely chopped
50 ml red wine vinegar
2 ml brown sugar
½ bunch fresh coriander leaves, chopped

Mix together the mango, chilli, onion, vinegar and brown sugar. Cover and set aside for 3-4 hours for the flavours to mingle. Just before serving, stir in the coriander. SERVES 8

AFRICAN BANANA CHUTNEY

125 ml sugar
250 ml white wine vinegar
1 dried chilli, sliced
2 cardamom pods, lightly crushed
2 ml cumin seeds
1 bay leaf
4 nearly ripe bananas, peeled and sliced

Combine the sugar, vinegar, chilli, cardamom, cumin and bay leaf in a medium saucepan. Heat slowly, stirring until the sugar dissolves. Cover and simmer for about 5 minutes for the flavours to infuse. Add the banana and simmer uncovered for about 3 minutes until the bananas are soft and the syrup has thickened. Bottle in a hot, sterilized jar. MAKES ABOUT 500 ml

PAWPAW DACQUIRI

6 tots light rum
juice of 1 lime
60 ml Vanilla Sugar Syrup (page 137)
¼ pawpaw, peeled, pipped and puréed

Place all the ingredients in a cocktail shaker, over crushed ice. Shake well and pour into cocktail glasses. SERVES 4

WARM BEEF SALAD WITH BACON AND BLUE CHEESE DRESSING

500 g fillet steak, cut into 4 steaks
salad leaves
Ghee (page 135)
1 avocado
croûtons
BACON AND BLUE CHEESE DRESSING
6 rashers rindless streaky bacon, chopped
125 ml olive oil
45 ml wine vinegar
50 g blue cheese, crumbled
salt, milled black pepper

Breakfast with a difference: Muesli layered with yoghurt; Sausage Stacks with Corn and Cheese Cakes; Mango and Chilli Relish; African Banana Chutney.

BACON AND BLUE CHEESE DRESSING
Fry the bacon until crisp in a little ghee. Drain and crumble into a jug. Mix in the olive oil, vinegar and blue cheese, and season with salt and pepper.
TO SERVE Arrange salad leaves on four plates. Grill or panfry the steaks in a little ghee for 2-3 minutes on each side until cooked to the desired degree. Place on the leaves and garnish with avocado and croûtons. Pour over the dressing. SERVES 4

MARINATED TOMATO WITH CHILLI, MINT AND MOZZARELLA

6-7 plum tomatoes
18-21 slices mozzarella cheese
CHILLI MINT DRESSING
60 ml chopped fresh mint
2-3 red chillies sliced, seeded and finely chopped
30 ml balsamic vinegar
100 ml olive oil
salt, milled black pepper

CHILLI MINT DRESSING Mix together the mint, chilli, balsamic vinegar and olive oil and season with salt and pepper.
TO SERVE Slice the tomatoes in three, cutting only three-quarters of the way through. Tuck mozzarella into the cuts of the tomatoes and arrange on a plate. Pour over the dressing and set aside to marinate for about 2 hours before serving. SERVES 6

> **WINE** Serve well-chilled sparkling wine with the breakfast spread, even if pawpaw daquiris are part of the line-up. JC le Roux Pinot Noir, a complex Méthod Cap Classique with a biscuity flavour, will be delicious. A full-bodied oaked chardonnay is needed by the beef salad, especially to cope with the blue cheese in the dressing. Offer rich and toasty Hamilton Russell Chardonnay. However, if you are serving the tomato and butternut salads as well, perhaps an easy-drinking blended wine would be a better idea: Buitenverwachting Buiten Blanc or Vergelegen Vin de Florence.

ROASTED BUTTERNUT AND CORN SALAD

Pumpkin may be used instead of butternut in this recipe.

500 g butternut peeled, seeded and sliced
olive oil, balsamic vinegar
salt, cracked black pepper
2 corn on the cob, sliced
salad leaves
45 ml chopped fresh oregano

Set the oven at 180°C. Arrange the butternut in a baking dish. Drizzle olive oil and balsamic vinegar over and season with salt and cracked pepper. Bake uncovered for about 35 minutes until golden and tender.
　Cook the corn slices in salted water for about 10 minutes until tender. Drain. Arrange the corn, butternut and salad leaves on a plate. Garnish with oregano. Dress with a little olive oil and balsamic vinegar. SERVES 6-8

Warm Beef Salad with Bacon and Blue Cheese Dressing; Marinated Tomato with Chilli, Mint and Mozzarella; Roasted Butternut and Corn Salad.

PHINDA PRIVATE GAME RESERVE ◆ 109

KAROO VETKOEK SCHWARMAS

'Fat cakes', may be served with apricot jam. At Dennehof they are served as picnic fare, and for a light meal.

sliced cold lamb, chicken or fish
vegetable oil
VETKOEK
500 ml white bread flour
10 g (1 sachet) instant dried yeast
15 ml sugar
2 ml salt
300 ml warm water
15 ml wine vinegar
15 ml vegetable oil
MID-EASTERN YOGHURT SAUCE
250 g cream cheese
80 ml plain yoghurt
30 ml lemon juice
15 ml olive oil
2 garlic cloves, peeled and crushed
2 ml salt
2 ml dried oregano
2 ml cumin seeds

VETKOEK Sift the flour, yeast, sugar and salt into a bowl. Add the warm water, vinegar and oil and mix to form a soft dough. Add a little extra warm water if necessary. Place the dough in a warm, oiled bowl, cover and set aside in a warm spot until doubled in bulk.
MID-EASTERN YOGHURT SAUCE Mix together all the ingredients in a small bowl. Cover and chill.
TO SERVE Heat vegetable oil in a large frying pan. Drop in generous spoonfuls of dough and shallow fry over gentle heat for 5-6 minutes until golden and cooked through, turning frequently. Drain well on kitchen paper and keep warm. Slice open and fill with lamb and yoghurt sauce.
SERVES 6

WINE Enjoy Glen Carlou Pinot Noir with both these dishes, it will meet the demands of the olives and lemon in the chicken, as well as the spices in the vetkoek schwarmas.

CHICKEN WITH GREEN OLIVES AND PRESERVED LEMONS

1 large chicken, trimmed and portioned
olive oil
5 ml ground ginger
5 ml ground cumin
5 ml ground paprika
2 ml turmeric
2-4 garlic cloves, peeled and crushed
3 onions, roughly chopped
250 ml hot Chicken Stock (page 134)
60 ml chopped fresh parsley
salt, milled black pepper
juice of 2 lemons
peel from one large Preserved Lemon cut into strips (page 135), or substitute lemon juice and thin strips of lemon rind
250 ml pitted green olives

Place the chicken portions in a flat dish. Combine 60 ml olive oil, ginger, cumin, paprika, turmeric and garlic in a small saucepan. Warm gently. Pour over the chicken. Cover and set aside for several hours, or overnight in the fridge.

Brown the onion in olive oil in a large saucepan. Remove from the pan and set aside. Add the chicken pieces and marinade and fry until golden. Return the onion to the pan with the stock and parsley, and season with salt and pepper. Cover and simmer for 40 minutes. Turn the chicken occasionally. Add the lemon juice, lemon and olives and simmer for 15 minutes until the chicken is cooked.

Lift the chicken pieces and onion onto a warm dish. Skim the sauce and pour over. Serve with couscous or rice. SERVES 4

DENNEHOF KAROO GUEST HOUSE

PRINCE ALBERT, GREAT KAROO

In 1835 a young countrywoman, just married, moved into the new farmhouse built for her by her husband Gert Bothma. Surrounded by aged cypress trees, it was named Dennehof (cypress place). It stood at the foothills of the awesome Swartberg mountains, on the fringe of a tiny Karoo village laid out in a green and fertile valley – Prince Albert.

The young couple planted vines and fruit orchards, soon building a reputation for wine, brandy and fine vinegars as well as the potent distillation "witblits." Karoo hospitality being what it is, many a visitor must have gone on his way nursing an unforgettable hangover.

Mrs Bothma was the granddaughter of the founder of Prince Albert, Zacharias de Beer – an ancestor of the late DP leader Zach de Beer – who was granted a loan farm in 1762 and named it "Qweeckvalleij", the valley of cultivation. Today the town is still renowned for its superb Karoo lamb and fruit, including olives, as well as its warm-hearted hospitality towards travellers crossing the great spaces of this vast land.

And so too, at Dennehof, which has recently become a National Monument and Prince Albert's first Satour-accredited guesthouse. Mrs Bothma's barn and dairy have been converted into simple guest cottages where visitors may enjoy high-quality budget accommodation in surroundings of utter tranquility.

The Dennehof cottage, the Wagon Shed and the Olive House next door have crisp, simple furnishings evocative of Greek island homes, and have become a favourite Karoo location for food and fashion crews. Although most of her guests self-cater, owner Elaine Hurford will, between writing travel books, prepare meals for small groups booked well in advance. While making good use of local produce such as lamb, olives, feta cheese, figs or apricots, it is invariably presented with a middle-Eastern or Mediterranean twist.

ROZENHOF RESTAURANT

GARDENS, CAPE TOWN

ABOVE *The team who have been at Rozenhof since the restaurant opened: Rachel, Sindiswa, Liziwe, Robert Mulders with Louisa Malherbe (seated in front), Nosisa and Lilly.*

ROZENHOF RESTAURANT IS IN PICTURESQUE KLOOF STREET, the heart of 'old' Cape Town adjoining the original gardens of the Dutch East India Company. Established by Jan van Riebeeck in 1652, the Company's Garden was a vast orchard and vegetable garden which supplied fresh provisions not only to the company's small band of settlers, but also to ships rounding the southernmost tip of Africa. Fresh drinking water was abundant, crops flourished, and soon demand outstripped supply. So began the legendary hospitality which gave Cape Town its earliest name: Tavern of the Seas.

In the eighteenth century, the city's aristocrats resided alongside gracious canals in fine Victorian and Georgian houses in the areas today known as the Gardens, Long Street, Kloof Street and the Heerengracht. Long Street, the hub of the hospitality area, was lined with hotels, bottle stores and tiny shops even then offering a cosmopolitan range of fare including Greek, Swiss, Portuguese, Italian and Austrian. Streets in the Gardens are still imbued with a sense of history from the architectural gems that abound. Rozenhof occupies one of them, an authentic Cape Georgian house with title deeds dating back to 1852.

Before opening as a restaurant in November 1984, the characterful building had served as a private residence, a hostel for young ladies and a brothel. At one time it was a boarding house run by Evelyne Ford Malan, mother of Group Captain Aaolphus Gysbert "Sailor" Malan, the first South African to win the D.S.O. in the Second World War. The building has retained its beautiful origins with yellowwood ceilings, brass chandeliers and original artworks contributing to an elegant, welcoming atmosphere.

Robert Mulders is a charming host who runs the front-of-house operation, while in the kitchen Louisa Malherbe creates innovative, seasonally-slanted, continental menus with a team headed by Lilly Mbazwana. Only the freshest ingredients are used at Rozenhof, which ensures a consistently high standard of cuisine, and amply reflects the natural bounty of the Cape.

TOMATO AND BOCCONCINI SALAD WITH HERB PESTO

large bunch rocket leaves
6 tomatoes, sliced
250 g bocconcini
Mixed Herb Pesto (page 138)

Arrange rocket on a plate. Top with sliced tomatoes, bocconcini and pesto. SERVES 6

BABY CHICKENS WITH ROASTED GARLIC AND PANCETTA, AND ROSEMARY DEMI-GLACE

6 small baby chickens
1 onion, roughly chopped
olive oil
375 ml dry white wine
500 ml light Chicken Stock (page 134)
2 sprigs fresh rosemary
24 garlic cloves, peeled
salt, milled black pepper
24 thin slices pancetta
Rosemary Demi-Glace (Page 140)

Cut the chickens in half. Fry the onion in olive oil in a roaster on the stovetop until translucent. Remove from the pan and set aside. Add the chickens and brown gently. Remove from the pan and set aside. Stir the wine and chicken stock into the pan and bring to the boil. Add the onion, chickens and rosemary. Cover and simmer for about 20 minutes until the chickens are cooked.

Cool the chickens in the pan juices. Remove the breast bones. (Add bones and roasting juices to the demi-glace.)

Place the garlic cloves in a small saucepan and add cold water to cover. Cover and simmer for 15 minutes. Drain.
TO SERVE Set the oven at 200°C. Place the chickens skin side up in a lightly oiled roaster. Season lightly with salt and pepper. Cover each bird with two slices of pancetta. Scatter the garlic around and bake uncovered for about 20 minutes until the pancetta is crisp, the chickens are hot and the garlic is golden.

Pool sauce on warm plates, top with a chicken and scatter garlic around. SERVES 6

WINE With the tomato and bocconcini salad, serve an unwooded chardonnay or cinsaut, slightly chilled. Chicken calls for a New World shiraz with upfront fruit, or a good, fruity unwooded pinotage like Simonsig Pinotage, which has the warm spiciness of the reds of southern France. As it's not over-sweet, the dessert would be well served by sparkling wine such as Villiera Tradition Brut.

LEMON AND BASIL MOUSSE WITH STRAWBERRY SALAD

100 ml castor sugar
200 ml water
100 ml finely chopped fresh basil leaves
finely grated zest of 3 lemons
45 ml lemon juice
10 g (15 ml) gelatine
375 ml cream
350 g strawberries
60 ml smooth apricot jam

Stir the castor sugar and half the water together in a saucepan over low heat until dissolved. Boil for 1 minute. Reserve half the syrup. Set aside 15 ml of the chopped basil. Add the remainder and the lemon zest to the other half of the syrup. Cool.

Sprinkle the gelatine onto the lemon juice in a cup. Place in a pan of simmering water and stir to dissolve. Pour into the basil lemon syrup.

Whip the cream to soft peaks and fold in the gelatine mixture. Slice the strawberries. Place a few slices in six moulds. Spoon in the mousse, cover and refrigerate for about 4 hours until set.

Melt together the apricot jam and remaining water. Strain into a bowl. Add the reserved basil and syrup.
TO SERVE Unmould the mousses onto plates. Drizzle with apricot glaze and surround with strawberries. SERVES 6

 THE PRIVATELY-OWNED SABI SAND RESERVE, proclaimed a wildlife conservation area even before the Kruger Park, boasts a colourful and turbulent past. The ghosts which roam its history were traders in ivory and slaves, big game hunters, prospectors, raiding bandits and fortune-seekers. Their paths were engraved in the African landscape, showing the way for the Voortrekkers and their wagons in the 1830s and later, the transport riders carrying supplies from the coast to the eastern Transvaal goldfields.

Singita, meaning "miracle" in the local Shangaan language, was designed around the theme of the original hunting lodge on the site. Today, two luxurious lodges, Ebony and Boulders, blend perfectly with the surrounding African bush. Ebony Lodge has nine double suites with private swimming pools overlooking the Sand River. Sophisticated colonial interiors are complemented by interesting relics which include antique furnishings from the old lodge. There's a sumptuous library lounge with fireplace and a walk-in wine cellar. Bookshelves are lined with Africana, and a computer allows guests to access e-mail, or keep up with world events on the Internet.

SINGITA PRIVATE GAME RESERVE

SABI SAND, MPUMALANGA

The luxurious contemporary African Boulders Lodge is just 500 metres downstream. The nine suites offer floor-to-ceiling views of open plains across private swimming pools. A 12 000 bottle underground wine cellar entices guests to make personal selections of wine to accompany their meals. Between game safaris, a resident healthcare specialist will minister to your needs on the private deck beside your pool, offering a massage, aromatherapy or reflexology treatment.

Today, Singita is one of the most exclusive private game reserves in southern Africa offering stunning viewing of the Big Five. Occupying a vast 18 000 hectares, guests are ensured one of the lowest population densities in the Mpumalanga lowveld. To experience Singita is to savour Africa in its original form, and to depart – all too soon – unforgettably enriched.

ABOVE *Sundowners and snacks served deep in the bush on the evening game drive.*
BELOW *The formal dining room at Boulders Lodge.*

CUMIN-GRILLED PORK FILLET ON PEANUT SAMP AND BEANS AND BUTTERED SPINACH WITH CITRUS-GINGER GLAZE

6 large pork fillets (about 1,5 kg)
7 ml dried chillies
7 ml ground cumin
1 cinnamon stick
6 whole cloves
10 ml milled black pepper
125 ml soy sauce
1 onion, peeled and roughly chopped
4 garlic cloves, peeled
125 ml olive oil, extra for cooking
CITRUS-GINGER GLAZE
1 litre orange juice
250 ml golden syrup
10 ml cumin seeds
20 ml crushed garlic
20 ml crushed green ginger
3 red chillies, seeded and finely chopped
salt, milled black pepper
segments cut from 1 peeled orange
TO SERVE
Buttered Spinach (page 144)
Peanut Samp and Beans (page 142)
Zhug (page 139)

Place the pork fillets in a flattish dish. Roast the chillies, cumin, cinnamon and cloves in a dry frying pan over gentle heat. Grind in a pestle and mortar. Mix in the pepper and soy sauce. Fry the onion and garlic in olive oil until golden. Add to the soy sauce mixture. Whizz in a food processor until well blended. Slowly add the olive oil. Pour the marinade over the pork fillets and set aside for about 24 hours to marinate.
CITRUS-GINGER GLAZE Boil the orange juice uncovered in a medium saucepan until reduced to 250 ml. Add the golden syrup, cumin, garlic and ginger and simmer gently uncovered for a further 3-4 minutes. Add the chilli and orange segments.
TO SERVE Grill or panfry the pork fillets until done to the desired degree (they should still be pink in the centre). Form hot samp and beans into 10 cm rounds on plates. Top with hot buttered spinach. Slice the pork and arrange on top. Pour the glaze around. Offer zhug separately. SERVES 8

SESAME BEEF SALAD

400 g rump or sirloin steak
15 ml crushed garlic
15 ml ground coriander
5 ml cracked black pepper
45 ml olive oil
250 ml sesame seeds
butter, vegetable oil
mixed salad leaves
½ cucumber, finely sliced
1 tomato, finely cubed
1 small onion, finely sliced and deep-fried
leaves from ½ bunch fresh coriander
CHILLI DRESSING
30 ml fish sauce
30 ml lime or lemon juice
½ red or green chilli, seeded and finely chopped
10 ml brown sugar

Trim the steak. Combine the garlic, coriander, pepper, olive oil and sesame seeds in a food processor and blend smoothly. Spread evenly onto the steak. Fry in hot butter and vegetable oil until done to the desired degree. Cool.
TO SERVE Arrange salad leaves, cucumber and tomatoes on plates. Slice the steak thinly and arrange on the salads. Blend together the dressing ingredients, drizzle over the salad and garnish with deep-fried onion and coriander leaves. SERVES 4

> **WINE** Blended white and red wines would enhance the pleasure of the sesame beef salad. Opt for Warwick Trilogy (usually a fine merging of cabernet sauvignon, merlot and cabernet franc) or Stellenzicht Blanc-Semillon, a sophisticated, unusual blend.

POTATO, SPINACH AND FETA PIE

4 potatoes (about 500 g)
1 bunch spinach, well washed
2 onions, sliced
salt, milled black pepper
2 bunches leeks, sliced
olive oil
10 ml dried oregano
15 ml Garam Masala (Page 136)
10 ml turmeric
5 sheets phyllo pastry
100 g butter, melted
2 wheels feta cheese
60 ml sesame seeds

Boil the potatoes in their jackets. Peel and slice fairly thickly. Drain the spinach, cut out the tough stems and tear the leaves into small pieces.

Fry the onions and leeks in olive oil until golden. Add the oregano, garam masala and turmeric. Remove from the heat and add the potato, spinach and crumbled feta. Season with salt and pepper.

Butter a small frying pan with a metal handle. Layer in the phyllo sheets, brushing them with butter, and allowing plenty of overhang. Spoon in the filling and wrap up. Brush with remaining melted butter and sprinkle with sesame seeds.
TO SERVE Set the oven at 180°C. Bake the pie for about 20 minutes until crisp, golden and piping hot. SERVES 8

Zhug (page 139, foreground). On the tray: Potato, Spinach and Feta Pie; Cumin-Grilled Pork Fillet on Peanut Samp and Beans and Buttered Spinach with a Citrus and Ginger Glaze; Sweet Potato Pudding.

SWEET POTATO PUDDING

BISCUIT CRUST
100 g cashew nuts
400 g crunchy biscuits
125 g butter, melted
FILLING
250 g sweet potato, skinned and cubed
200 g cashew nuts
finely grated zest of 1 lemon
500 ml castor sugar
15 ml sifted cocoa powder
8 eggs, separated
PASSIONFRUIT COULIS
pulp of 6 passionfruit (granadillas)
   (or 2 X 115 g cans)
15 ml castor sugar
15 ml cornflour
30 ml cold water

BISCUIT CRUST Set the oven at 180°C. Whizz the nuts and biscuits in a food processor until finely crumbled. Mix in the butter. Press the mixture into a large, greased quiche tin. To make individual desserts, press into greased 7 cm ring moulds set on a greased baking sheet. Bake for about 10 minutes until lightly browned.

FILLING Cook the sweet potato in boiling water until tender. Drain. Whizz the cashew nuts in a food processor until finely crumbled. Blend in the sweet potato, lemon zest, castor sugar, cocoa, butter and egg yolks.

Whip the egg white stiffly and fold in. Pour into the quiche tin or moulds. Bake for 20 minutes. Reduce the oven temperature to 160°C and bake for about 15 minutes more until set. A large tart will require an extra 20-30 minutes' cooking time.
PASSIONFRUIT COULIS Mix the passionfruit pulp and sugar in a saucepan and bring to the boil. Mix together the cornflour and water, stir in and simmer until the sauce thickens. Cool.
TO SERVE Turn out or slice the pudding and serve with whipped cream, sugared lemon rind and passionfruit coulis. SERVES 12

> **WINE** Pork fillet teamed with such a rich, tangy sauce would be delicious with a pinotage such as those made by Bellingham and Kanonkop. Sip Pongrácz Méthode Cap Classique made by the house of JC le Roux with the sweet potato pudding.

SINGITA PRVATE GAME RESERVE ◆ 117

CLOETE'S AT ALPHEN

CONSTANTIA, CAPE PENINSULA

ABOVE *Nicky and Dudley Cloete-Hopkins in front of the historical wine cellars on the Alphen estate.*

Alphen estate, an elegant cluster of historical buildings, nestles in lush parklands at the gateway to the Constantia valley, birthplace of South African wines. The estate has been owned by the Cloete family since 1850 and is presently in the care of Nicky and Dudley Cloete-Hopkins.

Cloete's Restaurant extends through several rooms of the double-storey Manor House, one of the great houses of the Cape: the formal Agterkamer, the Heerenkamer, hung with French paintings and engravings, and the Cullinan Room, a private dining room which accommodates parties of up to ten. Warm and generous hospitality has reigned supreme here since the house was built in the mid-1700s. Other buildings on the estate include an even older Jonkershuis, the Victorian Dower House, and the long, whitewashed wine cellars that overlook lawns and aged oak trees.

Wandering through Alphen's grand antique-filled rooms, gleaming with the patina of polished wood or strolling in the dappled shade of ancient oaks and plane trees, it's not hard to conjure up images of ghosts of the past. There's Lord Charles Somerset, mounted on a stallion with hounds baying at his heels, arriving for the hunt breakfast; army doctor, Dr James Barry, fighting a pistol duel with Sir Josias Cloete on the back steps (they both missed, and at her death Barry was discovered to be a woman!) Other distinguished visitors who have passed through Anton Anreith's carved and marbled front door include Princess (later Queen) Frederika of Greece, who arrived with Jan Smuts, Prime Minister of South Africa and a Cloete family friend, writers Mark Twain and George Bernard Shaw, and statesman Cecil Rhodes.

Squirrels still frolic in oaks standing proud in manicured gardens, just as they did in days gone by. In Cloete's Restaurant old fashioned values merge with today's global culinary trends in fine haute cuisine prepared from the freshest produce the Cape has to offer.

TARTARE OF FISH WITH OLIVE OIL AND LIME JUICE

600 g filleted fish, trimmed
1 onion, very finely chopped
15 ml snipped fresh chives
15 ml finely chopped spring onion
1 tomato, blanched, peeled, seeded and diced
juice of 4 limes
100 ml olive oil
Tabasco, salt, milled black pepper
grapefruit slices

Pull out all the fish bones with tweezers. Chop fish into 5 mm cubes and place in a bowl. Mix in the onion, chives, spring onion, tomato, lime juice and olive oil, and season with a few drops of Tabasco, salt and pepper. Cover and chill for 1-2 hours.
TO SERVE Drain the tartare and plate in circular moulds on plates. Garnish with grapefruit. SERVES 4

PROVENÇAL LAMB RACKS WITH TOMATO AND ROSEMARY SAUCE

2 x 8-rib lamb racks, trimmed
salt, milled black pepper, vegetable oil
200 g fresh white breadcrumbs
15 ml finely chopped fresh parsley
15 ml finely chopped garlic
Dijon mustard
TOMATO AND ROSEMARY SAUCE
1 large onion, finely sliced
3 garlic cloves, peeled and finely sliced
olive oil
1 large sprig fresh rosemary
4 large tomatoes, blanched, peeled, seeded and chopped
15 ml tomato paste
250 ml water

Season the lamb with salt and pepper. Seal in vegetable oil in a frying pan, make sure it is still raw inside.
  Mix together breadcrumbs, parsley and garlic. Using a pastry brush, coat the racks with a thin layer of Dijon mustard. Press on a layer of crumb mixture. Place in a roaster.

TOMATO AND ROSEMARY SAUCE Fry the onion and garlic in olive oil in a frying pan until translucent. Add the rosemary, tomato, tomato paste and water, and season with salt and pepper. Simmer uncovered, stirring occasionally, for about 15 minutes until richly coloured and slightly thickened.
TO SERVE Set the oven at 250°C. Roast the lamb uncovered for 20-25 minutes, depending on size of chops. Remove from the oven and allow to rest for 10 minutes. Slice into portions. Spoon tomato and rosemary sauce onto warm plates, top with lamb and garnish with rosemary. Serve with Potatoes with Fresh Thyme, page 142. SERVES 4

> **WINE** Serve Sémillon Reserve from Constantia Uitsig with the tartare of fish; it will not be overwhelmed by the citrus flavour of the limes and has an aftertaste which complements the fish. Klein Constantia Marlbrook, a wooded Bordeaux-style blend of merlot and cabernet, is vigorous enough to complement the strong flavours of tomato and herbs in the lamb recipe.

ORANGE BLOSSOM CREME BRULEE

6 egg yolks
100 ml castor sugar
500 ml cream
100 ml milk
10 drops orange essence
brown sugar

Set the oven at 140°C. Lightly whisk together the egg yolks and castor sugar. Whisk in the cream, milk and orange essence. Strain into individual ramekins. Bake in a bain-marie for about 45 minutes until set. Chill for at least 1 hour.
TO SERVE Sprinkle the crème brûlée with brown sugar and caramelize under the oven griller. SERVES 4

> **WINE** Buitenverwachting Rhine Reisling has a smooth, soft finish to go with the creaminess of the crème brûlée. It is also low in sugar, which is perfect for the delicate nuance of the orange essence.

CLOETE'S AT ALPHEN

STEEPED IN TRADITION AND HISTORY, THE COACH HOUSE IS SET IN 500 HECTARES of rolling farmlands on the Agatha hills at the foot of the majestic Drakensberg (dragon mountains). The hotel stands on the site of what was once a coaching halt used by transport riders of the Zeederberg Coach Company. They carried supplies from the railhead at Pietersburg to the Leydsdorp goldfields during the gold rush of the 1880s. Thrilling stories of half-forgotten journeys are legion, often involving intrepid, well fortified drivers – sometimes carrying equally inebriated passengers – who braved swollen rivers and awesome mountain passes, not to mention attacks by lion, buffalo and thieving highwaymen. These tortuous routes were the only way open to public transport before the advent of the railways in 1916, when the Selati Line was built.

The original rough and ready wayside inn belonged to two gentlemen, Messrs Plange and Altenroxel, and consisted of a small farmhouse and several rondavels. The guests' 'bathroom' was a hollowed-out tree trunk, the kitchen was open to the elements, and most of the meals were cooked in three-legged potjies! John Buchan, secretary to Lord Milner, is believed to have stayed and written The African Colony here after the end of the Anglo-Boer conflict. Some years later the hotel's name changed from Altenroxel's to Strachan's Hotel, in deference to its new owner, Mrs Strachan. In 1983 the old building was transformed into the Coach House, which proudly offers gracious comfort and understated elegance to travellers on the old coach road en route to the Lowveld game farms and the Kruger Park.

More mangoes, lychees, avocados, papayas, macadamias, bananas, tea and coffee are produced in the Northern Province than in any other part of the country. This abundance of fresh produce finds its way into the hotel kitchen, where the commendable principle of simple but delicious food, impeccably prepared and offered at a fair price, is applied. The Coach House is a fine hotel set in one of the most beautiful parts of Africa.

THE COACH HOUSE

AGATHA,
NEAR TZANEEN,
NORTHERN PROVINCE

ABOVE *Guy and Jane Matthews, owners of The Coach House, with long-time chef Lucas Ndlovu.*
ABOVE LEFT *The walk-in wine cellar is a wine-lovers dream, edge to edge with bins of neatly labelled bottles.*
OPPOSITE PAGE TOP *Mango and Prawn Bava (page 122)*

BUTTER FRIED TROUT WITH MACADAMIA AND MUSHROOM STUFFING AND PECAN LEMON BUTTER

6 medium trout, boned from the stomach
salt, milled black pepper, butter
MACADAMIA AND MUSHROOM STUFFING
100 g macadamia nuts, chopped
150 g button mushrooms, wiped and finely sliced
2 garlic cloves, peeled and crushed
finely chopped fresh herbs: parsley, dill, thyme
PECAN LEMON BUTTER
200 g butter
45 ml lemon juice
50 g pecan nuts, chopped

Rinse the trout, pat dry and season inside and out with salt and pepper.
MACADAMIA AND MUSHROOM STUFFING Fry the macadamia nuts and mushrooms in a little butter in a medium saucepan until the nuts are golden and the mushrooms are soft. Add the garlic and herbs, season with salt and pepper, and cook for 30 seconds.
  Heat 150 g butter in a clean frying pan until sizzling. Lay in the trout open side down, and fry until the butter browns. Turn fish onto their sides, and fill the cavities with a little of the stuffing. Cook for 2-4 minutes on each side over moderate heat until cooked through.
PECAN LEMON BUTTER While the trout are cooking, melt the butter in a medium saucepan. Stir in the lemon juice and pecan nuts and sizzle until golden.
TO SERVE Lift the trout onto warm plates and serve on rocket leaves with hot pecan lemon butter. SERVES 6

MANGO AND PRAWN BAVA

3 ripe mangoes, halved and pipped
36-48 cooked, deveined prawns
cayenne pepper, lemon wedges
CURRIED MAYONNAISE
15 ml finely chopped onion
1 garlic clove, crushed
olive oil
15 ml curry powder
5 ml tomato paste
5 ml apricot jam or mango chutney
250 ml Mayonanaise (page 138)

Cut the mangoes round the equators and remove the pips. Shell the prawns.
CURRIED MAYONNAISE Gently fry the onion and garlic in olive oil in a small saucepan until translucent. Add the curry powder. Remove from the heat. Stir in the tomato paste and apricot jam or chutney. Mix in the mayonnaise.
TO SERVE Place the mangoes on plates. Fill the hollows with a few prawns and top with a little mayonnaise. Add more prawns and mayonnaise. Dust with cayenne pepper and place lemon wedges alongside. SERVES 6

> **WINE** A lively, sparkling start to the meal would be Pongrácz, a fine Méthode Cap Classique made by the house of JC le Roux, which would meet the fruity demands of the mango bava. Ken Forrester Chenin Blanc, a "just-dry food wine with serious intent" would be delicious with the trout, balancing both the flavour of the fish and the richness of the pecan lemon butter. Roast beef deserves a flavorsome red such as Welgemeend Estate Reserve, a wine with long lasting flavours. Finally, procure Nederburg Private Bin S354 to accompany the macadamia pie. A blend of weisser riesling and gewürztraminer, it has a ripe but uncloying sweetness to compliment a nutty desert.

RARE ROAST BEEF WITH YORKSHIRE PUDDING AND MANGO SALSA

2 kg beef sirloin on the bone, wiped
4 garlic cloves, peeled and crushed
cake flour, salt, milled black pepper
butter, vegetable oil
375 ml Beef Sock (page 134)
125 ml red wine

Set the oven at 180°C. Rub the meat with crushed garlic, dust with flour and season with salt and pepper. Heat butter and oil in a roaster on the stove-top and brown the meat all over. Roast uncovered in the oven for 60 minutes (if the weight of your joint varies, calculate 20 minutes per 500 g).

Remove the meat from the roaster, tent with foil and keep warm while preparing the gravy. Pour off all but a film of fat, and blend in a little flour. Stir in the stock and red wine and boil, stirring constantly, for 5-6 minutes until smooth and thickened. Season with salt and pepper. Strain into a gravy boat and keep hot.
TO SERVE Slice the beef and serve with hot gravy, Yorkshire pudding and mango salsa. SERVES 6-8

MANGO SALSA

2 large, ripe mangoes, peeled and diced
30 ml finely chopped spring onion
1-2 small red chillies, sliced and seeded
60 ml shredded fresh basil leaves
20 ml chopped mango atjar
salt, milled black pepper

Mix ingredients together in a bowl. Cover and chill. SERVES 6

MACADAMIA PIE

Rich Shortcrust Pastry (page 145)
200 g macadamia nuts, roughly chopped and roasted in a dry pan
60 ml cake flour, sifted
125 ml castor sugar
60 ml maple syrup
2 eggs
100 g butter, melted
30 ml icing sugar

Roll out the pastry on a floured surface and line a 26 cm flan tin. Place in the fridge while preparing the filling. Set the oven at 180°C.

Set aside quarter of the nuts for the topping. Mix together the remaining nuts with the flour, castor sugar, maple syrup and eggs. Mix in half the butter. Pour into the pastry case and bake for about 30 minutes until set.

Brush the tart with the remaining melted butter and scatter over the remaining nuts. Sift the icing sugar on top. Brown under the oven grill until golden and glazed; watch carefully, as the sugar may burn. Serve with ice-cream or whipped cream. SERVES 8-10

YORKSHIRE PUDDING

150 ml cake flour
1 ml salt
3 eggs
250 ml milk
dripping or vegetable oil

Set the oven at 200°C. Sift the flour and salt into a bowl. Blend in the eggs and milk until smooth. Pour into a jug.

Pour a little dripping or oil into patty pans and place in the oven until smoking hot. Pour batter into the moulds until two-thirds full and bake for about 15-20 minutes until well risen and golden. 15 minutes will make them creamy in the middle. Bake longer for crisper puddings. Turn out and serve with the roast beef. SERVES 8

THE COACH HOUSE ◆ 123

RHEBOKSKLOOF
PAARL, CAPE WINELANDS

RHEBOKSKLOOF IS ONE OF THE MOST PICTURESQUE WINE FARMS IN THE WESTERN CAPE. Its vineyards straddle two small valleys at the north-west end of the Paarlberg, with blue and gold views of the Swartland and the mountains towering above Wellington. The nearby Paarl Nature Reserve is home to the endemic antelope, the grey rhebok (also called vaalribbok), for which the estate is named.

The first owner of the property, Dirk van Schalkwyk, was granted the title deeds by Cape governer Simon van der Stel on 19 August 1692. An early dwelling erected at about this time has been meticulously restored as the main homestead (photographed left). A later dwelling, built by Petrus van der Merwe in 1797 and now restored to original Cape Dutch splendour by Daljosaphat Restorations, serves as the estate's guesthouse. The distinctive gable bears the initials of van der Merwe and his wife.

Between the first and second World Wars, the farm was split up into several smaller estates which were happily re-consolidated in September 1986 by a proud new owner. The farms of Waterpoel, St Felix, St Peters, St Martin and Bonne Espoire were restored to their heritage and once more became part of the great history of Rhebokskloof. Today's Rhebokskloof is one of the few privately owned independent wine estates in South Africa. It extends over 415 hectares, of which 92 hectares are under vines for wines, and another 45 hectares are cultivated for table grapes. Sensible diversification led to the planting of stone fruit orchards, and in 1991 the first consignment of apricots was exported, with plums being sold to an enthusiastic local market.

Rhebokskloof's motto – 'A Journey of the Senses' – precisely sums up the visitor's experience. Guests are invited to taste top quality wines in special tasting rooms housed in the majestic cellars (photographed below), or to dine at the estate's two restaurants, the Victorian and the Cape Dutch. Both are named for the architectural style of the buildings they occupy.

In appropriate harmony with the seasons, guests dine indoors in winter, and out of doors in summer. Winter dinners offer gourmet delights in intimate and cosy dining rooms; in summer the backdrop changes to soaring mountains and lush vineyards, with beautiful gardens and ponds dotted with ducks in the foreground.

ABOVE *Fish Tournedos with Mussel Risotto Dumplings (page 125).*

TRIO OF ROSTI WITH RATATOUILLE AND CAMEMBERT, SMOKED SALMON TARTARE AND CHICKEN AND MUSHROOM RAGOUT

mixed salad leaves and herbs
cherry tomatoes
Sun-Dried Tomato Vinaigrette (page 138)
ROSTI
7 large potatoes
2 eggs
1 onion, grated
salt, milled black pepper, grated nutmeg
vegetable oil
SMOKED SALMON TARTARE
150 g smoked salmon, cut into thin strips
60 ml Crème Fraîche (page 135) or sour cream
6-8 spring onions, finely chopped
15 ml finely chopped onion
15 ml finely chopped gherkins
5 ml chopped capers
lemon juice
RATATOUILLE
1 onion, chopped
olive oil
½ aubergine, diced
1 courgette, diced
½ each red, green and yellow pepper, diced
15 ml tomato paste
2 ml crushed garlic
15 ml chopped fresh thyme
1 large tomato blanched, skinned and chopped
50 g camembert cheese, sliced
CHICKEN AND MUSHROOM RAGOUT
1 filleted skinless chicken breast, finely diced
100 g button mushrooms, finely chopped
4 spring onions, finely chopped
125 ml cream
30 ml chopped fresh parsley

SMOKED SALMON TARTARE Mix the ingredients together and season with salt, pepper and lemon juice. Cover and chill.
RATATOUILLE Fry the onion in olive oil in a medium saucepan until translucent. Add the aubergine, courgette and pepper, cover and sweat for about 5 minutes until tender. Add the tomato paste, garlic and thyme, and season with salt and pepper. Cover and cook gently for 5 minutes more. Add the chopped tomato. Keep warm.
MUSHROOM AND CHICKEN RAGOUT Fry the chicken, mushroom and spring onion in vegetable oil in a medium saucepan for 2-3 minutes. Add the cream and cook uncovered until thickened. Add the parsley and season with salt and pepper. Keep warm.
ROSTI Shortly before serving peel and grate the potatoes. Drain well in a strainer set over a bowl. Mix in the eggs and onion, and season with salt, pepper and nutmeg. Divide the mixture into eighteen balls and shallow fry in hot oil for about 5 minutes on each side until golden and cooked through. Drain well on kitchen paper.
TO SERVE Arrange salad leaves on plates. Top six rösti with ratatouille and a slice of camembert and gratinate under the oven grill. Place alongside the salad. Add two more rösti to each serving. Top one with smoked salmon tartare and the other with warm chicken and mushroom ragoût.

Garnish with cherry tomatoes and fresh herbs. Drizzle with sun-dried tomato vinaigrette. SERVES 6

WINE Menus at the Victorian Restaurant have been composed to enhance the estate's wines. Serve Rhebokskloof Chardonnay Grande Reserve with the rösti, and Chardonnay Sur Lie with the fish.

FISH TOURNEDOS WITH MUSSEL RISOTTO DUMPLINGS

2 fillets fish, each about 800 g, skinned (choose one red and one white fish fillet)
30 ml chopped fresh fennel
30 ml chopped fresh coriander
lemon juice, sea salt
vegetable oil, butter
carrot pearls (from carrot butter sauce)
TO SERVE
Mussel Risotto Dumplings (page 143)
Deep-Fried Vegetables (page 144)
Carrot Butter Sauce (page 140)

If the fish fillets are too thick to roll up, cut a slice off the thickest part. Place one fillet on a piece of plastic wrap. Scatter over the fennel and coriander and season with lemon juice and sea salt. Place another fish fillet on top. Roll tightly in plastic wrap, then in foil. Freeze for 3-4 hours until firm. Unwrap and cut into tournedos about 2 cm thick. Tie securely with string.
TO SERVE Heat oil and butter in a large frying pan and fry the fish tournedos until golden brown and cooked through (about 3-4 minutes on each side).

Arrange fish, risotto dumplings and deep fried vegetables on warm plates. Drizzle with carrot butter sauce and garnish with carrot pearls. SERVES 6

GARONGA SAFARI CAMP

MAKALALI WILD LIFE CONSERVANCY, NORTHERN PROVINCE

A CENTURY AGO THE KARONGA PEOPLE SPOKE OF GARONGA, the big tusked one "who roamed this land before man's fences blocked his path". Now, with fences coming down, elephant walk this land again, along with rhino, lion, kudu, waterbuck and countless other creatures. It is as if this land, in all its abundance, is celebrating new life.

In 1996 Bernardo Smith set about finding an ideal location for setting up an exclusive safari camp. He found it here, near Hoedspruit in South Africa's Northern Province. In June 1997 Garonga took down the fences bordering neighbouring Makalali Private Game Reserve and opened its doors not only for guests, but also for the free migration of animals.

Garonga nestles in a bushveld haven below the Drakensberg. Knobthorn, jackalberry and marula trees grow in profusion. There are no lights by night and no traffic noise by day. Garonga is a place to nourish the soul and its owners delight in sharing the abundance of this African sanctuary.

The design has evolved around the natural flow of African living. There are six luxurious en-suite half tent, half hacienda rooms, each with its own deck overlooking a water course and

indoor and outdoor showers. The use of earthen columns recreates the crumbled spires of termite mounds and roughly plastered walls reflect the sands of a North African oasis, redefining the age-old meaning of a place where travelers may stop in peace and enjoy the shelter of a natural haven. For the ultimate luxury, the Hambledon Suite offers a private pool and sala with unsurpassed bushveld views. Its interior is a fusion of Africa and the East, combining a strong Indonesian/Balinese theme with colonial accents.

Guests find inspiration in nature, tracking wildlife before dawn or by moonlight, learning the names of trees and the habits of birds. They are encouraged to walk close to the animals, to sleep out on open platforms in the treetops, and to observe the constellations in the vast African sky. Time spent here is time to replenish lost energy. Others come simply to anchor themselves to the earth, empty their minds, eat wonderful food, sleep deeply and unwind in the aromatherapy sala.

Garonga's elegant, modern cuisine suits all palates and caters for all types of diets. Good use is made of local, seasonal produce, including wild fruits, berries and game such as impala, wildebeest and guinea fowl. The land is beautiful. The soil is rich and deep. It gives life – and this life-giving force is celebrated each day as guests watch the changing seasons at Garonga, and experience the kind of holistic wildlife experience many come to Africa to find. If each guest takes a deeper understanding of wilderness away with them, then the owners of this special place will have fulfilled their ambition to share their place of peace.

BREAD WITH ROASTED VEGETABLES

1,5 litres cake flour
125 ml grated parmesan cheese
10 g (1 sachet) instant dried yeast
5 ml salt
10 ml sugar
60 ml olive oil
250 ml warm milk
375 ml warm water
1 red and 1 yellow pepper, seeded and cut into large pieces
2 courgettes, sliced
6 baby corn, cut in half lengthwise
6 sun-dried tomatoes in oil
grated parmesan cheese
EGGWASH
1 egg
30 ml milk

Sift the flour into a bowl. Stir in the parmesan cheese, yeast, salt, sugar and olive oil. Stir in the warm milk and enough of the warm water to make a soft, pliable dough. Cover and place in a warm spot until doubled in bulk.

Set the oven at 180°C. Grease a 26 cm ring cake tin. Knock down the dough and roll into a 26 cm rectangle. Arrange the vegetables on top, with the tops sticking over the edge. Fold over the lower edge to secure the vegetables like an envelope. Roll into a circle and place in the baking tin. Cover and set aside to rise until doubled in bulk. Mix together the egg and milk and brush onto the dough. Sprinkle with parmesan cheese. Bake for about 50 minutes until the loaf is golden and crisp, and sounds hollow when tapped. Cool on a rack.
MAKES 1 LOAF

POACHED FRUIT FLAVOURED WITH LEMONGRASS AND STAR ANISE WITH CINNAMON-HONEY YOGHURT

750 ml water
250 ml sugar
30 ml whole star anise
1 cinnamon stick
2 stalks lemongrass, cut in half lengthwise
½ pineapple, peeled and halved
6 kiwi fruit, peeled and sliced
250 g melon balls
CINNAMON-HONEY YOGHURT
350 ml Greek yoghurt
15 ml honey
5 ml ground cinnamon

Whisk the water and sugar together in a medium saucepan over medium heat until the sugar has dissolved. Add the star anise, cinnamon and lemongrass and boil for 5 minutes.

Add the pineapple and simmer uncovered for about 5 minutes until tender. Cool to room temperature.

Add the kiwi fruit and melon. Set aside for 2-3 hours before serving, to allow the flavours to be absorbed.
CINNAMON-HONEY YOGHURT Mix the ingredients together and chill.
TO SERVE Tip the fruit and syrup into a serving bowl. Serve the cinnamon-honey yoghurt separately. SERVES 6

> **WINE** If you like things spicy and decide to increase the chilli in the fish recipe, select an off-dry gewürztraminer such as the one from Neethlingshof to do the honours. Alternatively, a crisp, lively, aromatic white blend would be delicious. Offer Van Loveren Colombard-Chardonnay.

FISH BAKED IN BANANA LEAVES WITH CHILLI, LEMONGRASS AND CORIANDER, WITH RED PEPPER AND COCONUT CREAM SAUCE

6 portions filleted fish, each about 140 g
salt, milled black pepper, lemon juice
400 g can coconut cream
1 lemon, sliced
5 ml cornflour
CHILLI, PEPPER AND COCONUT PASTE
1 red pepper, cored and roughly chopped
2 spring onions, trimmed and roughly chopped
2 large garlic cloves, peeled
2 cm piece green ginger, peeled
½ red chilli, seeded and chopped
1 stalk lemongrass, roughly chopped
small bunch fresh coriander

Set the oven at 200°C. Cut 12 pieces of banana leaves, approximately 8 cm x 20 cm. Place on a worktop in the form of six crosses. Cut a few diagonal slits into each portion of fish and place on the leaves. Season with salt, pepper and lemon juice.
CHILLI, PEPPER AND COCONUT PASTE Place all the ingredients into a food processor and whizz to form a fairly smooth paste. Add about 100 ml of the coconut cream; reserve the remainder for the sauce.

Spread a little of the paste on the fish and top with slices of lemon. Wrap the fish securely in the banana leaves and tie the parcels with raffia or string. Place in a baking dish and bake uncovered for approximately 20 minutes until the fish is cooked.

Meanwhile pour the remaining paste into a small saucepan. Mix the cornflour into the remaining coconut cream, add to the pan and cook, stirring for about 5 minutes until thickened. Season with salt and pepper.
TO SERVE Place the fish parcels on warm plates and offer the hot sauce separately.
SERVES 6

HIGHGROVE HOUSE
HAZYVIEW, MPUMALANGA

The spectacular Mpumalanga Lowveld is an unspoiled world of gentle country pursuits and rural tranquillity. This physically diverse region stretches from the urban sprawl of Gauteng through misty hills and undulating vales of the Eastern Highlands, past rugged escarpments and majestic mountains of the high-lying plateaux, to the sparse bushveld and savannahs of big game country and luxurious game reserves.

These peaceful places once echoed with the clattering ox wagons of Voortrekkers, rang with sounds of battle during the Anglo-Boer war, witnessed the plunder (and ultimate demise) of slave traders, pioneering gold-diggers, raiding bandits, fortune seekers and ivory hunters. Wild, wonderful, desperate times; gone, though not forgotten, as tales of those early days are told and retold round crackling bushveld fires.

In the heart of this beautiful area, near Hazyview, a graceful country inn has been established on the edge of the escarpment, just four hours' drive from Gauteng. With remarkable foresight, Peter and Mary Terry (left) recognized the potential of the property when Highgrove Farm came up for sale in 1989. Around the turn of the last century it was a chilli farm, hacked from the untamed bushveld and lovingly nurtured by one Colonel Wicks, whose ghostly presence may still be felt in the historical main buildings on still evenings. Today the crops that grow in the lush soil are avocados and bananas.

The old farmstead has been masterfully restored and transformed into an elegant country lodge, with delightful garden suites added, and the surroundings landscaped into gardens perfumed by nature's ambrosial scents. Aged jacaranda trees (above left) provide an enchanting entrance avenue.

There is a wonderful atmosphere of congeniality, created by the warm greeting of friendly staff who combine attentive service with friendliness and care. A fine collection of antiques and Persian carpets adorns the reception rooms, warmed by crackling log fires when winter's chill sets in. To further pander to the senses, the aromas of good living fill the air with fragrances of flowers, herbs, cooking and fine wines.

Pause a while in the intimate bar or on the spacious colonial verandah before entering the romantic, candle-lit dining room for a gourmet experience. Each meal is memorable, as specialities of the house are exquisitely created and served with South Africa's finest wines. Old world charm and courtesy are the order of the day in this gracious country home from home.

SMOKED SALMON ON CRISP NOODLE CAKES WITH AVOCADO AND HORSERADISH CREAM

2 avocados
200 g sliced smoked salmon
salmon caviar, fresh coriander sprigs, toasted sesame seeds
NOODLE CAKES
100 g egg noodles
vegetable oil
salt, milled black pepper
VEGETABLE JULIENNE
1 red onion, finely sliced
sesame oil
1 carrot, finely sliced
½ red pepper, seeded, and finely sliced
½ green pepper, seeded, and finely sliced
12 mangetout, sliced into julienne strips
HORSERADISH CREAM
150 ml Crème Fraîche (page 135)
50 ml cream cheese
15 ml creamed horseradish
15 ml chopped fresh parsley

NOODLE CAKES Cook the noodles in salted boiling water until just tender. Drain and dry. Divide into four bundles and fry in vegetable oil in a frying pan until crisp on both sides. Drain on kitchen paper. Season with salt and pepper and keep warm.
VEGETABLE JULIENNE Stir-fry the onion in sesame oil in a hot wok or frying pan until translucent. Add the remaining vegetables and stir-fry until limp. Remove from the heat and season with salt and pepper. Cool.
HORSERADISH CREAM Mix together all the ingredients and season with salt and pepper.
TO SERVE Peel, stone and fan the avocados on four plates. Place noodle cakes in the centre. Top with horseradish cream, vegetables and smoked salmon. Garnish with caviar, coriander, and sesame seeds. SERVES 4

> **WINE** Smoked salmon and sauvignon blanc have a natural affinity; offer Steenberg Sauvignon Blanc Reserve with this starter. To accompany the duck you couldn't do better than to serve Hamilton Russell Pinot Noir.

ROASTED BREAST OF DUCK ON A WARM SALAD OF TOMATOES, BEANS AND PEAS

4 pekin duck breasts, skin on, trimmed
100 ml Basil Pesto (page 138)
olive oil
15 ml chopped fresh thyme leaves
salt, milled black pepper

WARM SALAD OF TOMATOES, BEANS AND PEAS
2 red onions, finely sliced
2 garlic cloves, peeled and crushed
16 cherry tomatoes, halved
100 g cooked green peas
100 g canned red kidney beans
8 fresh basil leaves, shredded
TO SERVE
Thyme Jus (page 140)

Set the oven at 180°C. Lift the duck breast skins and spread pesto underneath. Rub with olive oil and prick all over to release excess fat. Sear in a hot frying pan to seal on both sides. Place in a roasting dish and season with thyme, salt and pepper. Roast uncovered for about 20 minutes; the breasts should still be pink inside.
WARM SALAD OF TOMATOES, BEANS AND PEAS Fry the onion and garlic in olive oil in a frying pan until translucent. Add the remaining vegetables and basil and heat through. Season with salt and pepper.
TO SERVE Spoon salad onto warm plates. Slice duck breasts and arrange on top. Drizzle thyme jus around. SERVES 4

SPICY BLACK MUSHROOM SOUP WITH PESTO

150 g chopped onion
2 garlic cloves, peeled and crushed
50 g butter
30 ml cake flour
7 ml curry powder
15 ml tomato purée
15 ml fruit chutney
300 g large black mushrooms, sliced
1 Granny Smith apple, peeled, cored and chopped
1 litre Beef Stock (page 134)
250 ml red wine
salt, milled black pepper
TO SERVE
Basil Pesto (page 138)

Fry the onion and garlic in the butter in a medium saucepan until golden brown. Stir in the flour and curry powder. Add the tomato purée, chutney, mushrooms and apple. Pour in the beef stock and red wine, and season with salt and pepper. Cover and simmer for 45 minutes until the vegetables are tender.
TO SERVE Ladle the soup into bowls and garnish with basil pesto and croûtons. SERVES 4-6

VEGETABLE TOWER TOPPED WITH CAMEMBERT, AND RED PEPPER SAUCE

4 red or yellow peppers, seeded and sliced
4 medium courgettes
4 large black mushrooms, wiped and peeled
1 medium aubergine, sliced
4 large pattipans, sliced
olive oil
125 g camembert cheese
TO SERVE
Roasted Red Pepper Sauce (page 140)

Preheat the oven griller. Arrange the vegetables in a roasting pan and brush generously with olive oil. Grill until golden brown and lightly charred; remove as and when ready. Peel the skin from the peppers. Set the oven at 180°C.
TO SERVE Stack the vegetables on four plates. Top with a wedge of camembert. Bake until the cheese melts. Serve with roasted red pepper sauce. SERVES 4

WINE The spiciness of the soup is brilliantly offset by Vergelegen Mill Race Red Bordeaux blend, a wine with attractive plummy, ripe berry and wood vanilla flavours.

ICED DARK CHOCOLATE AND HAZELNUT PARFAIT WITH ORANGE CRÈME ANGLAISE

100 g dark chocolate, roughly chopped
50 g butter
30 ml honey
30 ml dark, strong coffee
60 ml cocoa powder
6 egg yolks
100 ml castor sugar
250 ml cream
50 g hazelnuts, chopped and toasted in a dry pan
TO SERVE
Orange Crème Anglaise (page 146)

Melt together the chocolate, butter, honey, coffee and sifted cocoa in a bowl over simmering water. Stir well and cool. Whip together the egg yolks and castor sugar until thick and pale. Mix into the chocolate. Whip the cream to soft peaks and fold in with the nuts. Divide into six dariole moulds and freeze for 4-5 hours until set.
TO SERVE Unmould the parfaits onto plates and pour orange crème anglaise around. Serve, if you wish, with crisp tuille biscuits and strawberries. SERVES 6

WINE Vergelegen Sauvignon Blanc, with its classic ripe fig, green pepper, grass and guava undertones, deliciously draws together the myriad flavours in the vegetable tower.

VERGELEGEN

SOMERSET WEST, CAPE WINELANDS

The story of Vergelegen is almost as old as the tale of the Cape itself, embodying the romance, charm and history of this magical part of the world. No trip to the Cape's winelands is complete without a visit to this beautiful property in the shadow of the towering Hottentots Holland Mountains.

Vergelegen, meaning "situated far away", was originally granted to the Governor of the Cape, Willem Adriaan van der Stel, in 1700. Within a very short time van der Stel had developed the property into a profitable farm with extensive vineyards, orchards and cattle.

During its three centuries of history, Vergelegen has seen many owners and changes in fortune; there were times when it was sadly run down and neglected. But, without doubt, the period which saw the most changes was the twenty-year tenure of Sir Lionel and Lady Florence Phillips. Lady Phillips was responsible for extensive alterations to the historic homestead and adjacent library, and she also introduced innovative farming methods to the area.

The most memorable sight on Vergelegen is the row of five camphor trees which were planted by van der Stel in 1700. Declared National Monuments in 1942, these trees shadow the simple but impressive gable of the homestead. Situated alongside the trees and homestead is The Lady Phillips Restaurant where guests can enjoy the sounds of the ever-flowing Lourens River while sampling the culinary delights produced by the resident chef.

The new winery, completed in 1992, gives visitors a totally different architectural aspect. Designed by a French partnership, *Architectes Associes*, the four-storey winery is built into the side of a hill with commanding views across False Bay and majestic Table Mountain in the distance.

Visitors are encouraged to spend a day on this superb property taking in the natural beauty, strolling through the beautifully landscaped gardens and grounds, touring the winery and, of course, tasting the wines. There is also an old-world library, tiny museum and gift shop on the property.

ABOVE *The north elevation of the homestead tranquilly reflected in a pond in the 'white garden' adjacent to the Lady Phillips Restaurant.*

THE GOURMET PANTRY

STOCKS & OTHER BASIC RECIPES

COURT BOUILLON

A gently-flavoured stock in which to poach vegetables and seafood.

1 litre water
250 ml dry white wine
1 onion, sliced
1 carrot, sliced
1 fresh or dried bouquet garni
   (parsley, thyme, bay leaf, fennel)
6 black peppercorns
5 ml salt
60 ml lemon juice

Combine the ingredients in a large saucepan, cover and bring to the boil. Reduce the heat and simmer uncovered for 20 minutes. Strain before using. Court bouillon may be prepared up the 3 days ahead and chilled. Alternatively freeze for up to 3 months. MAKES 1 litre

CHICKEN STOCK

2 litres cold water
1 raw chicken carcass, with trimmings and
   giblets (not the liver)
1 onion or 4 leeks, roughly sliced
1 stalk celery with leaves, roughly chopped
1-2 carrots, roughly chopped
1 fresh or dried bouquet garni
   (parsley, thyme, bay leaf)
2 ml black peppercorns

Combine all the ingredients in a large saucepan, cover and bring to the boil. Reduce the heat and simmer very gently for 2-3 hours. Strain into a clean saucepan, pressing on the solids to extract as much of the liquid as possible. Check the flavour. If you wish, concentrate the stock by boiling uncovered. Chill for up to 3 days or freeze for up to 3 months. MAKES ABOUT 1 litre

FISH STOCK

1 kg white fish trimmings
1,5 litres cold water
1 onion, quartered
1 carrot, roughly chopped
1 stalk celery with leaves, roughly chopped
1 fresh or dried bouquet garni
   (parsley, fennel, bay leaf)
1 strip lemon rind
12 black peppercorns

Rinse the fish trimmings very well. Discard gills and entrails, which will impart a bitter flavour. Place in a large saucepan. Add the remaining ingredients, cover and bring to the boil. Move the lid aside to partially cover the saucepan and simmer very, very gently for 30 minutes. Strain into a bowl through a colander lined with muslin or 'kitchen wipes'. Press on the solids to extract as much of the liquid as possible. Chill for up to 3 days or freeze for up to 3 months. MAKES ABOUT 1 litre

MEAT STOCK
(VEAL, BEEF, LAMB, VENISON)

This is a standard recipe for veal, beef, lamb or venison stock. Vary the bones accordingly.

1,5 kg veal, beef, lamb or venison bones
2 onions, quartered
2 carrots, quartered
2-3 stalks celery with leaves, roughly
   chopped
125 ml vegetable oil
100 g can tomato paste
300 ml dry red wine
2 litres cold water
1 fresh or dried bouquet garni
   (parsley, thyme, bay leaf, oregano)

Set the oven at 170°C. Place the bones in a roaster with the onions, carrots and celery. Pour over the oil, mix in lightly and roast uncovered for about 3 hours until well browned. Turn the ingredients occasionally, and watch that they don't burn; reduce the oven temperature if this happens.

Transfer the bones and vegetables to a large saucepan. Mix together the tomato paste and red wine, and stir into the roaster to deglaze. Add to the saucepan with the water and herbs. Cover and simmer gently for 3-4 hours.

Skim the surface and boil uncovered until reduced by two-thirds. Strain into a bowl, pressing on the solids to extract as much of the liquid as possible. Chill for up to 3 days or freeze for up to 3 months. MAKES ABOUT 750 ml

RED WINE MARINADE

A basic marinade for venison, and good with beef too.

750 ml dry red wine
2 large tomatoes, seeded and diced
4 carrots, peeled and sliced
1 onion, sliced
4 sprigs fresh parsley
2 stalks celery, chopped
2 bay leaves
8 sprigs fresh thyme
2 garlic cloves, peeled and chopped
5 ml black peppercorns

Combine the ingredients in a non-metal dish. Use to marinate up to 2 kg venison or beef. MAKES ABOUT 1 litre

GHEE

Clarified butter is best for frying. It may be heated to a very high temperature without burning and gives a rich, distinctive flavour. Ghee will keep in the fridge for up to 4 months.

500 g butter

Place the butter in a deep saucepan and boil gently uncovered for 10-15 minutes. As the moisture evaporates the butter will bubble, and a frothy layer will rise to the surface. Remove from the heat, scoop off the froth and pour the melted ghee into a bowl. Cool to room temperature then chill in the fridge to set. Discard the solids in the pan. Heat the ghee again and strain through muslin (or a 'kitchen wipe') to remove any remaining impurities.
MAKES 350 g

CREME FRAICHE

Thick cream which is partially soured doesn't separate when cooking. You will need to make it a day ahead; it will keep in the fridge for up to a month.

500 ml cream
60 ml buttermilk

Sterilize a glass jar. Pour in the cream. Stir in the buttermilk, close with the lid and stand at room temperature for the crème fraîche to develop. This may take anything from 14-24 hours, depending on the freshness of the cream and the room temperature. When the mixture is lovely and thick, store in the fridge. The flavour will become stronger and the consistency thicker as time goes by. If you wish, add more fresh cream to dilute the mixture and to continue the culture. MAKES 500 ml

ROASTED GARLIC

Plump, toasty garlic is wonderful as an accompaniment to meat or as a garnish for meat or vegetables. When puréed, the smooth, golden paste is used to flavour vegetables and sauces.

4 large, plump garlic heads
sprigs of fresh rosemary and thyme
olive oil

Set the oven at 180°C. Cut the top quarter off the garlic heads and discard. Arrange the garlic in a baking dish to fit fairly snugly. Scatter over the rosemary and thyme and sprinkle generously with olive oil. Cover with foil and roast for about 45-60 minutes until very tender. Uncover and grill until the garlic is golden brown.

Serve whole heads, or break into cloves, peel and use as a garnish. Or, to make roasted garlic purée, mash the peeled garlic cloves with a fork with the olive oil it baked in. Cover and chill for up to a week.
SERVES 4-8. MAKES ABOUT 80 ml PUREE

GARLIC CONFIT

2 heads garlic
olive oil

Break open the garlic heads and separate the cloves. Bring three pots of water to the boil. Blanch the garlic cloves in the first pot for 30 seconds. Drain. Refresh with cold water. Drain. Repeat the process in the second and third saucepans.

Peel the cloves and fry gently in olive oil in a frying pan for about 20 minutes until very tender and golden. Serve as a garnish for meat and vegetables. SERVES 3-4

CHARGRILLED LIMES

Charring imparts a subtle smoky flavour to limes, which may be served with seafood or the juice squeezed into salad dressing. They also look rustic and different as a garnish. If limes are hard to find, substitute small lemons.

limes
olive oil

Cut limes into halves or quarters. Brush lightly with olive oil. Grill on a flat-topped grill or in a heavy frying pan until well coloured and lightly charred. They may be covered and refrigerated for up to 5 days. Alternatively, cover left-over chargrilled limes with olive oil and use the flavoured oil for cooking.

PRESERVED LEMONS

The skin of preserved lemons is delicious in African and middle-eastern dishes. Jars may be stored for up to a year, so they make lovely gifts or display items in the pantry.

lemons
sea salt

Sterilize wide-mouthed pickling jars. Wash lemons in hot water. Hold them firmly and cut a deep cross from top to bottom, to within about 2 cm from the base; they should fall open but not fall apart. Open out and sprinkle about 30 ml sea salt onto each lemon. Press back into shape and pack in the jars. Add another handful of salt.

Fill the jars with boiling water. Allow to stand at room temperature for 3-4 weeks before using. Refrigerate after opening and use within a few days.

TAMARIND WATER

Tamarind, the pasty dried fruit of an Indian tree, is a flavouring frequently used in South African cooking, especially in curries. If you cannot find it, add a dash of good wine vinegar which lends a similar sourish note, but will not be as aromatic and spicy.

50 g dried tamarind seed
hot water

Soak the tamarind seed for about 1 hour in hot water to cover. Drain well. Discard the seed and mash the tamarind pulp into the water. SERVES 6-8

HARISSA PASTE

This North African spice mix adds unique flavour to a wide variety of dishes.

125 ml coriander seeds
6 garlic cloves, peeled and chopped
50 ml coarse sea salt
100 g red chillies, halved lengthways and seeded
125 ml olive oil

Roast the coriander seeds in a dry frying pan until golden and aromatic. Whizz in a food processor or pass through a fine sieve. Discard the hard outer parts. Mash the garlic with half the sea salt. Blanch the chillies in boiling water. Drain and mash with the remaining salt. Mix into the garlic with the coriander.

Add the olive oil a spoonful at a time, stirring constantly to form a paste. Spoon into a sterilized jar, cover with a film of olive oil, seal and refrigerate for up to 3 months. MAKES ABOUT 200 ml

GARAM MASALA

The word garam (or gharum) means 'warm' or 'hot', and describes spice mixes which may vary, depending on the personal preferences of the cook. To retain the fresh flavour always add garam masala at the end of the cooking time – preferably shortly before serving the dish.

15 g whole cloves
25 g cumin seeds
25 g coriander seeds
30 g black peppercorns
30 g cardamom pods, lightly crushed
2 cinnamon sticks, broken into small pieces

Roast all the spices in a dry frying pan to intensify the flavours. Grind fairly finely in a pestle and mortar or coffee grinder. Store in an airtight container in a cool cupboard for 2-3 weeks, or in the fridge or freezer for up to 3 months. MAKES ABOUT 130 g

ROASTED MASALA

Like most spicings, masalas are available ready-made, but home-made blends are much fresher and more piquantly spiced. If you wish, use roasted masala instead of commercial curry powder.

150 g coriander seeds
125 g cumin seeds
50 g dried red chillies
25 g black peppercorns
2 small cassia sticks, broken into pieces
5 g whole cloves
15 ml cardamom pods, lightly crushed
25 g turmeric
25 g ground ginger

Roast the coriander, cumin, chillies, peppercorns, cassia, cloves and cardamom in a dry frying pan, tossing until aromatic. Remove from the heat and mix in the turmeric and ginger. Cool. Grind fairly finely in a pestle and mortar or coffee grinder. Store in a screw-topped jar in a cool cupboard for 2-3 weeks, or in the fridge or freezer for up to 3 months. MAKES 400 g

CAPE-MALAY SPICE MIX

A gentle spice mix for curried meat or vegetables.

20 g curry powder
10 g Roasted Masala (page 136)
10 g turmeric
10 g ground coriander

Mix all the ingredients together. Store in a bottle in the fridge for up to 3 months. MAKES 50 g

SRI LANKAN SPICE MIX

A very gentle, complex mix of spices for any type of curry, whether meat, fish or vegetable.

125 ml coriander seeds
30 ml cumin seeds
15 ml fennel seeds
5 ml fenugreek
1 small cinnamon stick
6 green cardamom pods, seeded
6 whole cloves
6 fresh curry leaves
15 ml turmeric
5 ml cayenne pepper

Place the coriander, cumin, fennel, fenugreek, cinnamon, cardamom and cloves in a dry frying pan and stir-fry over medium heat until the aroma of the spices fills the air. Remove from heat and mix in the curry leaves, turmeric and cayenne pepper. Cool.

Grind with a pestle and mortar. Sift gently so that only the finest of the powder passes through. Discard the rest. Store in an airtight container in the fridge for 4-6 weeks. MAKES 100 ml

FENNEL, MUSHROOM AND MACADAMIA STUFFING

A delicious stuffing for any bird, from quail to chicken, duck and turkey.

50 g wild mushrooms (preferably morels), or 100 g black mushrooms, wiped and chopped
250 ml port
2 large shallots or spring onions, finely chopped
30 ml finely chopped baby fennel
50 g butter
50 g fresh breadcrumbs
50 g finely chopped macadamia nuts
salt, milled black pepper

Soak the mushrooms in the port for about 1 hour. Drain in a sieve and gently press out the excess moisture. Retain the liquid for use in the sauce. Fry the mushrooms, shallots or spring onion and fennel in the butter in a frying pan until tender. Mix in the crumbs and macadamia nuts. Season with salt and pepper. Cool. SUFFICIENT FOR 4 QUAIL OR 1 CHICKEN

VANILLA SUGAR SYRUP

A sweet base for drinks, desserts and sweet sauces.

60 ml sugar
80 ml water
1 vanilla pod, split in half lengthwise

Combine the ingredients in a small saucepan. Heat gently, stirring constantly until the sugar dissolves. Boil uncovered until reduced to a light syrup. Discard the vanilla pod. Bottle and store in the fridge for up to 4 weeks. MAKES ABOUT 100 ml

SPICED SUGAR SYRUP

The base of several chutneys used in this book.

250 ml sugar
500 ml water
2 cinnamon sticks
juice of 1 lemon

Combine the ingredients in a medium saucepan. Heat gently, stirring constantly until the sugar dissolves. Boil for approximately 2-3 minutes until reduced to a light syrup. Bottle and store in the fridge for up to a month. MAKES ABOUT 500 ml

COLD SAUCES, CHUTNEYS & PRESERVES

VINAIGRETTE

250 ml vegetable or olive oil (or half and half)
60 ml lemon juice
60 ml red or white wine vinegar
5 ml dry English mustard
salt, milled black pepper

Whisk all the ingredients together. Bottle and store in the fridge for up to a week. If you wish, add crushed fresh garlic, chopped fresh herbs or a little honey for a change of pace. MAKES 375 ml

PINE NUT VINAIGRETTE

60 ml tomato juice
20 ml balsamic vinegar
125 ml olive oil
30 ml pine nut oil

Whisk the ingredients together. Bottle and store in the fridge for up to 5 days. MAKES 200 ml

MUSTARD SEED VINAIGRETTE

200 ml olive oil
80 ml wine vinegar
3 garlic cloves, peeled
15 ml yellow mustard seeds
1 ml salt

Whizz the ingredients in a blender or food processor until well blended. Bottle and store in the fridge for up to a month. If the flavour of the mustard seeds becomes too dominant, add a little extra olive oil and vinegar. A little honey adds a lovely flavour dimension if you wish to ring the changes. MAKES 200 ml

SUN-DRIED TOMATO VINAIGRETTE

30 g sun-dried tomatoes
125 ml olive oil
45 ml balsamic vinegar
1 spring onion, finely sliced
15 ml finely shredded fresh basil leaves
salt, milled black pepper

Place sun-dried tomatoes in a bowl, cover with water and set aside to plump for about 1 hour. Drain and press out as much liquid was possible.

Purée the sun-dried tomato, olive oil and balsamic vinegar in a food processor or blender. Mix in the spring onion and basil, and season with salt and pepper. Store in the fridge for up to 2 weeks. MAKES 200 ml

BASIL PESTO

Pesto is delicious on pasta, spread on salty biscuits and spooned into fresh vegetable soup or Mediterranean-style fish stew. It's also great with a salad of tomatoes, mozzarella cheese, and rocket leaves. Or use as a spread for sliced roasted aubergine and sizzle under the grill. For a change, stir pesto into mayonnaise to accompany smoked fish or as a topping for steak.

100 g fresh basil leaves
50 g pine nuts
2 garlic cloves, peeled
125 ml olive oil
50 g grated parmesan cheese
salt

Whizz together the basil, pine nuts and garlic in a food processor until fairly finely chopped. Blend in the olive oil and parmesan cheese and season with salt. Use immediately, or cover with a layer of olive oil and chill for up to a month in the fridge. MAKES ABOUT 250 ml

CORIANDER PESTO

Coriander lends a completely different flavour to the more traditional basil pesto.

50 g fresh coriander leaves
30 g pine nuts
1 clove garlic, peeled
100 ml olive oil
finely grated zest of ½ small lemon
2 ml salt

Whizz together the coriander, pine nuts and garlic in a food processor until fairly finely chopped. Blend in the olive oil and lemon zest and season with salt. Use immediately, or cover with a film of olive oil and chill for up to a month in the fridge. MAKES ABOUT 125 ml

MIXED HERB PESTO

This pesto has a more robust, gutsy flavour than pesto prepared with just one herb.

500 ml firmly packed fresh basil leaves
125 ml firmly packed fresh parsley leaves
60 ml firmly packed fresh mint leaves
100 g pine nuts
3-4 garlic cloves, peeled
250 ml olive oil
80 ml balsamic vinegar
100 ml grated parmesan cheese
salt, milled black pepper

Whizz together the herbs, pine nuts and garlic in a food processor until roughly chopped. With the motor running, gradually add the olive oil and balsamic vinegar until well combined. Mix in the parmesan cheese and season with salt and pepper. Use immediately, or cover with a film of olive oil and chill for up to a month in the fridge. SERVES 6-8

MAYONNAISE

For perfect mayonnaise ensure all ingredients are at room temperature.

2 whole eggs
2 egg yolks
5 ml dry English mustard
5 ml salt
2 ml white pepper
30 ml wine vinegar
30 ml lemon juice
750 ml vegetable oil

In a food processor or with an electric mixer whisk the whole eggs, egg yolks, mustard, salt and pepper until pale and thick. With the machine running, gradually add the vinegar and lemon juice, then pour in the oil in a thin stream. (If you add the oil too quickly, mayonnaise may separate.) Cover and store in the fridge for up to 3 weeks. MAKES 1 litre

HARISSA MAYONNAISE

150 ml Mayonnaise (page 138)
30 ml Harissa Sauce (page 138)
lemon juice, salt, milled black pepper

Mix together the mayonnaise and harissa sauce in a bowl. Season with lemon juice, salt and pepper. Cover and chill for up to 8 hours before serving for the flavours to develop. Store in the fridge for up to a week. MAKES 200 ml

HARISSA SAUCE

2 Roasted Red Peppers (page 141)
5 dried red chillies
2 garlic cloves, peeled
1 small onion, roughly chopped
1 cinnamon stick
1 bunch fresh coriander
1 bunch fresh mint
15 ml ground cumin
15 ml ground fenugreek
15 ml ground cardamom

Whizz the ingredients together in a food processor or liquidizer until well blended. Bottle and store in the fridge for up to 2 weeks. To prolong storage for up to 2 months, add 50 ml wine vinegar or lemon juice. MAKES ABOUT 400 ml

HUMMUS

400 g can chick peas, drained
2 ml crushed garlic
juice of 1-2 lemons
125 ml tahini (sesame paste)
100 ml olive oil
salt, paprika

Purée the ingredients until smooth and well blended in a food processor or liquidizer. Transfer into a serving bowl. Garnish with a sprinkling of paprika. Store in the fridge for up to 2 weeks. SERVES 8-10

GRAPE CHUTNEY

2,25 kg seedless grapes, washed
3 onions, finely chopped
500 ml white wine

Place the grapes in a large saucepan with the onions and wine. Simmer uncovered for 3-4 hours over very low heat until the mixture is thick and pulpy, stirring occasionally. Should the chutney still seem a little too runny, boil off the excess liquid. Cool slightly, then spoon into warm, sterilized jars. Store in a cool, dark place. MAKES ABOUT 500 ml

CRANBERRY APRICOT CHUTNEY

250 g dried or sun-dried apricots
2 onions, chopped
1 garlic clove, peeled and chopped
olive oil
250 ml red wine
10 ml balsamic vinegar
454 g can cranberry sauce

If using dried apricots, soak in hot water until soft. Slice finely. Fry the onion and garlic in olive oil in a medium saucepan until golden. Add the red wine, balsamic vinegar, cranberry sauce and apricots. Cover and simmer for 10-15 minutes. Spoon into hot sterilized jars. Store in the fridge for up to 2 months. SERVES 8

FRESH CORIANDER CHUTNEY

100 g (1 large bunch) fresh coriander, washed and dried
5 ml Harissa Paste (page 136)
2 garlic cloves, peeled
2 ml salt
2 ml ground cumin
30 ml lemon juice

Whizz all the ingredients in a food processor or blender and store in the fridge in an airtight container. MAKES ABOUT 250 ml

PEACH CHUTNEY

8 cling peaches, peeled
1 onion, finely chopped
vegetable oil
7 ml curry powder
2 ml ground ginger
125 ml sugar
200 ml Spiced Sugar Syrup (page 137)
100 ml white wine vinegar
salt

Finely slice the peaches from the pips. Gently fry the onion in oil in a medium saucepan until translucent. Stir in the curry powder and ginger. Add the sugar, sugar syrup, vinegar and peaches. Simmer uncovered for about 20 minutes until the peaches are translucent and the syrup has thickened slightly.
Check the flavour and add a little salt. Spoon into hot, sterilized jars. Store in the fridge for up to 3 months.
MAKES ABOUT 750 ml

RED CURRANT AND APPLE PRESERVE

1 onion, finely sliced
50 g butter
375 g Granny Smith apples, peeled, cored and sliced
250 g red currants
2 ml whole cloves
1 cinnamon stick
125 ml red wine vinegar
125 ml brown sugar

Gently sweat the onion in the butter in a large, covered saucepan over low heat until translucent. Add the apples and cook uncovered for 3-4 minutes until tender. Add the remaining ingredients, stirring until the sugar dissolves. Simmer gently uncovered over medium-low heat, stirring occasionally for about 20 minutes until the sauce is syrupy. Cover and chill before serving. If you wish to store the preserve for longer, bottle in sterilized jars and refrigerate. MAKES 500 ml

ZHUG

A delicious chilli condiment to serve with meat.

200 g dried chillies
5 ml black peppercorns
10 ml cardamom seeds
20 garlic cloves, peeled
1 bunch fresh coriander
15 ml salt
125 ml olive oil
30 ml tomato sauce

Pour boiling water over the chillies and set aside to soak for 30 minutes. Drain; reserve the soaking water. Trim and seed the chillies.
Roast the peppercorns and cardamom in a dry frying pan until aromatic. Grind in a pestle and mortar. Whizz the seeded chillies, garlic, coriander, spices, salt, olive oil and tomato sauce to a thick paste in a food processor. If the mixture is too thick, add a little of the soaking water. Store covered with olive oil in the fridge for up to a month. MAKES ABOUT 250 ml

HOT SAUCES

BEEF JUS (VENISON JUS)

750 ml Beef or Venison Stock (page 134)
50 g cold butter, cut into cubes
salt, milled black pepper

In a medium saucepan boil the stock uncovered until reduced by half and slightly thickened. Just before serving whisk in the butter. Season with salt and pepper if necessary. MAKES ABOUT 400 ml

PORT JUS

750 ml Beef Stock (page 134)
150 ml port
50 g cold butter, cut into cubes
salt, milled black pepper

In a medium saucepan boil the stock uncovered until reduced by half and slightly thickened. In a separate saucepan boil the port uncovered until reduced by half. Stir the port into the stock. Just before serving whisk in the butter. Season with salt and pepper. MAKES ABOUT 500 ml

THYME JUS

4 large sprigs fresh thyme
3-4 shallots or spring onions, finely sliced
vegetable oil
200 ml white wine
5 ml white wine vinegar
250 ml Beef Stock (page 134)
salt, milled black pepper
30 g (30 ml) cold butter

Soften the thyme and shallot or spring onion in oil in a covered medium saucepan. Add the wine and vinegar and boil uncovered until reduced by half. Add the stock and simmer uncovered until reduced by half and thickened. Season with salt and pepper. Strain into a clean saucepan. Just before serving reheat and whisk in the butter. SERVES 4

ROSEMARY DEMI-GLACE

300 g finely chopped celery, carrot and onion
olive oil
500 ml dry white wine
45 ml tomato paste
2 litres light Chicken Stock (page 134)

Fry the celery, carrot and onion in olive oil in a medium saucepan until lightly browned. Stir in the white wine, tomato paste and chicken stock. Simmer uncovered until reduced by half. Strain and cool. Remove and discard the surface fat. Just before serving simmer again uncovered until slightly thickened. SERVES 6

BECHAMEL SAUCE

50 g butter
45 ml cake flour
500 ml milk, or milk and cream
1 ml dry English mustard
salt, milled black pepper

Melt the butter in a medium saucepan. Remove from the heat and blend in the flour. Slowly add the milk (or milk and cream), stirring until smooth. Season with mustard, salt and pepper. Cook, still stirring, for a couple of minutes until the sauce thickens. MAKES ABOUT 500 ml

LEMON BUTTER

A baste for barbecuing or grilling vegetables and seafood, and a simple sauce to serve it with. If you wish, add crushed garlic and chopped fresh herbs.

200 g butter
juice of 2 lemons
salt, milled black pepper

Melt the butter in a small saucepan, add the lemon juice and heat through. Season with salt and pepper. MAKES ABOUT 200 ml

ROASTED RED PEPPER SAUCE

1 onion, chopped
3 garlic cloves, peeled and crushed
olive oil
4 Roasted Red Peppers (page 141), roughly chopped
250 ml milk
250 ml cream
salt, milled black pepper

Fry the onion and garlic in olive oil in a medium saucepan until translucent. Add the peppers, milk and cream and season with salt and pepper. Cover and simmer for about 20 minutes. Purée until smooth in a food processor or liquidizer. Reheat before serving. SERVES 4

RED PEPPER COMPOTE

250 ml water
1 onion, finely chopped
3 Roasted Red Peppers (page 141), sliced
60 ml balsamic vinegar
60 ml sugar

Bring the water to the boil in a medium saucepan. Add the onion, cover and simmer for about 10 minutes until soft. Add the peppers, vinegar and sugar and simmer uncovered until the sauce is syrupy. Serve warm or cool. SERVES 8

CARROT BUTTER SAUCE

150 g peeled carrots
vegetable or olive oil
1 onion, finely chopped
100 ml white wine
250 ml cream
salt, lemon juice
30 g (30 ml) cold butter
30 ml Noilly Prat

Cut tiny carrot pearls from the peeled carrots. Set aside; they will be used to garnish the completed dish. Finely chop the carrot off-cuts. Sweat the offcuts and onion in oil in a medium saucepan for about 10 minutes until soft. Add the white wine and cook uncovered until reduced by half. Add the cream and simmer uncovered until reduced by half. Season with salt and lemon juice.

Purée the sauce in a food processor or liquidizer until smooth and creamy. Strain back into a clean saucepan. Just before serving, reheat the sauce, mix in the cold butter and add the Noilly Prat. Serve hot SERVES 6

SALADS, VEGETABLES & SIDE DISHES

ROASTED RED PEPPERS

These may be used as a salad or in a sauce. Yellow, green and black peppers may be used as well.

olive oil
6-8 large, plump red peppers
salt, milled black pepper

Line a baking tray with foil. Brush lightly with olive oil. Core the peppers, cut into quarters and place skin-up on the tray. Grill under a preheated oven griller until charred and blistered. Place in a plastic bag and leave to cool.

Gently remove the skin from the peppers. Arrange on a plate. Pour over a little olive oil and season with salt and pepper. If you wish, add a dash of balsamic vinegar. SERVES 6-8

MARINATED TOMATOES

2-3 firm, ripe tomatoes
1 onion, finely chopped
125 ml finely shredded fresh basil leaves
2 garlic cloves, peeled and crushed
salt, milled black pepper
125 ml olive oil

Slice the tomatoes. Mix together the onion, basil and garlic, and season with salt and pepper. Put a layer of tomato slices in a glass dish, sprinkle onion mixture evenly on top, then add another layer of tomatoes. Continue until the ingredients are used up. Pour over the olive oil, cover and set aside at room temperature for about 1 hour. SERVES 4-6

PICKLED CUCUMBER

1 English cucumber
1 bay leaf
6 black peppercorns
125 ml sugar
125 ml white wine vinegar
125 ml water
5 ml salt

Slice the cucumber finely into a glass bowl. Tie the bay leaf and peppercorns in a small piece of muslin. Mix together the sugar, vinegar, water and salt in a medium saucepan, add the spice bag, cover and simmer for 10 minutes. Cool. Pour the pickling mixture over the cucumber and set aside at room temperature to marinate for 1 hour. SERVES 4-6

CREAMED AVOCADO

2 avocados
60 ml cream cheese
lemon juice, salt, milled black pepper

Peel, stone and mash the avocados. Blend in the cream cheese and season with lemon juice, salt and pepper. SERVES 4-6

WATERCRESS GNOCCHI

500 ml water
120 g butter
salt, milled black pepper
500 ml cake flour, extra cake flour for coating
150 g grated mozzarella cheese
100 g watercress, roughly chopped
4 eggs
2 litres water
vegetable oil

Bring the water and butter to the boil in a medium saucepan. Season with salt and pepper. Remove from the heat and add the flour all at once, stirring with a wooden spoon until smooth. Return to the heat and stir briskly until the dough comes away from the sides of the pot. Cool to room temperature. Stir in the mozzarella cheese, watercress and eggs. Shape into walnut-sized balls and roll in flour.

Bring the water and 5 ml salt to simmering point in a large saucepan. Drop in a few gnocchi balls at a time and simmer uncovered until they float to the top. Remove from the pot with a slotted spoon, refresh in a bowl of iced water and drain. TO SERVE Roll the gnocchi in a little flour. Deep fry in hot oil until golden. Drain well on kitchen paper. Serve hot. SERVES 8

GARLIC CREAMED POTATO

1 kg potatoes, peeled and quartered
100 g unsalted butter
50-80 ml Roasted Garlic purée (page 135)
125 ml cream or milk
salt, milled white pepper, grated nutmeg

Boil the potatoes in salted water for about 25 minutes until cooked. Drain, cover with the lid and shake the pan to break up the potatoes. Mash in the butter, garlic purée and cream or milk. Season with salt, pepper and nutmeg. SERVES 6

POTATOES WITH FRESH THYME

1 kg small potatoes, peeled and washed
1 large onion, peeled and roughly sliced
3 large garlic cloves, peeled
olive oil
coarse salt, black peppercorns
100 ml white wine
1 bunch fresh thyme
3 bay leaves
chopped fresh parsley to garnish

Fry the potatoes, onion and garlic in hot olive oil in a wide saucepan until golden brown. Season with salt and peppercorns. Deglaze the pan with white wine. Add the thyme and bay leaves, cover and simmer gently for 15-20 minutes until the potatoes are cooked. Add a little extra wine if necessary, to ensure the vegetables don't become too dry.

Uncover the pan and cook away any remaining moisture, swirling to coat the vegetables in the pan juices. Discard the thyme and bay leaves, tip the vegetables into a warm bowl and garnish with chopped parsley. SERVES 6

CHATEAU POTATOES

1 kg potatoes
75 g clarified duck or beef fat
salt, milled black pepper
30 g (30 ml) butter
chopped fresh parsley

Set the oven at 200°C. Peel the potatoes, cut into sections and turn into barrel shapes about 5 cm in length. Heat the fat in a roasting dish in the oven. Add the potatoes, season with salt and pepper and turn until well coated. Roast uncovered, turning once or twice, for 40-50 minutes until golden brown and soft. Drain well on kitchen paper. Toss in melted butter and parsley. SERVES 6

POTATO CROQUETTES

These keep hot in the oven for up to an hour before serving.

500 g potatoes, peeled and cubed
2 egg yolks
30 ml butter
30 ml cream
salt, milled black pepper
COATING
2 eggs, lightly beaten
30 ml milk
flour, toasted breadcrumbs

Cook the potatoes in salted water until soft. Drain and mash with the egg yolks, butter and cream. Season with salt and pepper. Chill until firm enough to handle then form into croquettes with floured hands.

Chill once more. Mix together eggs and milk. Roll croquettes in flour, dip in egg-and-milk mix then in crumbs or crushed flaked almonds. Refrigerate until just before serving.

Deep fry in hot oil for about 5 minutes until brown and hot right through. Be very careful not to crowd the pan: the temperature will drop and the croquettes will burst. MAKES 10

POTATO AND PISTACHIO WAFERS

2 large potatoes
salt, milled black pepper, grated nutmeg
50 g shelled pistachio nuts
50 g butter, melted
lightly toasted sesame seeds

Parboil the potatoes in their jackets. Drain and refrigerate overnight to develop the natural starch.

Set the oven at 180°C. Skin and grate the potatoes coarsely into long strips. Season with salt, pepper and nutmeg. Press loosely into rounds on a baking tray or onto moulds so that the mixture resembles lace. Lightly press pistachio nuts into the surface. Dribble over the melted butter and sprinkle with sesame seeds. Bake for about 25 minutes until crisp. MAKES ABOUT 8

GLAZED SWEET POTATOES

1 kg sweet potatoes, skinned and cubed
1-2 cinnamon sticks
strips of rind from 1 orange
2-3 slices green ginger
60 ml honey
125 ml brown sugar
100 g butter, cut into small blocks
60 ml water

Set the oven at 180°C. Arrange the sweet potato in a baking dish with the cinnamon sticks, orange rind and ginger. Drizzle over the honey. Sprinkle with brown sugar. Dot with butter. Add the water. Cover with the lid or foil and bake for about 60 minutes until almost tender. Turn the potatoes halfway through the baking time. Uncover, turn on the oven grill and grill until nicely browned. SERVES 6

PEANUT SAMP AND BEANS

Samp and Beans is a daily staple in South Africa's black community. Any dried beans may be used. The addition of peanuts adds a delicious dimension of flavour. If you wish, add also the kernels of a couple of cooked corn or can of whole kernel corn.

200 ml dried kidney beans
250 ml samp, rinsed
100 g raw or roasted peanuts, finely crushed
10 ml salt, milled black pepper
30 g (30 ml) butter

Soak the beans and samp in plenty of cold water for about 8 hours. Drain. Bring 1,2 litres of water to the boil in a medium saucepan. Add the samp and beans, cover and simmer for about 1½ hours until the vegetables are very tender. Season with salt and pepper, add the butter and peanuts and cook uncovered until the mixture thickens. SERVES 8

YELLOW RICE WITH RAISINS

Rice is an important dish on the Cape-Dutch table, and this recipe is a particular favourite with all sections of the community; it is always served with bobotie and curry. Its popular name, begrafnisrys (funeral rice), comes from the fact that it was always part of the meal served after funerals, a tradition of both Dutch and Malays.

250 ml white rice
60 ml seedless raisins
6 whole cloves
5 ml salt
2 ml turmeric
1-2 slices green ginger
625 ml cold water
30 g (30 ml) butter
50 g slivered almonds, toasted in a dry pan

Combine the rice, raisins, cloves, salt, turmeric, ginger and water in a medium saucepan. Cover and simmer gently until the rice is tender and all the liquid has been absorbed. Add the butter, fluff up with a fork and discard the ginger. Tip the rice into a warm bowl and garnish with toasted almonds. SERVES 8

WILD RICE PILAF

250 ml wild rice
1 onion, finely chopped
30 g (30 ml) butter
250 ml white rice
500 ml Chicken Stock (page 134)
salt

Cook the wild rice in boiling salted water for 20 minutes. Drain. Fry the onion in the butter in a medium saucepan until translucent. Stir in the white rice and drained wild rice. Add the chicken stock and season with salt. Cover and simmer gently for about 20 minutes until the rice is cooked and the stock has been absorbed. Fluff up with a fork and tip the pilaf into a warm bowl. SERVES 6

COUSCOUS WITH ROASTED VEGETABLES

300 g couscous
400 ml boiling water
olive oil
1 garlic clove, peeled and crushed
5 ml salt, milled black pepper
100 g flaked almonds, toasted in a dry pan
ROASTED VEGETABLES
½ red pepper, cored and cut into strips
½ yellow pepper, cored and cut into strips
1 red onion, cut into wedges
1 small aubergine, cut into cubes

Place the couscous in a bowl and pour over the boiling water. Allow to plump and absorb the water for about 5 minutes. Mix in 15 ml olive oil and garlic, and season with salt and pepper.

Set the oven at 200°C. Place the vegetables into a roasting pan and drizzle with olive oil. Roast uncovered for about 20 minutes until golden and tender. Mix in the couscous and heat through. Transfer to a warm bowl. Just before serving scatter with roasted almonds. SERVES 6

MUSSEL RISOTTO DUMPLINGS

8 black mussels, well scrubbed
4-6 shallots or large spring onions, finely chopped
olive oil, vegetable oil
180 g arborio rice (risotto rice)
100 ml white wine
1 litre hot vegetable stock
30 ml chopped fresh thyme
salt
2 egg yolks
15 ml cornflour
cake flour or fresh breadcrumbs for coating

Steam open the mussels in a pot of boiling water. Drain. Remove shells and beards and chop the mussel meat finely.

Sweat the shallot or spring onion in olive oil in a medium saucepan until translucent. Stir in the arborio rice. Stir in the white wine and cook until it has been absorbed. Add the vegetable stock little by little, stirring each time until absorbed, and the rice is soft yet still firm to the bite. Remove from the heat and flavour with thyme and salt. Spread on a tray to cool. Mix in the chopped mussels, egg yolks and cornflour. TO SERVE Form the rice mixture into about 24 small dumplings, and roll in cake flour or breadcrumbs. Deep fry in hot vegetable oil for 3-4 minutes until golden brown. Drain on kitchen paper. MAKES 24; SERVES 6

PAP

Maize meal is a traditional South African dish, served for breakfast as well as with a meat main dish.

1 litre water
5 ml salt
500 ml maize meal or polenta
30 g (30 ml) butter

Bring the water and salt to the boil in a large, heavy saucepan. Tip in the maize meal or polenta all in one go, mix quickly, cover and cook undisturbed over very gentle heat for about 15 minutes. Mix in the butter. Serve hot. SERVES 8

SPINACH WITH PEANUTS

1 kg baby spinach leaves, well washed and drained
1 onion, finely sliced
butter
5 ml salt
2 ml bicarbonate of soda
4 tomatoes, chopped
100 g crushed peanuts

Roughly chop the spinach. Fry the onion in butter in a medium saucepan until golden. Add the spinach, 250 ml water, salt and bicarb, and bring to the boil. Cook for about 5 minutes. Drain in a colander. Tip into a clean saucepan. Add 125 ml water, tomato and peanuts. Cover and simmer gently for about 20 minutes, stirring occasionally. Uncover to cook off the excess moisture. SERVES 6-8

BUTTERED SPINACH

2 bunches spinach, well washed and drained
100 g butter
salt, milled black pepper

Trim the spinach stems and tear leaves into small pieces. Heat the butter in a wide saucepan, add the spinach, cover and steam gently for a few minutes until limp. Season with salt and pepper. SERVES 6

CORN PANCAKES

African maize recipes are as old as most cooks can remember (the plants were brought to Europe from America following the travels of Colombus, and Portuguese seafarers brought it to the coast of Africa at the start of the 16th century). It was called 'milho' from which the word 'mealie' is derived. You may slice the kernels from corn cobs for these pancakes (also called 'fritters' and 'vetkoek'); a can of whole kernel corn or cream-style sweetcorn may be substituted.

4 sweetcorn, or 400 g can whole
    kernel corn, drained
2 eggs, separated
125 ml cake flour
2 ml baking powder
1 ml salt
grated nutmeg, milled black pepper
vegetable oil

Cut the kernels from the corn and chop coarsely (by hand or in a food processor). Mix in the egg yolks. Sift in the flour and baking powder, add a little salt, nutmeg and pepper and mix well. Beat the egg white until stiff but not dry, and fold in.

Fry spoonfuls of the mixture in hot oil until crispy brown on both sides. Take care: if insufficiently cooked the fritters will be runny in the middle. Drain very well on several layers of kitchen paper laid on a wad of newspaper then arrange on a warmed serving plate. Continue cooking the fritters until all the batter has been used up. MAKES ABOUT 24

CONFIT OF BABY ONIONS

20 pickling onions
200 ml white wine
200 ml white wine vinegar
50 g butter
30 ml sugar
salt, milled black pepper

Place all the ingredients in a medium saucepan. Partially cover with the lid and simmer for about 20 minutes until the onions are tender. Uncover and cook for a few minutes more until the sauce thickens. Serve hot. SERVES 6-8

ROASTED VEGETABLES

Mix and match your favourite vegetable for this recipe; this list is only a suggestion.

1 onion, quartered or 8 shallots or large
    spring onions, trimmed
2 small aubergines, quartered lengthwise
4 courgettes, halved
1 red and 1 yellow pepper, seeded and cut
    into big flat pieces
4 brown mushrooms
olive oil
sea salt, freshly milled black pepper

Toss the prepared vegetables liberally in olive oil in a baking dish. Season with salt and pepper. Grill slowly at first to soften vegetables, then fiercely to char the edges. The total cooking time is 10-15 minutes. Tip the vegetables into a hot serving dish, season with extra salt, pepper and olive oil if you wish. SERVES 6

BABY BEANS WITH TOMATOES AND FETA

500 g slim green beans, topped and tailed
200 g cocktail tomatoes
1 wheel feta cheese, crumbled
salt

Steam the beans or blanch in a saucepan of salted boiling water until crisp-tender. Drain, pile into a warm serving bowl and top with cherry tomatoes and crumbled feta cheese. Salt lightly and serve hot or cool. SERVES 6

DEEP-FRIED VEGETABLES

250 g vegetables (carrots, broccoli, baby
    beans, mangetout)
vegetable oil
TEMPURA BATTER
125 ml cake flour
salt, milled black pepper
3 egg whites
100 ml water

Prepare the vegetables by slicing or cutting into small florets.
TEMPURA BATTER Sift the flour into a bowl. Season with salt and pepper. Blend in the egg whites and milk or water to form a thin batter.
TO SERVE Dip the vegetable pieces in the batter and deep fry in hot oil until puffed and golden. Drain on kitchen paper. SERVES 4

BRAISED RED CABBAGE

1 small red cabbage, cored and finely
    shredded (about 400 g)
vegetable oil
60 ml sugar
100 ml balsamic vinegar
50 ml red wine
30 ml reducurrant jelly
salt, milled black pepper

Stir-fry the cabbage in oil in a medium saucepan for about 5 minutes. Add the remaining ingredients, cover and cook for about 60 minutes until the cabbage is soft and the sauce has thickened to a glaze. Season with salt and pepper. SERVES 6-8

RED BEAN AND MANGETOUT TARTLETS

4 thick slices white bread
100 g butter, melted
100 g mangetout
100 g canned red kidney beans

Set the oven at 220°C. Flatten the bread with a rolling pin. Brush both sides liberally with melted butter and line tartlet moulds. Press down with smaller moulds to form a cup. Bake for about 5 minutes until crisp and golden. Keep warm.
  Just before serving, stir-fry the mangetout and red kidney beans in the remaining butter until cooked and piping hot. Place toast cups on warm plates and fill with vegetables. SERVES 4

BUTTERNUT AND ROCKET RISOTTO WITH TRUFFLE-SCENTED MUSHROOMS

500 g butternut, peeled, pipped and cut into small dice
olive oil, salt, milled black pepper
125 ml chopped fresh herbs (parsley, sage, oregano, thyme)
1 onion, finely chopped
50 g butter
300 g arborio rice (risotto rice)
1½ litres vegetable or Chicken Stock (page 134)
1 bunch rocket, washed and roughly chopped
50 g grated parmesan cheese
250 g button mushrooms, wiped
truffle oil

Set the oven at 200°C. Spread the butternut in a roaster, sprinkle generously with olive oil and season with salt and pepper. Scatter over the herbs and roast uncovered for about 30 minutes until tender and lightly charred.
  Fry the onion in the butter in a medium saucepan until translucent. Stir in the arborio rice. Add a cupful of the stock and stir until it has been absorbed. Continue in this way, stirring in the stock little by little until the rice is tender and cooked through, but firm to the bite and no more liquid remains. Stir in the roasted butternut, rocket and parmesan cheese. Fry the mushrooms in truffle oil in a frying pan until tender. Season with salt and pepper. TO SERVE Spoon the risotto onto warm plates and garnish with mushrooms. SERVES 6

BREADS & PASTRIES

RICH SHORTCRUST PASTRY

500 ml cake flour, sifted
1 ml salt
60 ml castor sugar
100 g cold butter, cut into small blocks
3 egg yolks
5 ml vanilla essence
60 ml chilled water (approximate amount)

Mix together the flour, salt and castor sugar. Rub in the butter until the mixture is finely crumbled. Mix together the egg yolks, vanilla essence and chilled water and mix into the dry ingredients to make a soft dough. (Add additional water if necessary.) Wrap in waxed paper and chill in the fridge for an hour or two.
TO BAKE BLIND Set the oven at 180°C. Roll out the pastry on a floured surface and line a 26 cm baking tin. Press lightly oiled heavy foil into the pastry and bake for 10 minutes. Remove the foil and bake for about 5 minutes more to crisp slightly. Cool before adding the filling.

BRIOCHE

1,5 litres cake flour
20 ml salt
50 ml sugar
20 g (2 sachets) instant dry yeast
250 ml milk
250 g butter, cut into blocks
5 eggs, lightly beaten

Sift the flour and salt into a large bowl. Mix in the sugar and yeast. Warm the milk in a medium saucepan. Remove from the heat, add the butter and stir until melted. Add to the dry ingredients with the eggs. Mix well to form a soft dough.
  Transfer the dough to a clean, oiled bowl, cover and set aside in a warm, draught-free spot until doubled in bulk. Knock down, knead lightly again and put into a large greased loaf tin or two small tins. Bake at 180ºC for about 30 minutes. Cool on a rack. MAKES 1 LARGE OR 2 SMALL LOAVES

GARLIC CROSTINI

8 slices French bread
1 garlic clove, peeled
30 ml olive oil

Toast the French bread, rub with garlic and drizzle with olive oil. SERVES 4

CHEESE STRAWS

400 g puff pastry
prepared English mustard
cayenne pepper, paprika
1 egg, lightly beaten
sesame seeds

Set the oven at 200°C. Roll out the pastry to a thickness of approximately 50 mm. Smear with mustard, and season with cayenne pepper and paprika. Fold into three, turn clockwise and roll out into a rectangle. Brush the pastry with egg and sprinkle with sesame seeds. Cut into strips, twist and place on a baking tray. Bake for about 15 minutes until crisp and golden. SERVES 4

SWEET THINGS & ICE-CREAM

CHOCOLATE LEAVES

leaves
vegetable oil spray
100 g dark chocolate, roughly chopped
100 g milk chocolate, roughly chopped

Select pretty leaves from the garden (for obvious reasons avoid the leaves of poisonous plants). Spray the back of each leaf – the prettier side – lightly with oil. Melt together dark and light chocolates in a bowl over simmering water. Dip the oiled sides of the leaves into the chocolate to coat thinly and place in a baking sheet. Refrigerate until the chocolate hardens, then carefully peel off and discard the leaves. Use to garnish desserts or cakes.

RASPBERRY COULIS

Any berries may be used in this sauce.

250 g raspberries
80 ml water
5 ml cornflour
80 ml sugar

Whizz the raspberries in a food processor. Pour into a medium saucepan. Mix together the water and cornflour. Stir into the purée and cook until the coulis thickens. Stir in the sugar. Cool. SERVES 8

VAN DER HUM SAUCE

If Van der Hum is unavailable, substitute any citrus-based liqueur of your choice.

250 ml Spiced Sugar Syrup (page 137)
15 ml potato flour
30 ml cold water
30 ml Van der Hum

Bring the spiced sugar syrup to the boil in a small saucepan. Mix together the potato flour and water to form a smooth paste. Stir into the syrup and boil for 1-2 minutes until thickened and clear. Remove from the heat and add the Van der Hum. Serve cool. MAKES 250 ml

LEMON COULIS

finely grated zest of 2 lemons
juice of 3 lemons (about 100 ml)
200 ml water
15 ml cornflour
125 ml castor sugar

Mix together all the ingredients until well blended. Pour into a small saucepan. Bring to the boil, stirring constantly. Boil for 1-2 minutes until thickened and clear. Cool. MAKES ABOUT 350 ml

DARK CHOCOLATE SAUCE

200 g dark chocolate, roughly chopped
400 ml cream
30 g (30 ml) butter

Melt the chocolate in a bowl over simmering water. Heat the cream to just below boiling point. Stir into the melted chocolate with the butter. Serve warm over vanilla ice-cream. SERVES 6-8

CARAMEL SAUCE

200 g sugar
60 ml water
500 ml cream

Dissolve the sugar in the water over very low heat in a medium saucepan. Simmer uncovered, tilting the pan to and fro, until caramelized. Remove from the heat and stir in the cream. Cook, stirring, until slightly thickened. Pour into a jug and cool. SERVES 8

BUTTERSCOTCH SAUCE

250 ml sugar
100 g butter
125 ml cream
60 ml milk

Combine the sugar and butter in a medium, deep saucepan. Heat gently, stirring constantly, until the sugar dissolves. Increase the heat and boil uncovered until the sauce caramelizes to a pale golden brown. Remove from the heat and stir in the cream and milk. Boil for 1-2 minutes. Pour into a jug and cool. SERVES 6

CREME ANGLAISE

3 egg yolks
30 ml castor sugar
125 ml milk
200 ml cream
15 ml vanilla essence

Combine the egg yolks, castor sugar, milk and cream in a medium saucepan. Cook over medium heat, stirring constantly, just until custard thickens and coats the back of a spoon. Remove from heat and stir in the vanilla essence. Pour into a jug and cool. SERVES 6-8

ORANGE CREME ANGLAISE

Crème Anglaise (page 146)
15 ml finely grated orange zest
15 ml Cointreau

Prepare the crème anglaise. Remove from heat and stir in the orange zest and Cointreau. Pour into a jug and cool. SERVES 6-8

ROOIBOS CRÈME ANGLAISE

Crème Anglaise (page 146)
2 rooibos tea bags

Prepare the crème anglaise, adding the rooibos bags to the ingredients for making the custard. Discard the bags before adding the vanilla essence. SERVES 6-8

BRANDIED FIGS

6 nearly ripe figs
Vanilla Sugar Syrup (page 137)
brandy

Sterilize large jars to hold the figs. Pack in the figs while the jars are still hot.

Bring the sugar syrup to the boil and pour over the figs to cover by half. Top up with brandy. Seal the jar and store in the fridge. If possible, keep for a month or two before using for the flavour to develop. SERVES 6

ALMOND PRALINE

A delicious garnish for ice-cream or a chocolate dessert.

50 g slivered almonds
200 ml sugar
80 ml water

Toast the almonds in a dry frying pan until golden and aromatic. Spread evenly onto a clean, ungreased baking sheet.

Combine the sugar and water in a small saucepan and bring to the boil, stirring. Make sure the sugar dissolves before the syrup reaches boiling point. Boil until the syrup is golden brown, tipping the pan to and fro. Pour the syrup over the nuts in a thin stream, coating them as evenly as possible. When cold, lift the praline off the tray and break into shards. SERVES 6

VANILLA ICE-CREAM

600 ml milk
250 ml cream
2 vanilla pods, split in half lengthwise
6 egg yolks
200 ml castor sugar

Bring the milk, cream and vanilla pods to the boil in a medium saucepan. Beat together the egg yolks and castor sugar until thick and pale. Add to the saucepan. Cook, stirring constantly, until the custard thickens and coats the spoon. Cool. Remove the vanilla pod. Freeze in an ice-cream machine. If you don't have an ice-cream machine transfer the mixture to a metal bowl (which speeds up the chilling process) and place in the freezer. Stir at intervals during the chilling process to freeze evenly. The ice-cream will eventually become very thick, and should be re-whipped in a food processor or with an electric mixture to make it smooth, creamy and free of icicles. Freeze and rewhip as necessary. SERVES 6-8

FENNEL AND HONEY ICE-CREAM

500 ml cream
500 ml milk
10 ml fennel seeds
125 ml sugar
9 egg yolks
15 ml honey

Combine the cream, milk, fennel seeds and sugar in a medium saucepan and bring to just below boiling point. Set aside for 15-20 minutes for the flavours to infuse. Lightly whisk the egg yolks in a clean saucepan. Bring the cream mixture to boiling point and pour into the egg. Cook over medium-low heat, stirring constantly, until the custard thickens and coats the spoon. Stir in the honey. Strain into an ice-cream machine and freeze, or use the manual freezing and whipping process as described for Vanilla Ice-Cream (page 147). SERVES 8-10

CAPE VELVET ICE-CREAM

250 ml milk
250 ml cream
125 ml Cape Velvet liqueur
100 g milk chocolate, roughly chopped
6 egg yolks
125 g (150 ml) sugar

Bring the milk, cream and liqueur to just below boiling point in a medium saucepan. Remove from the heat, add the chocolate and stir until melted.

Whisk together the egg yolks and sugar until thick and frothy. Stir into the saucepan. Cook, stirring constantly, until the custard thickens and coats the spoon. Freeze in an ice-cream machine or use the manual whipping and freezing process as described for Vanilla Ice-Cream (page 147). SERVES 6-8

CINNAMON ICE-CREAM

5 egg yolks
150 ml sugar
250 ml milk
30 g (30 ml) butter
250 ml cream
10 ml vanilla extract
15 ml freshly ground cinnamon bark

Beat together the egg yolks and sugar until well blended. Pour into a double boiler. Stir in the milk and cook over boiling water, stirring constantly, until the mixture thickens and coats the spoon. Remove from the heat and stir in the butter. Cool, stirring occasionally, until the mixture reaches room temperature.

Stir in the cream, vanilla extract and cinnamon. Freeze in an ice-cream machine or use the manual whipping and freezing process as described for Vanilla Ice-Cream (page 147). SERVES 8

APRICOT AND ALMOND ICE-CREAM

4 egg yolks
250 ml castor sugar
500 ml cream
250 ml diced dried or sun-dried apricots
200 g flaked almonds, toasted in a dry pan

Whisk together the yolks and castor sugar until pale and thick. Whip the cream stiffly and fold in with the apricots and almonds. Pour into a container and freeze. SERVES 8

DOUBLE CHOCOLATE COFFEE ICE-CREAM

50 g walnuts, finely chopped
250 ml castor sugar
250 ml cocoa powder
125 ml strong black coffee
4 egg yolks
250 ml cream
TOPPING
Crème Fraîche (page 135)
grated dark chococlate

Toast the walnuts in a dry frying pan until aromatic. Cool. In a small saucepan, combine the castor sugar, cocoa and coffee. Stir over a low heat until well mixed and smooth. Whip the egg yolks until pale and thickened, then whip in the chocolate mixture. Cool to room temperature.

Whip the cream until it holds soft peaks, then fold into the chocolate mixture with chopped walnuts. Divide the mixture between six serving bowls or glasses, cover and freeze for at least 6 hours. It may be frozen for up to 2 months.
TO SERVE Top each serving of ice-cream with crème fraîche and plenty of grated chocolate. SERVES 6

QUICK CASSATA WITH RASPBERRY COULIS

The perfect make-ahead pudding for summer entertaining, especially as there's no need to rewhip the ice-cream as it freezes.

100 g glacé cherries
45 ml brandy
100 g flaked almonds
6 eggs, separated
15 ml vanilla essence
397 g can condensed milk
500 ml cream
TO SERVE
Raspberry Coulis (page 146)

Quarter or halve the cherries, place in a small bowl and pour over the brandy. Toast the almonds in a dry non-stick frying pan until aromatic and golden. Cool.

In a large bowl beat the egg yolks, vanilla essence and condensed milk until smooth and creamy. Whip the cream stiffly and fold in. Whip the egg white stiffly and fold in. Pour two-thirds of the mixture into a large loaf tin and place in the freezer with the remaining mixture in a separate bowl. Freeze until the ice-cream is firm but still malleable.

Press a hollow into the ice-cream in the loaf tin. Mix the cherries (with the brandy) and almonds into the remaining ice-cream and spoon into the hollow. Freeze for 6-8 hours until firm.
TO SERVE Unmould the cassata onto a long platter and serve in slices with raspberry coulis or another sauce of your choice. SERVES 10-12

LEMON AND GREEN PEPPERCORN ICE-CREAM

Make your own crème fraîche for this ice-cream. Alternatively, purchase commercial crème fraîche. In this case, it's not necessary to whip it prior to folding it into the ice-cream base.

2-3 lemons
10 egg yolks
2 whole eggs
80 ml sugar
45 ml green peppercorns
45 ml lemon vodka
500 ml Crème Fraîche (page 135)
60 ml ginger liqueur
10 ml vanilla essence

Finely grate the lemon zest. Squeeze the juice. In a double boiler combine the egg yolks, eggs, sugar, lemon zest and half the juice. Beat over simmering water until pale and thick, and the eggs are cooked.

Purée the peppercorns with the remaining lemon juice and lemon vodka in a food processor or liquidizer until smooth. Remove the ice-cream base from the heat and pour into a clean, cold container. Cool. Stir in the peppercorn pulp.

If using home-made crème fraîche, beat to soft peaks. Add the ginger liqueur and vanilla essence and beat until stiff peaks form. Fold one-third of the crème fraîche into the ice cream base, then fold in the rest. If using commercial crème fraîche, simply fold it into the ice-cream base with the ginger liqueur and vanilla essence. Spoon into a plastic (not metal) freezer-friendly container. Freeze. SERVES 6-8

METRIC CONVERSION CHART

In this book, metric measurements have been given. Conversion to standard imperial measures are given below. Please remember that the equivalents are not exact, as measurements have been rounded out. Use either metric or imperial measurements, but not a mixture of both.

VOLUME AND LIQUID MEASURES

1 litre	4 cups		
750 ml	3 cups		
500 ml	2 cups		
375 ml	1½ cups		
300 ml	1¼ cups		
250 ml	1 cup		
200 ml	¾ cup		
150 ml	⅔ cup		
125 ml	½ cup		
80 ml	⅓ cup		
60 ml	¼ cup		
45 ml	3 tablespoons		
30 ml	2 tablespoons		
20 ml	4 teaspoons		
15 ml	1 tablespoon		
10 ml	2 teaspoons		
7 ml	1½ teaspoons		
5 ml	1 teaspoon		
2 ml	½ teaspoon		
1 ml	¼ teaspoon		

WEIGHTS

1000 grams	2¼ pounds
900 grams	2 pounds
450 grams	16 oz / 1 pound
350 grams	12 oz / ¾ pound
270 grams	9 oz
230 grams	8 oz / ½ pound
200 grams	7 oz
180 grams	6 oz
140 grams	5 oz
115 grams	4 oz / ¼ pound
90 grams	3 oz
60 grams	2 oz
30 grams	½ oz

OVEN TEMPERATURE EQUIVALENTS

Celcius	Fahrenheit	Gas mark	Heat of oven
100	200	¼	very cool
120	250	½	very cool
140	275	1	cool
150	300	2	cool
160	325	3	moderate
180	350	4	moderate
200	400	5	fairly hot
220	425	6	hot
230	450	8	very hot
250	475	9	very hot

CONTACT DETAILS

96 WINERY ROAD PAGE 28
Zandberg Farm, Winery Road,
  Somerset West, Western Cape
PO Box 5012 Helderview 7130
Tel (021) 842-2020. Fax (021) 842-2050
E-mail wineryrd@mweb.co.za

AUBERGINE PAGE 38
39 Barnet Street, Gardens,
  Western Cape 8001
Tel (021) 465-4909. Fax (021) 461-3781
E-mail aubergin@mweb.co.za

AU JARDIN AT THE VINEYARD
PAGE 104
Vineyard Hotel, Colinton Road,
  Newlands, Western Cape
PO Box 151 Newlands 7725
Tel (021) 683-1520. Fax (021) 683-3365
E-mail hotel@vineyard.co.za
Website www.vineyard.co.za

BARTHOLOMEUS KLIP FARMHOUSE
PAGE 12
Elandsberg Farm, Hermon,
  Western Cape
PO Box 36 Hermon 7308
Tel (022) 448-1820. Fax (022) 448-1829
E-mail bartholomeusklip@icon.co.za
Website www.parksgroup.co.za

THE BLUE TRAIN PAGE 40
PO Box 2671 Joubert Park, Gauteng 2044
Tel (012) 334-8459. Fax (012) 334-8464
E-mail bluetrain@transnet.co.za
Website www.bluetrain.co.za

BOSCHENDAL PAGE 94
R310, Pniel Road, Groot Drakenstein,
  Western Cape
PO Groot Drakenstein 7680
Tel (021) 870-4274. Fax (021) 874-2137
E-mail reservations@boschendal.com
Website www.boschendal.com

BUSHMANS KLOOF WILDERNESS
RESERVE PAGE 30
Jacaranda House, Forest Avenue,
  Bishopscourt, Western Cape
PO Box 53405 Kenilworth 7745
Lodge: PO Box 267 Clanwilliam 8135
Reservations: Tel (021) 797-0990. Fax (021)
  761-5551. Lodge: (027) 482-2627
E-mail info@bushmanskloof.co.za
Website www.bushmanskloof.co.za

CAPE MALAY RESTAURANT
PAGE 44
The Cellars-Hohenort, 93 Brommersvlei
  Road, Constantia, Western Cape
PO Box 270 Constantia 7848
Tel (021) 794-2137. Fax (021) 794-2149
E-mail cellars@ct.lia.net
Website www.cellars-hohenort.com

CARRIGANS COUNTRY ESTATE
PAGE 64
Off R40 between White River and
  Hazyview, Mpumalanga
PO Box 19 Kiepersol 1241
Tel (013) 764-1713. Fax (013) 764-1714

THE CELLARS-HOHENORT
PAGE 52
93 Brommersvlei Road, Constantia Valley,
  Western Cape
PO Box 270 Constantia 7848
Tel (021) 794-2137. Fax (021) 794-2149
E-mail cellars@ct.lia.net
Website www.cellars-hohenort.com

CLOETE'S AT ALPHEN PAGE 118
Alphen Drive, Constantia, Western Cape
PO Box 35 Constantia 7848
Tel (021) 794-5011. Fax (021) 794-5710
E-mail reservations@alphen.co.za
Website www.alphen.co.za

THE COACH HOUSE PAGE 120
PO Box 544 Tzaneen, Northern
  Province 0850
Tel (015) 307-3641. Fax (015) 307-1466
E-mail coachhouse@mweb.co.za
Website www.coachhouse.co.za

CYBELE FOREST LODGE PAGE 98
Off R40 between White River and
  Hazyview, Mpumalanga
PO Box 346 White River 1240
Tel (013) 764-1823. Fax (013) 764-1810
E-mail cybele@iafrica.com
Website www.cybele.co.za

DENNEHOF KAROO GUEST HOUSE
PAGE 110
Off Christina de Wit Street, Prince Albert,
  Western Cape
PO Box 123 Prince Albert 6930
Tel (023) 541-1227. Fax (023) 541-1158
E-mail hurford@gem.co.za
  elaineh@intekom.co.za
Website www7.50megs.com/dennehof

EMILY'S BISTRO PAGE 76
77 Roodebloem Road, Woodstock,
  Western Cape 7925
Tel (021) 448-2366. Fax (021) 761-7631
E-mail caia@mweb.co.za

FANCOURT HOTEL AND COUNTRY
CLUB PAGE 66
Montagu Street, Blanco, George,
  Western Cape
PO Box 2266 George 6530
Tel (044) 804-0000. Fax (044) 804-0700
E-mail hotel@fancourt.co.za
Website www.fancourt.co.za

GAMETRACKERS PAGE 46
Eagle Island Camp, Xaxaba Island,
  Okavango Delta, Botswana
Khwai River Lodge, Moremi Wildlife
  Reserve, Botswana
Savute Elephant Camp, Chobe National
  Park, Botswana
PO Box 786432 Sandton 2146
Tel (011) 481-6052. Fax (011) 481-6065
E-mail gtres@iafrica.com
Website www.gametrackers.orient-
  express.com

GARONGA SAFARI CAMP PAGE 126
Near Mica, Makalali Wild Life
  Conservancy, Northern Province
PO Box 2058 Parklands 2121
Tel (011) 233-8821. Fax (011) 233-8829
E-mail tsa@wn.apc.org
Website www.garonga.com

GLENSHIEL COUNTRY LODGE
PAGE 72
R71 Magoebaskloof, Northern Province
PO Box 55 Haenertsburg 0730
Tel (015) 276-6000. Fax (015) 276-6001
E-mail gm@glenshiel.threecities.co.za
Website www.threecities.co.za

GRANDE ROCHE HOTEL PAGE 16
Plantasie Street, Paarl, Western Cape
PO Box 6038 Paarl 7622
Tel (021) 863-2727. Fax (021) 863-2220
E-mail reserve@granderoche.co.za
Website www.granderoche.com

HAZENDAL ESTATE PAGE 74
Bottelary Road, Kuils River, Western Cape
PO Box 336 Stellenbosch 7599
Tel (012) 903-5112. Fax (012) 903-0057
E-mail info@hazendal.co.za
Website www.wine.co.za

HIGHGROVE HOUSE PAGE 130
R40 between White River and Hazyview, Mpumalanga
PO Box 46 Kiepersol 1241
Tel (013) 764-1844. Fax (013) 764-1855
E-mail highgrove@mweb.co.za
Website www.highgrove.co.za

LE QUARTIER FRANÇAIS PAGE 34
16 Huguenot Road, Franschhoek, Western Cape
PO Box 237 Franschhoek 7690
Tel (021) 876-2151. Fax (021) 876-3105
E-mail res@lqf.co.za
Website www.lqf.co.za

THE MARINE PAGE 82
Marine Drive, Hermanus, Western Cape
PO Box 9 Hermanus 7200
Tel (028) 313-1000. Fax (028) 313-0160
E-mail marine@hermanus.co.za
Website www.marine-hermanus.co.za

THE MOUNT NELSON HOTEL PAGE 56
76 Orange Street, Gardens, Cape Town, Western Cape
PO Box 2608 Cape Town 8000
Tel (021) 483-1000. Fax (021) 424-7472
E-mail reservations@mountnelson.co.za
Website www.mountnelsonhotel.orient-express.com

NGALA PRIVATE GAME RESERVE PAGE 18
Kruger National Park, Northern Province
CCAfrica, Bateleur House, Pinmill Farm, Katherine Avenue, Sandown, Gauteng
Private Bag X27 Benmore 2010
Tel (011) 809-4447. Fax (011) 809-4400
E-mail reservations@ccafrica.com
Website www.ccafrica.com

OLD JOE'S KAIA PAGE 50
Schoemanskloof Valley Road, Mpumalanga
PO Box 108 Schagen 1207
Tel (013) 733-3045/6. Fax (013) 733-3777
Website www.oldjoes.co.za

PARKS PAGE 22
114 Constantia Road, Constantia, Western Cape
PO Box 100 Constantia 7848
Tel (021) 797-8202. Fax (021) 797-8233.
E-mail bibendum@iafrica.com
Website www.parksgroup.co.za

PHINDA PRIVATE GAME RESERVE PAGE 106
Mkuze, KwaZulu-Natal
CCAfrica, Bateleur House, Pinmill Farm, Katherine Avenue, Sandown, Gauteng
Private Bag X27 Benmore 2010
Tel (011) 809-4447. Fax (011) 809-4400
E-mail reservations@ccafrica.com
Website www.ccafrica.com

THE PLETTENBERG PAGE 24
40 Church Street, Plettenberg Bay, Western Cape
PO Box 719 Plettenberg Bay 6600
Tel (044) 533-2030. Fax (044) 533-2074
E-mail plettenberg@pixie.co.za
Website www.plettenberg.com

PRUE LEITH COLLEGE OF FOOD AND WINE PAGE 58
262 Rhino Street, Hennopspark Ext. 2, Centurion, Gauteng
PO Box 10731 Centurion 0046
Tel (012) 654-5203 / 660-3260. Fax (012) 660-3246
E-mail pleith@global.co.za
Website: www.prueleith.co.za

RHEBOKSKLOOF PAGE 124
Paarl, Western Cape
PO Box 7141 Noorder Paarl 7623
Tel (021) 863-8386. Fax (021) 863-8504
E-mail rhebok@iafrica.com
Website www.rhebokskloof.co.za

ROGGELAND COUNTRY HOUSE PAGE 60
Dal Josafat Valley, Northern Paarl, Western Cape
PO Box 7210 Northern Paarl 7623
Tel (021) 868-2501. Fax (021) 868-2113
E-mail rog@iafrica.com
Website www.exploreafrica.com/roggeland

ROSENHOF COUNTRY LODGE PAGE 80
264 Baron van Rheede Street, Oudtshoorn, Western Cape
PO Box 378 Oudtshoorn 6620
Tel (044) 272-2232. Fax (044) 279-1793
E-mail rosenhof@xsinet.co.za
Website www.theportfolio.co.za

ROZENHOF RESTAURANT PAGE 112
18 Kloof Street, Cape Town, Western Cape 8001
Tel (021) 424-1968. Fax (021) 423-6058
E-mail rozenhofrestaurant@mweb.co.za

SAVOY CABBAGE PAGE 88
101 Hout Street, Heritage Square, Cape Town, Western Cape
PO Box 15912 Vlaeberg 8018
Tel (021) 424-2626. Fax (021) 424-3366
E-mail savoycab@iafrica.com

SELATI LODGE AT SABI SABI PAGE 92
Sabi Sabi Private Game Reserve, Sabi Sand, Mpumalanga
PO Box 52665 Saxonwold 2132
Tel (011) 483-3939. Fax (011) 483-3799
E-mail com@sabisabi.com
Website www.sabisabi.com

SHANGANA CULTURAL VILLAGE PAGE 86
R535 Graskop Road, Hazyview, Mpumalanga
PO Box 2500 Hazyview 1242
Tel (013) 737-7000. Fax (013) 737-7007
E-mail shangana@fast.co.za
Website www.shangana.co.za

SINGITA PRIVATE GAME RESERVE PAGE 114
Sabi Sand, Mpumalanga
PO Box 650881 Benmore 2010
Tel (011) 234-0990. Fax (011) 234-0535
E-mail singita@singita.co.za
Website www.singita.co.za

SPIER ESTATE PAGE 100
Baden Powell Drive, Stellenbosch, Western Cape
PO Box 1078 Stellenbosch 7599
Tel (021) 809-1100. Fax (021) 881-3634
E-mail info@spier.co.za
Website www.spier.co.za

VERGELEGEN PAGE 132
Loursensford Road, Somerset West, Western Cape
PO Box 17 Somerset West 7129
Tel (021) 847-1334. Fax (021) 847-1608
E-mail jjohnson@vergelegen.co.za

THE WESTCLIFF HOTEL PAGE 70
67 Jan Smuts Avenue, Westcliff, Johannesburg, Gauteng
PO Box 2700 Saxonwold 2132
Tel (011) 646-2400. Fax (011) 646-3500
E-mail reservations@westcliff.co.za
Website www.westcliffhotel.orient-express.com

GLOSSARY OF COOKING TERMS, EQUIPMENT & INGREDIENTS

Allspice Also called pimento. A small, dried berry which is full of aroma and flavour combining the elements of cinnamon, cloves and nutmeg.

Amarula Liqueur Creamy liqueur made from the fruit of the marula tree.

Aroborio rice Short-grained rice used for making risotto, named after a village in the Piedmont region of northern Italy. While cooking the rice releases starch, giving a creamy texture to the dish.

Atjar Generic name for a variety of pickles.

Aubergine Firm, glossy-skinned vegetable available in different shapes and colours from purple to white with ivory flesh. Also called brinjal and eggplant.

Avocado Pear-shaped fruit native to tropical America. When ready to eat, the whole surface yields slightly to even pressure; there's extra softness around the stalk, which comes off easily when touched gently.

Bain-Marie Water bath with very hot water in which food is cooked. The water diffuses the direct heat of the oven so that the food cooks gently. Also used to keep food hot after cooking.

Baking Powder A mixture of baking soda (sodium bicarbonate) and cream of tartar used as a raising agent in baking. When baking powder is moistened it produces carbon dioxide which causes the mixture to expand and rise.

Balsamic Vinegar Dark, sweetish, mellow wine vinegar produced in Modena, Italy and used mainly as a dressing for salads and vegetables, but sometimes in cooking. The vinegar is aged in a series of oak and hickory barrels; the older it is, the sweeter and less acidic it becomes.

Barbecue Grilling meat, fish, vegetables and fruit over the coals of a fire. Known as braaiing in SA.

Basil Herb with soft green leaves. Sweet basil is the most common, but there are other varieties, like purple, bronze or opal basil, lettuce basil and small-leafed Greek basil. Basil has a warm, resinous, clove-like flavour and fragrance, and is delicious fresh or cooked. To preserve the taste add basil right at the end of the cooking time.

Bay Leaves From the bay or laurel tree. Essential ingredient in a bouquet garni.

Bean Sprouts Green mung beans are usually used for fresh bean sprouts. Excellent for garnishing salads, and for adding to stir-fries.

Beef Fillet Cut from the middle portion of the fillet. Known as tenderloin in the USA.

Beef Sirloin Cut from the larger part of the T-bone. Entrecôte is the French term for the large oblong muscle in the sirloin.

Bicarbonate of Soda Called Baking soda in the USA. Used as a raising agent in baking.

Biltong Traditional South African snack: salty, spicy dried meat which also makes a great garnish for salads, soups and vegetables.

Black Currants Round black berries, larger than red currants which grow as single berries. More savoury than sweet, they are good in savoury sauces.

Black Mussels Grow wild on rocks close to the seashore and are also cultivated and sold fresh, frozen and canned. When preparing fresh mussels, discard any with broken or cracked shells and those that remain open after you've tapped them.

Blanch A cooking technique where raw ingredients are plunged briefly into boiling water then drained and refreshed in cold water.

Blue Cheese Strong blue-veined cheese like French roquefort, English stilton and Italian gorgonzola.

Bobotie Traditional South African dish made from spiced, minced or finely chopped meat baked in a dish with a custard topping. See recipes for Duck Bobotie page 32 and Bobotie page 97.

Bocconcini Small balls of mozzarella cheese.

Boerewors "Farmer's sausage", a fairly coarse South African sausage made from a spicy mix of beef and pork, with coriander predominating.

Bok Choy "Choy" means "cabbage", and there are many types available, known as bok choy, pak choy, choy sum, choy sin, Chinese cabbage and more. They lend crisp texture and flavour to dishes.

Bouquet Garni "Herb bouquet", a bundle of aromatic herbs which should include parsley, thyme and bay leaves used to flavour stocks, soups, casseroles and stews. Also available dried.

Braise Cooking where very little liquid is added.

Brandy Distilled from grapes and matured in oak barrels; one of the great drinks of the world. Brandy is used frequently in cooking. It may be added to sauces and casseroles, or warmed, flamed and added to a dish at the end of cooking; the alcohol evaporates, but the flavour lingers.

Breyani/Biryani Spicy dish made with rice and lentils which forms a base for meat, fish or vegetables. **Breyani Masala** A special spice mix for the preparation of breyanis. Can be purchased ready-made.

Butter Both salted and unsalted butter are used in cooking. Unsalted butter is preferred for baking and desserts. However, as salt is a preserving agent, salted butter will last longer in the fridge. When frying in butter, don't use too high a heat, otherwise the butter will burn. To prevent this happening, add a dash of oil or fry in ghee. Recipe page 135.

Buttermilk The sourish liquid left over from churned cream when butter is being produced.

Butternut Like pumpkin, butternut is family of the gem squash, courgette and hubbard squash. Pumpkin may be substituted in all butternut recipes.

Calamari Also called squid, inkfish and chokka. Close cousin is the cuttlefish. Though both are called calamari on restaurant menus, they look quite different. Cuttlefish has a shorter head and tentacles, and a much larger body which yields steaks that are thick and tender.

Camembert Cheese Pale yellow, smooth soft French cheese which gets stronger as it ripens.

Capers The flower of the caper bush grows into an oval fruit or berry filled with tiny seeds. Sold in a brine or vinegar.

Caraway Seeds Aromatic, brown sickle-shaped seeds used in baking and cheese-making.

Cardamom The pods are the dried fruit of a plant of the ginger family containing tiny black seeds which are pungent and aromatic. Lightly crushed pods and seeds are used in savoury and sweet dishes.

Castor Sugar Fine granulated sugar used in baking and desserts. Also known as superfine sugar and caster sugar.

Cayenne Pepper Fine powder made by grinding various species of dried capsicum (chilli) pods. Also called chilli powder. Very hot, so use sparingly.

Celeriac Edible, turnip-type root, a variety of celery.

Celery A plant with long, crisp stalks and bushy leaves on the top. Both the leaves and stalks (ribs) may be used in cooking as well as in salads.

Cheddar Cheese Sharp-tasting English cheese.

Cherry Tomatoes Small red tomatoes.

Chicory Also called witloof, witlof and endive, chicory is the cultivated and developed form of wild chicory, the plant whose root was first used as a coffee substitute, or for adding to coffee. Chicory roots put out pale green shoots which form a conical head of crisp white, faintly bitter leaves.

Chilli/Chili Fresh and dried red and green chillies impart heat to dishes. There are many different types, the smaller the hotter, with seeds and ribs being the hottest parts. These may be discarded before use.

Chives A herb of the onion family with thin green stems. Snip and use in salads and omelettes.

Chutney Thick, sweet-spicy relish made with fruit or vegetables, used as a condiment and a sambal with curried dishes.

Cinnamon Trees from which cinnamon and cassia come from belong to the laurel family. Finely rolled cinnamon sticks are more gently spiced than sturdier cassia bark. Both add flavour to sweet and savoury dishes, though ground cinnamon is more often used in sweet dishes.

Cloves Whole cloves are the small, dark and spiky bud of the flower of an evergreen tropical tree native to Southeast Asia, which add a fairly pungent aroma to many dishes. Ground cloves may be used in savoury dishes as well as in baking and desserts.

Coconut Coconuts grow on tropical palms. The flesh may be dried and shredded into desiccated coconut. Coconut milk and cream is available in tins.

Coriander Yellowish-white whole seeds are aromatic and impart a lemony-sage flavour to savoury dishes. Ground coriander is an important flavouring for delicately spiced dishes, as well as in curry mixes. Aromatic coriander leaves (fresh coriander), the herb which grows from the seeds, is used as a garnish, though occasionally added to a dish at the end of cooking. Also called dhania, dhunia, cilantro and Chinese parsley.

Cornflour Fine flour made from corn. A quick thickener for sauces, gravies, casseroles and stews. Don't add directly to hot liquid, first mix to a paste with cold liquid, stir into the sauce and cook, stirring constantly, until it thickens. Also useful in desserts and, when mixed with cake flour, makes baking lighter. Also known as cornstarch and maizena. Substitute: arrowroot.

Courgettes Slim green vegetable with creamy flesh. Also called baby marrows and zucchini.

Couscous This North African staple is a form of pasta; semolina grains are dampened then rolled in flour. Par-cooked couscous merely needs to be moistened and steamed until piping not, then it's ready to eat. Butter or olive oil may be mixed in.

Cream Cheese Soft curd cheese with a mild flavour, more often used in cooking than on a cheese board.

Cream Fresh cream is the lighter, fattier portion of full cream milk, and contains all the major nutritional components of milk. Should it become sour, use in savoury dishes and to enrich casseroles, sauces and gravies.

Crème de Cassis Liqueur made from black currants.

Crème de Menthe Peppermint-flavoured liqueur.

Crème Fraîche Cream which has been allowed to ferment and thicken naturally and has a nutty, slightly sour flavour. Crème fraîche may also be made by mixing cream and buttermilk. Recipe page 135.

Crostini Thin slices of bread toasted and brushed with olive oil and garlic. Good in soups or as a crisp salad topping, as well as a base for canapés.

Croûtons Cubes of bread which are fried, grilled or baked. Good as a garnish for soups and salads.

Cumin Highly aromatic spice available as brownish seeds as well as ground to a fine powder. Adds distinctive flavouring to many savoury dishes.

Curry Powder Usually refers to a commercial mix of spices to flavour curries. It is preferable to mix, roast and grind your own spices. Recipes page 136.

Dariole Moulds Small cylindrical moulds, usually made of metal, used to bake or steam single portions of puddings, or in which to set puddings, ice-creams or mousses.

Dates Fruit of the date palm.

Deglaze The process of adding liquid to a pan in which food has been fried, whereby the coagulated juices are dissolved and incorporated into the sauce.

Demi-Glace Light brown sauce usually flavoured with madeira or sherry.

Dijon Mustard Superior aromatic mustard made in Dijon, the great mustard centre of France. Like pepper, mustard loses its flavour if it is cooked for any length of time, so add it towards the end of cooking.

Dill Delicate herb with feathery blue-green leaves, fine yellow flowers and flat, pale brown, oval seeds with a dark rib down the centre.

Fat Clarified duck or beef fat is made by the rendered fat of duck, beef or veal, which is then strained through a fine cloth. Store in a small container in the fridge for up to six months.

Fennel Flowering herb with a bulbous edible stem. The seeds, dried roots and anise-flavoured leaves may be used as flavouring, or added to salads. Known as "sweet cumin", fennel is a member of the same family. Available in seeds or in ground form.

Feta Cheese Classic, crumbly feta cheese is high in sodium because it's cured and stored in brine. Soak it in cold water to remove some of the salt if wished.

Fish Sauce Thin sour, salty sauce used in Asian cooking to bring out the flavour of other foods. Made from fermented anchovies.

Five Spice A reddish-brown powder popular in Chinese cooking; made from star anise, fennel, cinnamon, cloves and szechwan pepper.

Flour Most flour is made from wheat, of which there are two types – strong and soft. The former has a higher proportion of gluten-producing protein, which is essential for bread baking. Flour made from soft wheat does not rise as well, but it is higher in starch – perfect for cakes, scones and muffins. All-purpose flour is a mixture of soft and hard wheat. Wholewheat flour is made from the whole grain. Brown and cake flour is refined – brown has 85% of the grain; cake has about 70%. Self-raising flour has a raising agent added to make it nice and light.

Frying Pan Wide, flat pan in which to shallow-fry food. USA: skillet.

Game Big game in South Africa includes buffalo, zebra, kudu, gemsbok, hartebeest, wildebeest and eland. Small game includes the common duiker, steenbok, springbok, impala, ribbok, blesbok and bosbok. Wild boars such as bushpig and warthog are also regarded as game.

Ganache A mixture of melted chocolate and cream or butter used to make chocolate truffles or to use to fill or ice cakes.

Garam Masala A fresh spice mix used in making curry. The word garam (or gharum) means "warm" or "hot" and describes spice mixes which may vary, depending on the personal preferences of the cook. Recipe page 136.

Garlic Indispensable in cooking! Purchase firm, plump heads and separate into cloves to peel and crush or chop just before using. See also recipes for Garlic Confit and Roasted Garlic page 135.

Gelatine/Gelatin Available as granules and occasionally in sheet form. For 1 sheet, substitute 5 ml (1 tsp) granules. To dissolve, sprinkle gelatine onto cold liquid and warm in a pan of hot water. Alternatively, sprinkle onto warm liquid and stir in.

Ghee Clarified Butter may be heated to a very high temperature without burning, for example when frying. Recipe page 135.

Gherkins Small, young, pickled cucumbers.

Ginger Green or root ginger is important in Asian cooking, and any spicy or curried dishes. Purée a knob of green ginger in a food processor with a little oil, salt and water, or a dash of sherry as a preservative. Bottle and refrigerate for up to eight weeks. Dried ginger is used in curry spices as well as in a variety of recipes and drinks, from savoury to sweet.

Glacé Cherries Ripe cherries are picked, sorted, graded and stored in waxed underground tanks filled with brine. After rinsing, stalking and pitting, the cherries are subjected to a process of soaking in increasingly stronger sugar solutions during which all the natural fruit sugars are replaced by sucrose.

Gnocchi Small dumplings made of potatoes and other ingredients such as ricotta and spinach.

Goats' Cheese Chevre, or goats' milk cheese, is fine-textured and distinctively flavoured and may be used as is or lightly cooked.

Grand Marnier Citrus-based liqueur.

Granny Smith Apples Tart apples most often used in cooking.

Grill A method of cooking under a preheated oven griller, over a barbecue (called braai in South Africa) or in a frying pan, grill pan or skillet. USA: broil.

Harissa A paste made from chillies, olive oil and garlic, used in North African cooking or as a condiment. Recipe Harissa Paste page 136; Harissa Sauce page 138.

Horseradish A tall plant, a member of the mustard family, grown for its white, hot-flavoured root, which is ground and mixed with vinegar, salt and cream to form a paste known as creamed horseradish or horseradish cream.

Hummus Chick pea and sesame seed paste served as a spread or a dip with pita bread or vegetables.

Icing Sugar Finely ground sugar used for making cake icing. Known as powdered sugar or confectioners' sugar in the USA.

Julienne Strips Foods – most often vegetables – cut into fine strips about the size of matchsticks.

Juniper Berries Fruit of a shrub related to the cypress family, which lends special flavour to venison and game birds.

Ketjap Manis Indonesian dark, sweetened soy sauce which is more syrupy in texture to soy sauce.

Kiwi Fruit Oval, soft green fruit in a pale brown fuzzy skin. Also called Chinese gooseberry.

Lamb Meat from young sheep slaughtered anytime between birth and sixteen months. More tender though less flavourful than mutton, which comes from older animals.

Lemongrass A tall lemon-scented grass used in oriental cooking. Strip off the tough outer leaves and use the more tender root-end of the grass.

Lentils Nutritious, flattish leguminous seeds, a pulse, used in soups, salads and stews.

Maize Also called mealie, sweetcorn, corn on the cob. Portuguese seafarers introduced the corn via Europe to Africa many years ago. The local populace called it mealie. In recent years natural cloning of the starch-rich mealie has produced a new, sweet cultivar called sweetcorn.

Maize Meal Coarse "flour" ground from dried maize. Substitute: polenta.

Mangetout Also known as snow peas and sugar peas; small, bright green, flat pods containing embryo peas. They are cooked for only a brief time to retain their texture and colour.

Mango Tropical fruit with golden flesh and skin which ripens to orangey-red. Eaten fresh and dried. Delicious in fruit salads, and also in atjars and chutneys.

Marjoram Perennial herb of the mint family, with delicately scented and flavoured soft leaves.

Marzipan Sweet paste made from almonds and sugar, used for covering and decorating cakes.

Masala A mixture of spices cooked with a particular dish. Green masala, red masala and garam masala (mixed spice), is available commercially, but home-made is better. Recipes page 136.

Mascarpone Cheese Soft Italian curd-style cheese from cow's milk, similar is consistency to very thick cream. Serve with fruit or use fresh in a dessert.

Melon Soft fruit known variously as sweet melon, cantaloupe, rockmelon and winter melon.

Mint A popular garnish, especially for desserts and cakes. Great with peas and young potatoes, as well as other vegetables such as beans, carrots, beetroot, cabbage, spinach and mushrooms.

Mirin Sweetened rice wine from Japan which is used in sauces and marinades.

Mortar and Pestle A wooden, brass or stone set consisting of a bowl (mortar) and crusher (pestle) which is used for crushing spices and pulping softer ingredients such as nuts, garlic and ginger.

Mozzarella Soft, unripened curd cheese with a mild, creamy taste. Good for cooking, especially as a topping for pizza. Also smoked mozzarella which is gently smoked for added flavour.

Muscadel Red and white varieties of grapes used to make dessert wines. Also refers to the wine which is made from the grapes.

Mushrooms Many different mushrooms are used in cooking, including button (white), brown, black and oyster mushrooms, and wild mushrooms such as the shiitake, cep, morel and girolle. The button mushroom is small and closed. As it grows, brownish-pink gills open and it is called a cup mushroom. Large, flat, black mushrooms are fully ripe and have darker gills.

Mustard Seeds Reddish-brown seeds are highly nutritious and spicy-hot, adding pungency to savoury dishes and salad dressings.

Nutmeg The evergreen nutmeg tree bears a yellow fruit with a seed which, when dried, is called nutmeg, a popular spice. The seed is surrounded by a lacy red network which is dried and known as mace. For the best flavour, use freshly grated nutmeg rather than bottled ready-ground nutmeg.

Olive Oil Extra virgin olive oil is produced from the first cold pressing of olives which gives a strong distinctive flavour. Due to its lower yield, it tends to be more expensive than olive oil. Olive oil is a blend of extra virgin olive oil with oil that has been further refined to remove any impurities and improve the flavour.

Onions There are many types of onion, the most common being the brown and white onion. Red onions are milder and more sweetly flavoured.

Orange Essence Extract from oranges which is used in baking, desserts and ice-cream.

Oregano/Origanum Herb from a creeping perennial plant; essential in Mediterranean dishes.

Ostrich Fillet Ostrich meat is virtually fat-free, high in protein, and lower in calories, saturated fat and cholesterol than chicken, turkey, mutton, beef or pork. As ostrich meat has a high moisture content and so little fat compared with other meats, special care has to be taken in cooking.

Oysters Molluscs which are found along many parts of South Africa's coastline: KwaZulu-Natal (wild oysters in deep, oblong shells), Knysna (cultivated in the lagoon), Algoa Bay (cultivated on ropes in the deep sea), and the West Coast as far as Namibia, which are large and tasty.

Pancetta Strongly flavoured Italian streaky pork belly (bacon) that may be purchased raw or smoked. Usually rolled tightly and sliced across to form spirals. Unsmoked bacon may be substituted.

Papino See Pawpaw.

Paprika Dried spice from the sweet red pepper (capsicum). Good paprika should have a mild, sweet flavour, strong smell and a brilliant red colour.

Parmesan Cheese Hard Italian cheese made from cow's milk with granular texture and sharp flavour. Always served freshly grated or shaved.

Parsley Most useful herb in cooking. Several different varieties may be found: curly and the more flavoursome flat-leaf being the most prolific.

Passionfruit Also known as granadilla (grenadilla). Round, purple-skinned tropical fruit. Cut open and scoop out pulp and seeds.

Pâté A firm, savoury paste that may be prepared with various types of meat such as chicken and veal, and offal, such as chicken and duck livers. Usually of finer texture than a terrine.

Pattipans Member of the squash family, also called custard marrow. Creamy, yellow or striped skin, the edges scalloped. The smaller specimens are the best, being of superior flavour and texture.

Pawpaw/Papaya Tropical fruit introduced to tropical KwaZulu-Natal after an influx of Mauritians had settled there.

Peanuts The peanut or groundnut, a legume, was discovered in 950 BC by Incas who lived in the Peruvian mountains and jungles in South America. They were taken to Europe during the 13th and 14th centuries by the Spanish Conquistadors, and then to Asia, West Africa and other parts of the world, including southern Africa.

Pecorino Cheese Italian ewe's milk cheese which is available aged, dry and hard, or young a soft.

Pepper Black and white peppercorns, essential spicing in all savoury dishes, grow on a tropical vine. Black pepper is the whole berry, picked when green and dried. White pepper, milder in flavour, is the core of the berry. Peppercorns are available whole, cracked (partially crushed) and ground. Freshly milled peppercorns impart the very best flavour.

Peppers Red, yellow and black peppers are the mature stage of varieties of green peppers, the riper the sweeter. Members of the capsicum family. Also called sweet peppers, bell peppers and capsicums.

Pesto Literally "paste", usually of basil (or other herbs), garlic, pine nuts, olive oil and parmesan cheese. Recipes page 138.

Phyllo Pastry Sheets of fine pastry, available rolled and frozen. The layers should be brushed with melted butter before baking.

Pilaf Dish of cooked rice to which meat, fish or poultry may be added.

Pine Nuts Kernels of pine cones that are rich, oily and flavoursome. Used widely in Middle Eastern and Greek cooking, and an essential ingredient of pesto.

Plum Tomatoes Also known as egg, roma and pear tomatoes. Robust, fleshy and oval in shape and particularly suitable for making sauces.

Polenta Grains of dried ground corn or maize. The term refers both to the grains as well as the cooked dish. In South Africa maize meal may be substituted.

Poppy Seeds The seed capsule of poppy flowers contains tiny seeds which are used in baking and confectionery. They also yield an oil used in cooking and salad dressings.

Port This noble wine was produced for generations by Portuguese peasants in the Douro valley of Northern Portugal, refined by British wine traders and merchants in the 17th century, and today shipped around the world. With its viticultural heritage stretching back nearly three and a half centuries, the vineyards of the Cape have been producing Port-style wines for a good portion of this time.

Prawns These delicious shellfish are usually purchased fresh, frozen in blocks of ice or snap frozen. If they're to be cooked in the shell, first remove the alimentary canal (vein) down the back.

Puff Pastry Very light pastry that expands when baking and forms many different layers.

Pumpkin Although pumpkins grow to an enormous size, those weighing between 3 and 5 kilograms are best. Colours range from greenish white through yellow and ochre to bright orange. Pumpkin was one of the first crops to grow successfully in Jan van Riebeeck's vegetable garden after he landed at the Cape in 1652, although there is evidence that the vegetable had been enjoyed for centuries by resident black clans. Butternut (also family of the gem squash, courgette and hubbard squash) may be substituted.

Purée Food blended to a smooth paste.

Quail Small, migratory game bird related to the pheasant.

Ramekin A small ceramic dish used to bake or set food in.

Red Currants Small, roundish, bright red currants are tart and juicy. They grow on a bush in clumps like grapes.

Render A method of melting fat from meat by heating it until it melts away.

Rice Long grain rice: long and slender in shape which, when cooked, remain separate, light and fluffy. Medium grain rice: plump in shape. When cooked, the rice is more moist and tender than long grain rice. Short grain rice: almost round in shape, and clings together when cooked. Brown rice: rice from which only the hull has been removed. Basmati rice: top quality long grain rice. Basmati means "fragrant" in Hindi. See also Wild Rice.

Rice Paper Fine transparent 'paper' made from a paste of rice and water. Dip in water before using to make them pliable.

Risotto Short grain arborio rice is used for risotto, a creamy Italian dish that may be sweet or savoury.

Rock Lobster Also called lobster, crayfish and kreef. In South Africa the official name is Rock Lobster, to prevent international confusion; crayfish or crawfish are smaller types of lobster not found in our waters. Three types of rock lobster are fished here, each with its own habitat and each controlled by specific regulations pertaining to catch, bag and size limits.

Rocket Leaves of a plant related to the cress family, which are delicious in salads, as they impart a fresh, peppery flavour. Also called aragula.

Rooibos World-famous tannin-free rooibos ("red bush") grows along the Olifants River and high in the Cedarberg in the Western Cape, where its twigs and leaves are dried and made into a popular "tea". Today it is the preferred beverage of many South Africans and health-conscious folk in other parts of the world where rooibos is exported.

Rosemary Needle-shaped leaves of the sturdy rosemary bush. Popular in Italian cooking, and well suited to meat recipes in particular. It may also be tossed onto the glowing coals over which meat, fish and vegetables are barbecuing to impart a gentle herby flavour.

Rosewater Diluted essence extracted from rose petals by steam dilation. Essential ingredient in many Asian sweetmeats and desserts.

Rump Steak Cut from the centre part of the rump. Known as sirloin in the USA.

Saffron The world's most expensive spice, the orangey-yellow stigmas from a small purple crocus flower, each of which only produces three flowers. These are hand-picked and dried. Some 75 000 blossoms produce just 500 g of saffron. Saffron is usually soaked in warm water or milk to extract its brilliant colour and mildly bitter flavour. About 2 ml (½ tsp) of saffron filaments are sufficient to flavour and colour a meal for four to six.

Sage Called salvia in Italy, it has grey-green leaves which are suited to dishes containing beans and meat. Also good infused in butter and served as a sauce, and deep-fried and used as a garnish.

Sago Small white grains made from the stem of the sago palm. Used as a thickening agent and for milk puddings.

Sambals Traditional accompaniments to curries such as desiccated coconut, chopped cucumber mixed with yoghurt, finely chopped onion and tomato, and chutneys and relishes.

Samoosa Deep-fried triangular pastries stuffed with spicy vegetables, meat or fish served as snacks.

Semolina A wheat product known as "farina" in the USA. It comes in coarse, medium and fine grades.

Sesame Oil Oil extracted from toasted sesame seeds which gives wonderfully nutty flavour. Use only a small amount in cooking, as the flavour is strong.

Sesame Seeds Small, nutritious seeds add a wonderful nutty flavour to dishes, especially when roasted in a dry frying pan. Useful in flavouring both sweet and savoury dishes, and as a garnish for soups, salads and vegetable dishes.

Shallot A small member of the onion family with a pale brown skin. Not easily found in South Africa, which is why large spring onions are substituted.

Sherry A sweet fortified wine.

Shiitake Mushrooms Originally from Japan and Korea, shiitake mushrooms have brownish tops with a creamy underside and a distinctive meaty flavour and firm texture. Available fresh or dried, in which case they should be soaked in cold water for about 3 hours before use.

Smoked Fish Fish cured by either hot or cold smoking.

Soufflé Light, fluffy baked dish made by folding beaten egg white into other ingredients and baking in a hot oven.

Soy Sauce Indispenable in Asian cooking, this versatile sauce enhances many dishes. Different grades such as light and dark are available.

Spinach More correctly called Swiss chard, or blett in Europe and silverbeet in Australia and New Zealand. In South Africa you will also find morog (also called morogo or imfino) used in recipes calling for spinach. This is the leaves of more than a hundred different varieties of wild plant. The leaves, pods and tendrils vary in flavour and are carefully plucked so as not to damage the plant.

Spring Onions Member of the onion family, called scallion in the USA. They do not form as large a bulb as shallots, for which they may be substituted.

Springbok Medium-sized antelope; popular venison.

Springroll Pastry Thin white sheets of pastry sold frozen. Thaw and peel off one at a time and re-freeze left-overs. Substitute large wonton wrappers.

Star Anise Star-shaped, pungently flavoured seed pod of a plant widely grown in southern China. Used as a spice, and available whole and ground.

Sterilize Jars Wash thoroughly in hot soapy water and rinse well. Place on a baking tray in an oven preheated to 100ºC for 30 minutes. Fill and seal while still warm.

Sultanas Dried, golden-yellow, seedless grapes.

Sun-Dried Tomatoes Sliced tomatoes dried in the sun or oven, sometimes packed in olive oil. The flavour is concentrated, rich and lingering. Reconstitute dried tomatoes in water before use.

Sweat To cook ingredients slowly over medium or low heat with very little fat or liquid until soft. The pan may be covered or uncovered.

Sweet Potato Irregularly-shaped sweet-flavoured potatoes with a mealy texture and nutty flavour. Called kumara in Australia and New Zealand.

Szechwan Peppercorns Not peppercorns at all, but small, reddish-brown dried berries, native to the Chinese province of Szechwan, have a distinctive fragrance and flavour. Roast gently in a dry frying pan before crushing in a pestle and mortar. They give a pleasant tingling sensation on the tongue. Also called anise pepper and Chinese pepper.

Tabasco Pepper Sauce Hot and spicy sauce/condiment made in Louisianna, USA from chillies.

Tahini Thick, smooth paste made from lightly roasted and ground sesame seeds. Available in jars.

Tamarind The pasty dried fruit of the tamarind tree which grows in southeast Asia and India. Available as a compressed paste or as a semi-dried seed. To extract the juice soak 50 g in 125 ml boiling water. Set aside to soak for about one hour, strain off the liquid, pressing out as much flavour as possible. Use as required. Recipe for Tamarind Water page 136.

Tempura Flour Very light flour used to make a light, crisp batter.

Teriyaki Sauce Asian sauce made from sake (rice wine), soy sauce and sugar.

Terrine Spicy mixed minced meat of coarser texture than pâté. Also the name of the dish that it is cooked in.

Terroir A French term which refers to geographic influences on wine grapes, including the type of soil, altitude, sun, incline and water drainage.

Thyme Sturdy, well-flavoured herb with small leaves on a woody stem.

Tikka Spice Mix Hot and spicy Indian mixture available commercially, and used to coat meat prior to cooking.

Toasting Technique for bringing out the flavour of nuts, seeds and spices. Heat them in a dry frying pan until their fragrance is released. Seeds may pop, so take care.

Trout Prized freshwater fish farmed in many areas of South Africa. Processing the fish for smoking includes soaking in brine (a mixture of salt and water) for a couple of hours. Larger fillets are cold-smoked (curing only by smoke); smaller fish are hot-smoked where temperatures of about 70ºC cures them by a combination of cooking and smoking.

Tuna Of the many species of this migratory gamefish, twenty four are found in southern African waters. The best for eating: bluefin tuna, longfin tuna, yellowfish tuna, frigate tuna and skipjack. Much of the annual catch ends up in cans, and becomes one of South Africa's most important pantry standby's. In the East, of course, fresh tuna is a very important ingredient of sashimi.

Turmeric Dried rhizome of a perennial plant belonging to the ginger family, available ground to a powder and cornerstone of commercial curry powders. Also called borrie in South Africa, turmeric imparts colour and a pungent flavour, which can become overpowering if too much of the spice is used.

Van der Hum Famous South African liqueur flavoured with naartjie (tangerine) and spices. The liqueur is believed to have been named after Admiral Van der Hum of the V.O.C. fleet who was extremely fond of it.

Vanilla Essence/ Extract Extract from vanilla pods, used to add flavour in baking, desserts and ice-cream.

Vanilla Pod Also called vanilla bean. Long, dark dried seed pods of an orchid native to Mexico. The best vanilla pods are flexible and fragrant.

Vegetable Oil Oils derived from vegetables and nuts, including canola, peanuts, sesame seeds and olives.

Venison Officially the word venison means "the flesh of deer", but more modern usage has broadened the base to include all types of buck as well as furred game (such as rabbits) and game birds. See also Game.

Vermicelli Fine rice flour noodles which may be boiled for a minute or two or deep fried, in which case they swell up and turn white and crisp.

Vetkoek Literally "fat cakes" made from deep-fried dough and served in many different ways. Either with a savoury filling, or spread with jam or sprinkled with cinnamon and sugar. Loved by many generations of South Africans.

Vinegar The flavours of vinegar are as complex as the flavours of the finest wines. Best known as a preservative, for example in pickles and chutneys, and an important ingredient in salad dressings. Malt vinegar is made from soured ale (an unhopped beer), coloured with caramel, and distilled to increase the strength. Wine vinegar is as good (or as bad!) as the wine from which it is made. Cider vinegar, made from soured apple cider, takes on the nature of the fruit from which it is made. Flavoured vinegars such as raspberry vinegar and sherry vinegar are popular. See also Balsamic Vinegar.

Wasabi Knobbly green root of a Japanese plant as pungent as horseradish, and used in sushi and sashimi. Available in paste or powdered form, which is mixed with water.

Water Chestnuts Fresh water chestnuts are far superior to the more easily available tinned variety. If using the fresh product, boil for 10 minutes and peel off the dark skin before using.

Wholegrain Mustard Granular mustard, a condiment made from mustard seeds. Adds flavour as well as texture to sauces.

Wild Rice Not strictly rice at all, but the seed of an aquatic grass native to the USA. The kernel is surrounded by a tough husk and is long and purplish-black. It bursts open during cooking to display a pale interior. Wild rice may be mixed with other rices. Don't overcook wild rice, as it will lose its fragrance and characteristic firm texture.

Wok Rounded frying pan used for stir-frying and other Chinese recipes.

Worcestershire Sauce One of the most useful and widely used flavourings in the world, and similar to the multitude of spicy, hot, salty sauces made from recipes brought back by colonels stationed in India during Queen Victoria's time.

Yeast Used for leavening bread. Instant dried yeast is the simplest to use, as it doesn't have to be dissolved in water beforehand. Simply add it to the dry ingredients then add the liquid. Instant dry yeast comes in 10 g (15 ml) sachets.

Yoghurt One of the world's oldest processed foods, yoghurt is formed by the addition of two specific bacilli, either as a culture or by adding a portion of previously made yoghurt.

Zest The coloured, flavoured part of citrus fruit contains volatile oils which give fragrance and flavour. When removing the zest be careful to avoid the bitter white pith between the zest and the fruit.

RECIPE INDEX

A
African Banana Chutney 108
Almond
  Praline 147
  -Crusted Fish with Coconut Lemongrass Sauce 17
Angel Hair Pasta with Avocado and Bacon 51
Apple and Date Crunch Cake 21
Apricot
  and Almond Ice-Cream 148
  Sauce, Spiced 42
Aubergine Scallopine and Tomato Compôte with Pine Nut Vinaigrette 39
Avocado
  and Bacon with Angel Hair Pasta 51
  Chocolate Avocado Mousse 73
  Creamed 141
  Lavosh Flatbread with Avocado Dip 20
  Smoked Salmon on Crisp Noodle Cakes with Avocado and Horseradish Cream 131

B
Baby
  Beans with Tomatoes and Feta 144
  Chickens with Mango-Coriander Sauce 74
  Chickens with Roasted Garlic and Pancetta, and Rosemary Demi-Glace 113
Baked Beetroot with Harissa and Mustard Foam 78
Baking
  Apple and Date Crunch Cake 21
  Bread with Roasted Vegetables 128
  Brioche 145
  Chocolate Marzipan Layer Cake 15
  Chocolate Mousse Cake 63
  Karilinah's Bush Scones 21
  Lemon Tart 70
  Macadamia Pie 123
  Maize and Cheese Bread 87
  Mango and Peanut Shortbread 21
  Mille-Feuille Cheesecake 97
Banana
  Chutney, African 108
  Samoosas and Cape Velvet Ice-Cream with Coconut Foam 17
Basil Pesto 138

Beans
  Baby with Tomatoes and Feta 144
  Chilli 93
  Peanut Samp and Beans 142
  Red Beans and Mangetout Tartlets 145
Béchamel Sauce 140
Beef
  Fillet, Seared, with Parmesan and Rocket 99
  Jus 140
  Salad, Warm with Bacon and Blue Cheese Dressing 108
  Stock 134
  Rare Roast Beef with Yorkshire Pudding and Mango Salsa 123
  Sesame Beef Salad 116
Beetroot, Baked, with Harissa and Mustard Foam 78
Berry Soufflé with Passionfruit Coulis 85
Black Mussel and Potato Salad with Roasted Garlic-Mustard Dressing 32
Black Mussels with Smoorvis-Filled Cabbage Roses in Ginger Broth 90
Blinis, Russian, with Smoked Salmon 74
Blue Cheese, Double Baked Soufflé with Fried Watercress Gnocchi and Red Pepper Compôte 36
Bobotie 97
Bobotie, Duck 32
Boeber 103
Braised
  Lamb Shanks with Peppers, Onions and Tomato 14
  Red Cabbage 144
Brandied Figs 147
Bread and Butter Pudding with Van der Hum 69
Breads
  Brioche 145
  Lavosh Flatbread with Avocado Dip 20
  Garlic Crostini 145
  with Roasted Vegetables 128
  Maize and Cheese Bread 87
  Sesame-Chilli Breadsticks with Smoked Trout 20
Breakfast
  Chilli Beans 93
  Kuku, East African, with Tomato Chutney 93
  Poached Fruit Flavoured with Lemongrass and Star Anise with Cinnamon-Honey Yoghurt 128
  Sausage Stacks with Corn and Cheese Cakes 108
Breyani, Mutton 102
Brioche 145
Burger, Lamb on Focaccia with Creamed Avocado, Marinated Tomatoes and Pickled Cucumber 37
Butter, Lemon 140
Buttered Spinach 144
Butter Fried Trout with Macadamia and Mushroom Stuffing and Pecan Lemon Butter 122
Butternut and Rocket Risotto with Truffle-Scented Mushrooms 145
  Curried Butternut Soup 96
  Risotto Cakes with Roasted Vegetables, Smoked Mozzarella and Sage Butter 37
  Roasted, and Corn Salad 109
Butterscotch Sauce 146

C
Cabbage, Braised Red 144
Cakes see Baking
Cape Velvet Ice-Cream 147
Cape-Malay
  Chicken Curry 45
  Spice Mix 136
  Spiced Fish with Coconut and Lemongrass Broth 57
Caramel Sauce 146
Caramelized
  Onion and Tomato Tarte Tatin 62
  Onions with Biltong and Pecorino 29
Carpaccio
  Ostrich with Peach Chutney and Avocado Parfait 68
  Ostrich, with Pickled Ginger and Wasabi Oil 48
Carrot Butter Sauce 140
Cassata, Quick with Raspberry Coulis 148
Chargilled Limes 135
Chateau Potatoes 142
Cheese
  Cream Cheese Soufflé 63
  Double-Baked Blue Cheese Soufflé with Fried Watercress Gnocchi and Red Pepper Compôte 36
  Goats' Cheese Soufflé with Red Currant and Apple Preserve 22
  Maize and Cheese Bread 87
  Marinated Tomato with Chilli, Mint and Mozzarella 109
  Potato, Spinach and Feta Pie 117
  Straws 145
  Tomato and Bocconcini Salad with Herb Pesto 113
  Vegetable Tower Topped with Camembert and Red Pepper Sauce 132
  Warm Beef Salad with Bacon and Blue Cheese Dressing 108
Cheesecake, Mille-Feuille 97
Chicken
  and Duck Livers, Parfait, with Grape Chutney and Rooibos Jelly with Toasted Brioche 84
  Baby with Roasted Garlic and Pancetta, and Rosemary Demi-Glace 113
  Breasts with Macadamia Nut Stuffing and Spiced Apricot Sauce 42
  Curry, Cape-Malay 45
  Honey-Lemon, with Sweetcorn Pancakes 70
  Salad, Tandoori 48
  Stock 134
  Spicy Peanut 87
  Roast Baby, with Mango-Coriander Sauce 74
  with Green Olives and Preserved Lemons 110
Chilli Beans 93
Chocmint Ice-Cream 65
Chocolate
  Amarula Truffle with Raspberry Coulis and Apricot and Almond Ice-Cream 27
  and Hazelnut Parfait, Iced, with Orange Crème Anglaise 132
  Avocado Mousse 73
  Double Chocolate Coffee Ice-Cream 148
  Iced Dark Chocolate and Hazelnut Parfait with Orange Crème Anglaise 132
  Leaves 146
  Marzipan Layer Cake 15
  Mousse Cake 63
  Pudding, Sticky 49
  Sauce, Dark 146
Chutney
  African Banana 108
  Cranberry Apricot 139
  Fresh Coriander 139
  Grape 139
  Peach 139
  Tomato 93
Cinnamon Ice-Cream 147
Coal-Roasted Corn 87
Confit
  Garlic 135
  of Baby Onions 144
Coriander
  Chutney, Fresh 139
  Pesto 138
Corn
  Pancakes 144
  Coal-Roasted 87
Coulis
  Lemon 146
  Raspberry 146
Court Bouillon 134
Couscous with Roasted Vegetables 142
Cranberry Apricot Chutney 139
Cream Cheese Soufflé 63
Creamed
  Avocado 141
  Potato, Garlic 141
Crème
  Anglaise 146
  Anglaise, Orange 146
  Anglaise, Rooibos 147
  Brûlée Espresso with Seed Biscuits, Vanilla Ice-Cream and Butterscotch Sauce 55
  Brûlée, Orange Blossom 119
  Fraîche 135
Croquettes, Potato 142
Crostini, Garlic 145
Cucumber, Pickled 141
Cumin-Grilled Pork Fillet on Peanut Samp and Beans and Buttered Spinach with Citrus-Ginger Glaze 116
Curried Butternut Soup 96
Curries
  Bobotie 97
  Cape-Malay Chicken 45
  Duck Bobotie 32
  Mutton Breyani 102
  Pienangvleis 79
  Smoorsnoek 45

D
Dark Chocolate Sauce 146
Date Salad 103
Demi-Glace, Rosemary 140
Desserts see also Ice-Cream
  Banana Samoosas and Cape Velvet Ice-Cream with Coconut Foam 17
  Berry Soufflé with Passionfruit Coulis 85
  Boeber 103

Bread and Butter Pudding with Van der Hum 69
Chocolate Amarula Truffle with Raspberry Coulis and Apricot and Almond Ice-Cream 27
Chocolate Avocado Mousse 73
Crème Brûlée Espresso with Seed Biscuits, Vanilla Ice-Cream and Butterscotch Sauce 55
Grilled Pineapple with Buttered Mint Glaze 58
Hazelnut Meringues with Berries and Cream 99
Lemon and Basil Mousse with Strawberry Salad 113
Lemon Tart 70
Little Malva Puddings with Rooibos Crème Anglaise 33
Macadamia Pie 123
Mille-Feuille Cheesecake 97
Orange Blosson Crème Brûlée 119
Pan-Roasted Fruit Kebabs with Vanilla Rice 104
Pears in Red Wine with Cinnamon Mousse 43
Poached Fennel and Strawberries in Vanilla Syrup 91
Poached Fruit Flavoured with Lemongrass and Star Anise with Cinnamon-Honey Yoghurt 128
Poppy Seed Orange Cakes with Liqueur Oranges 81
Sticky Chocolate Pudding 49
Strawberries Steeped in Merlot and Black Pepper 29
Sweet Potato Pudding 117
Wine Jelly 79
Traditional Sweet Peanut Snacks 87
Double-Baked Blue Cheese Soufflé with Fried Watercress Gnocchi and Red Pepper Compôte 36
Drinks
 Pawpaw Daquiri 108
 Sparkling Mango 51
Duck
 Bobotie 32
 Roast with Oriental Sauce 62
 Roasted Breast, on a Warm Salad of Tomatoes, Beans and Peas 131

E
East African Breakfast Kuku with Tomato Chutney 93

F
Fennel
 and Honey Ice-Cream 147
 and Strawberries, Poached, in Vanilla Syrup 91
Fennel, Mushroom and Macadamia Stuffing 137
Figs, Brandied 147
Fish see also Seafood
 Almond-Crusted with Coconut Lemongrass Sauce 17
 Baked in Banana Leaves with Chilli, Lemongrass and Coriander, with Red Pepper and Coconut Cream Sauce 129
 Butter-Fried Trout with Macadamia and Mushroom Stuffing and Pecan Lemon Butter 122
 Cape-Malay Spiced with Coconut and Lemongrass Broth 57
 Frikkadels with Chilli Tartare Sauce 102
 Grilled Tuna in Lemongrass-Spiced Vegetable Minestrone with Coriander Pesto 39
 Plaited Salmon Trout with Two Sauces and Ribbon Vegetables 69
 Smoked Salmon on Crisp Noodle Cakes with Avocado and Horseradish Cream 131
 Smoked Snoek Pâté 96
 Smoked Trout Salad with Papino and Chilli Salsa 65
 Smoorsnoek 45
 Spiced on Pasta with Olives and Tomato 49
 Stock 134
 Timbale of Smoked Fish with Cucumber Zest 42
 Tournedos with Mussel Risotto Dumplings 125
 Tuna Brix with Harissa Mayonnaise 58
 Tartare, with Olive Oil and Lime Juice 119
 with Scalloped Potatoes and Lime and Tomato Confit 70
Flatbread, Lavosh with Avocado Dip 20
Fresh Coriander Chutney 139
Frikkadels, Fish, with Chilli Tartare Sauce 102
Fruit
 African Banana Chutney 108
 Banana Samoosas and Cape Velvet Ice-Cream with Coconut Foam 17
 Berry Soufflé with Passionfruit Coulis 85
 Grilled Pineapple with Buttered Mint Glaze 58
 Hazelnut Meringues with Berries and Cream 99
 Lemon and Basil Mousse with Strawberry Salad 113
 Mango and Chilli Relish 108
 Mango and Prawn Bava 122
 Pan-Roasted Fruit Kebabs with Vanilla Rice 104
 Pawpaw Daquiri 108
 Pears in Red Wine with Cinnamon Mousse 43
 Poached Fennel and Strawberries in Vanilla Syrup 91
 Poached Fruit Flavoured with Lemongrass and Star Anise with Cinnamon-Honey Yoghurt 128
 Salad with Smoked Meat and Spiced Pickled Pears 14
 Sparkling Mango 51
 Strawberries Steeped in Merlot and Black Pepper 29

G
Garam Masala 136
Garlic
 Confit 135
 Creamed Potato 141
 Crostini 145
 Roasted 135
Ghee 135
Glazed Sweet Potatoes 142
Gnocchi, Watercress 141
Goat's Cheese Soufflé with Red Currant and Apple Preserve 22
Grape Chutney 139
Grilled
 Pineapple with Buttered Mint Glaze 58
 Tuna in Lemongrass-Spiced Vegetable Minestrone with Coriander Pesto 39

H
Harissa
 Mayonnaise 138
 Paste 136
 Sauce 138
Hazelnut Meringues with Berries and Cream 99
Honey-Lemon Chicken with Sweetcorn Pancakes 70
Hummus 138

I
Ice-Cream
 Apricot and Almond 148
 Cape Velvet 147
 Chocmint Ice-Cream 65
 Cinnamon 147
 Double Chocolate Coffee 148
 Fennel and Honey 147
 Hazelnut Meringues with Berries and Cream 99
 Lemon and Basil Mousse with Strawberry Salad 113
 Mango and Chilli Relish 108
 Mango and Prawn Bava 122
 Pan-Roasted Fruit Kebabs with Vanilla Rice 104
 Pawpaw Daquiri 108
 Pears in Red Wine with Cinnamon Mousse 43
 Poached Fennel and Strawberries in Vanilla Syrup 91
 Poached Fruit Flavoured with Lemongrass and Star Anise with Cinnamon-Honey Yoghurt 128
 Salad with Smoked Meat and Spiced Pickled Pears 14
 Sparkling Mango 51
 Strawberries Steeped in Merlot and Black Pepper 29
Iced Dark Chocolate and Hazelnut Parfait with Orange Crème Anglaise 132
Lemon and Green Peppercorn 148
Quick Cassata with Raspberry Coulis 148
Vanilla 147
Iced Dark Chocolate and Hazelnut Parfait with Orange Crème Anglaise 132

J
Jelly
 Rooibos 84
 Wine 79
Jus
 Beef 140
 Port 140
 Thyme 140

K
Karilinah's Bush Scones 21
Karoo Vetkoek Schwarmas 110

L
Lamb
 Burger on Focaccia with Creamed Avocado, Marinated Tomatoes and Pickled Cucumber 37
 Karoo Vetkoek Schwarmas 110
 Loin, Roast Spiced, with Apricots and Rooibos 91
 Mutton Breyani 102
 Provençal Lamb Racks with Tomato and Rosemary Sauce 119
 Shanks, Braised with Peppers, Onions and Tomato 14
 Stock 134
 Roast Rack, with Ragoût of Mushrooms, Liver and Kidneys 85
 Pienangvleis 79
Lavosh Flatbread with Avocado Dip 20
Lemon
 and Basil Mousse with Strawberry Salad 113
 and Green Peppercorn Ice-Cream 148
 Butter 140
 Coulis 146
 Tart 70
 Preserved Lemons 135
Limes, Chargilled 135
Little Malva Puddings with Rooibos Crème Anglaise 33
Lobster Tempura with Jasmine Rice and Stir-Fried Fine Greens 26

M
Macadamia Pie 123
Maize
 and Cheese Bread 87
 Meal Wedges 15
Malva Puddings, Little with Rooibos Crème Anglaise 33
Mango
 and Chilli Relish 108
 and Peanut Shortbread 21
 and Prawn Bava 122
 Salsa 146
 Sparkling 51
Marinade, Red Wine 134
Marinated
 Tomato with Chilli, Mint and Mozzarella 109
 Tomatoes 141
Marinière of Seafood 104
Masala
 Garam 136
 Roasted 136
Mayonnaise 138
 Harissa 138
Meat see also Chicken and Poultry
 Bobotie 97
 Cumin-Grilled Pork Fillet on Peanut Samp and Beans and Buttered Spinach with Citrus-Ginger Glaze 116
 Lamb Burger on Focaccia with Creamed Avocado, Marinated Tomatoes and Pickled Cucumber 37
 Lamb Shanks, Braised with Peppers, Onions and Tomato 14
 Mutton Breyani 102
 Old Joe's Oxtail 51
 Ostrich Carpaccio with Peach Chutney and Avocado Parfait 68
 Ostrich Carpaccio with Pickled Ginger and Wasabi Oil 48
 Ostrich Fillet with Pesto and Beetroot and Spinach Salad 58
 Ostrich Medallions with Dijon Mustard Crust and Cape Velvet Sauce 73
 Ostrich Steaks with Country Mushroom Duxelle, Ginger Crisps and Port Jus 81
 Pienangvleis 79
 Provençal Lamb Racks with Tomato and Rosemary Sauce 119
 Rare Roast Beef with Yorkshire Pudding and Mango Salsa 123
 Roast Rack of Lamb with Ragoût of Mushrooms, Liver and Kidneys 85

Roast Spiced Loin of Lamb with Apricots and Rooibos 91
Roasted Springbok Fillet, Sweet Potato Tatin and Pickled Beetroot 54
Seared Beef Fillet with Parmesan and Rocket 99
Sesame Beef Salad 116
Springbok Steaks with Chilli-Roasted Onions 43
Stock 134
Venison on Red Cabbage with Black Currant and Apple Sauce 22
Venison Pie 96
Venison Steaks with Cranberry Apricot Chutney 33
Meringues, Hazelnut with Berries and Cream 99
Mille-Feuille Cheesecake 97
Mixed Herb Pesto 138
Mousse
  Chocolate Avocado 73
  Lemon and Basil, with Strawberry Salad 113
Mushroom Soup, Spicy with Pesto 132
Mussel Risotto Dumplings 143
Mussels, see Black Mussels
Mustard Seed Vinaigrette 137
Mutton Breyani 102

O
Offal
  Parfait of Chicken and Duck Livers with Grape Chutney and Rooibos Jelly with Toasted Brioche 84
  Roast Rack of Lamb with Ragoût of Mushrooms, Liver and Kidneys 85
Old Joe's Oxtail 51
Onions
  Caramelized with Biltong and Pecorino 29
  Confit of Baby 144
Orange
  Blossom Crème Brûlée 119
  Cakes, Poppy Seed, with Liqueur Oranges 81
  Crème Anglaise 146
Ostrich
  Carpaccio with Peach Chutney and Avocado Parfait 68
  Carpaccio with Pickled Ginger and Wasabi Oil 48
  Fillet with Pesto and Beetroot and Spinach Salad 58
  Medallions with Dijon Mustard Crust and Cape Velvet Sauce 73
  Steaks with Country Mushroom Duxelle, Ginger Crisps and Port Jus 81
Oxtail, Old Joe's 51

P
Pancakes, Corn 144
Pan-Roasted Fruit Kebabs with Vanilla Rice 104
Pap 143
Parfait
  Iced Dark Chocolate and Hazelnut Parfait with Orange Crème Anglaise 132
  of Chicken and Duck Livers with Grape Chutney and Rooibos Jelly with Toasted Brioche 84
Pasta, Angel Hair, with Avocado and Bacon 51
Pastry, Rich Shortcrust 145
Pâté, Smoked Snoek 96
Pawpaw Daquiri 108
Peach Chutney 139
Peanut
  Mango and Peanut Shortbread 21
  Samp and Beans 142
  Snacks, Traditional Sweet Peanut 87
  Spinach with Peanuts 143
Pears
  in Red Wine with Cinnamon Mousse 43
  Spiced Pickled Pears with Smoked Meat 14
Peppers
  Roasted Red Peppers 141
  Red Pepper Compôte 140
  Red Pepper Sauce, Roasted 140
  Terrine of Tomatoes, Red Pepper and Basil with Sultana and Caper Dressing 55
Pesto
  Basil 138
  Coriander 138
  Mixed Herb 138
  Pickled Cucumber 141
Pie
  Macadamia 123
  Potato, Spinch and Feta 117
  Venison 96
Pienangvleis 79
Pine Nut Vinaigrette 137
Pineapple, Grilled with Buttered Mint Glaze 58
Plaited Salmon Trout with Two Sauces and Ribbon Vegetables 69
Poached
  Fennel and Strawberries in Vanilla Syrup 91
  Fruit Flavoured with Lemongrass and Star Anise with Cinnamon-Honey Yoghurt 128
Poppy Seed Orange Cakes with Liqueur Oranges 81
Pork, Cumin-Grilled on Peanut Samp and Beans and Buttered Spinach with Citrus-Ginger Glaze 116
Port Jus 140
Potato/Potatoes
  and Pistachio Wafers 142
  Chateau 142
  Croquettes 142
  Garlic Creamed 141
  Glazed Sweet Potatoes 142
  Potato, Spinach and Feta Pie 117
  Sweet Potato Pudding 117
  Sweet Potato, Coriander and Buttermilk Soup 73
  Sweet Potato and Tomato Tarte Tatin with Chilli and Basil Dressing 29
  with Fresh Thyme 142
Poultry
  Baby Chickens with Roasted Garlic and Pancetta, and Rosemary Demi-Glace 113
  Cape-Malay Chicken Curry 45
  Chicken Breasts with Macadamia Nut Stuffing and Spiced Apricot Sauce 42
  Chicken with Green Olives and Preserved Lemons 110
  Duck Bobotie 32
  Honey-Lemon Chicken with Sweetcorn Pancakes 70
  Quail with Fennel, Mushroom and Macadamia Stuffing and Port Sauce 65
  Roast Baby Chickens with Mango-Coriander Sauce 74
  Roast Duck with Oriental Sauce 62
  Roasted Breast of Duck on a Warm Salad of Tomatoes, Beans and Peas 131
  Spicy Peanut Chicken 87
  Tandoori Chicken Salad 48
Praline, Almond 147
Prawns and Mango Bava 122
  Spicy Chickpea Battered with Lime and Coriander Vinaigrette 57
Preserve, Red Currant and Apple 139
Preserved Lemons 135
Provençal Lamb Racks with Tomato and Rosemary Sauce 119
Pudding
  see Dessert

Q
Quail with Fennel, Mushroom and Macadamia Stuffing and Port Sauce 65
Quick Cassata with Raspberry Coulis 148

R
Rare Roast Beef with Yorkshire Pudding and Mango Salsa 123
Raspberry Coulis 146
Red Bean and Mangetout Tartlets 144
Red Cabbage, Braised 144
Red Currant and Apple Preserve 139
Red Pepper Compôte 140
Red Pepper Sauce, Roasted 140
Red Peppers, Roasted 141
Red Wine Marinade 134
Relish, Mango and Chilli 108
Rice
  Butternut and Rocket Risotto with Truffle-Scented Mushrooms 145
  Butternut Risotto Cakes with Roasted Vegetables, Smoked Mozzarella and Sage Butter 37
  Wild Rice Pilaf 143
  Yellow Rice with Raisins 143
Rich Shortcrust Pastry 145
Risotto
  Butternut and Rocket Risotto with Truffle-Scented Mushrooms 145
  Cakes, Butternut with Roasted Vegetables, Smoked Mozzarella and Sage Butter 37
  Dumplings, Mussel 142
Roast
  Baby Chickens with Mango-Coriander Sauce 74
  Duck with Oriental Sauce 62
  Rack of Lamb with Ragoût of Mushrooms, Liver and Kidneys 85
  Spiced Loin of Lamb with Apricots and Rooibos 91
Roasted
  Breast of Duck on a Warm Salad of Tomatoes, Beans and Peas 131
  Butternut and Corn Salad 109
  Garlic 135
  Masala 136
  Red Pepper Sauce 140
  Red Peppers 141
  Springbok Fillet, Sweet Potato Tatin and Pickled Beetroot 54
  Vegetables 144

Rooibos
  Crème Anglaise 147
  Jelly 84
Rosemary Demi-Glace 140
Rösti, Trio, with Ratatouille and Camembert, Smoked Salmon Tartare and Chicken and Mushroom Ragout 125
Russian Blinis with Smoked Salmon 74

S
Salads
  Aubergine Scallopine and Tomato Compôte with Pine Nut Vinaigrette 39
  Black Mussel and Potato Salad with Roasted Garlic-Mustard Dressing 32
  Creamed Avocado 141
  Date 103
  Marinated Tomatoes 141
  Marinated Tomato with Chilli, Mint and Mozzarella 109
  Pickled Cucumber 141
  Roasted Butternut and Corn 109
  Roasted Red Peppers 141
  Sesame Beef 116
  Smoked Trout with Papino and Chilli Salsa 65
  Tandoori Chicken 48
  Terrine of Tomatoes, Red Pepper and Basil with Sultana and Caper Dressing 55
  Tomato and Bocconcini Salad with Herb Pesto 113
  Warm Beef, with Bacon and Blue Cheese Dressing 108
  with Smoked Meat and Spiced Pickled Pears 14
Salmon
  Trout, Poached with Two Sauces and Ribbon Vegetables 69
  Smoked, on Crisp Noodle Cakes with Avocado and Horseradish Cream 131
Salsa, Mango 123
Samoosas, Banana and Cape Velvet Ice-Cream with Coconut Foam 17
Samp and Beans, Peanut 142
Sauces, Savoury see also Chutney, Pesto and Vinaigrette
  Basil Pesto 138
  Béchamel Sauce 140
  Beef Jus (Venison Jus) 140
  Carrot Butter Sauce 140
  Harissa Mayonnaise 138
  Harissa Sauce 138
  Hummus 138

Lemon Butter 140
Mayonnaise 138
Port Jus 140
Red Currant and Apple
    Preserve 139
Red Pepper Compôte 140
Roasted Red Pepper Sauce 140
Rosemary Demi-Glace 140
Spiced Apricot 42
Thyme Jus 140
Vinaigrette 137
Zhug 139
Sausage Stacks with Corn and
    Cheese Cakes 108
Schwarmas, Karoo Vetkoek 110
Scones, Karilinah's Bush 21
Seafood see also Fish
    Black Mussel and Potato Salad
        with Roasted Garlic-Mustard
        Dressing 32
    Black Mussels with
        Smoorvis-Filled Cabbage Roses
        in Ginger Broth 90
    Lobster Tempura with Jasmine Rice
        and Stir-Fried Fine Greens 26
    Marinière of Seafood 104
    Mussel Risotto Dumplings 143
    Seafood Soup 26
    Spicy Chickpea Battered Prawns
        with Lime and Coriander
        Vinaigrette 57
Seared Beef Fillet with Parmesan
    and Rocket 99
Semolina Wedges, Spiced with
    Oriental Vegetables 68
Sesame
    Beef Salad 116
    -Chilli Breadsticks with Smoked
        Trout 20
Shortbread, Mango and Peanut 21
Smoked
    Fish Timbale with Cucumber
        Zest 42
    Salmon on Crisp Noodle Cakes
        with Avocado and Horseradish
        Cream 131
    Salmon with Russian Blinis 74
    Snoek Pâté 96
    Trout Salad with Papino and
        Chilli Salsa 65
    Trout with Sesame-Chilli
        Breadsticks 20
Smoorsnoek 45
Soufflés
    Berry with Passionfruit Coulis 85
    Cream Cheese 63
    Double-Baked Blue Cheese
        with Fried Watercress
        Gnocchi and Red Pepper
        Compôte 36
    Goats' Cheese, with Red Currant
        and Apple Preserve 22
Soups
    Spicy Black Mushroom Soup
        with Pesto 132
    Curried Butternut 96
    Seafood 26
    Sweet Potato, Coriander and
        Buttermilk 73
Sparkling Mango 51

Spice Mixes
    Cape-Malay 136
    Garam Masala 136
    Roasted Masala 136
    Sri Lankan 136
Spiced
    Apricot Sauce 42
    Fish on Pasta with Olives and
        Tomato 49
    Semolina Wedges with Oriental
        Vegetables 68
    Sugar Syrup 137
Spicy
    Black Mushroom Soup with
        Pesto 132
    Chickpea Battered Prawns with
        Lime and Coriander Vinaigrette
        57
    Peanut Chicken 87
Spinach
    Buttered 144
    with Peanuts 143
    Spinach, Potato and Feta Pie 117
Springbok
    Steaks with Chilli-Roasted
        Onions 43
    Roasted Fillet, Sweet Potato Tatin
        and Pickled Beetroot 54
Sri Lankan Spice Mix 136
Sticky Chocolate Pudding 49
Stir-Fried Fine Greens 27
Stocks
    Beef 134
    Chicken 134
    Court Bouillon 134
    Fish 134
    Lamb 134
    Meat 134
    Veal 134
    Venison 134
Strawberries Steeped in Merlot and
    Black Pepper 29
Stuffing, Fennel, Mushroom and
    Macadamia 137
Sun-Dried Tomato Vinaigrette 138
Sweet Peanut Snacks 87
Sweet Potato
    and Tomato Tarte Tatin with Chilli
        and Basil Dressing 29
    Glazed 142
    Pudding 117
    Sweet Potato, Coriander and
        Buttermilk Soup 73
Sweet Sauces
    Butterscotch Sauce 146
    Caramel Sauce 146
    Crème Anglaise 146
    Dark Chocolate Sauce 146
    Lemon Coulis 146
    Orange Crème Anglaise 146
    Raspberry Coulis 146
    Rooibos Crème Anglaise 147
    Van der Hum Sauce 146

T
Tamarind Water 136
Tandoori Chicken Salad 48
Tart, Lemon 70
Tartare of Fish with Olive Oil
    and Lime Juice 119

Tarte Tatin
    Caramelized Onion and Tomato 62
    Sweet Potato and Tomato with
        Chilli and Basil Dressing 29
    Tomato and Olive, with Feta and
        Basil Pesto 99
Tartlets, Red Bean and
    Mangetout 145
Terrine of Tomatoes, Red Pepper
    and Basil with Sultana and
    Caper Dressing 55
Thyme Jus 140
Timbale of Smoked Fish with
    Cucumber Zest 42
Tomato
    and Bocconcini Salad with Herb
        Pesto 113
    and Olive Tarte Tatin with Feta
        and Basil Pesto 99
    Caramelized Onion and Tomato 62
    Chutney 93
    Marinated with Chilli, Mint and
        Mozzarella 109
    Terrine of Tomatoes, Red Pepper
        and Basil with Sultana and
        Caper Dressing 55
Tomatoes, Marinated 141
Traditional Sweet Peanut Snacks 87
Trio of Rösti with Ratatouille and
    Camembert, Smoked Salmon
    Tartare and Chicken and
    Mushroom Ragout 125
Trout
    Butter-Fried with Macadamia and
        Mushroom Stuffing and Pecan
        Lemon Butter 122
    Smoked with Sesame-Chilli
        Breadsticks 20
    Smoked, Salad with Papino and
        Chilli Salsa 65
Tuna
    Brix with Harissa Mayonnaise 58
    Grilled, in Lemongrass-Spiced
        Vegetable Minestrone with
        Coriander Pesto 39

V
Van der Hum Sauce 146
Vanilla
    Ice-Cream 147
    Sugar Syrup 137
Veal Stock 134
Vegetable Tower Topped
    with Camembert and Red
    Pepper Sauce 132
Vegetables see also Potato
    Aubergine Scallopine and Tomato
        Compôte with Pine Nut
        Vinaigrette 39
    Baby Beans with Tomatoes
        and Feta 144
    Baked Beetroot with Harissa
        and Mustard Foam 78
    Braised Red Cabbage 144
    Buttered Spinach 144
    Butternut and Rocket Risotto with
        Truffle-Scented Mushrooms 145
    Butternut Risotto Cakes with
        Roasted Vegetables, Smoked
        Mozzarella and Sage Butter 37

    Caramelized Onion and Tomato
        Tarte Tatin 62
    Caramelized Onions with Biltong
        and Pecorino 29
    Chilli Beans 93
    Coal-Roasted Corn 87
    Confit of Baby Onions 144
    Corn Pancakes 144
    Couscous with Roasted
        Vegetables 143
    Deep-Fried Vegetables 144
    Maize Meal Wedges 15
    Marinated Tomato with Chilli, Mint
        and Mozzarella 109
    Mussel Risotto Dumplings 143
    Pap 143
    Peanut Samp and Beans 142
    Potato, Spinach and Feta Pie 117
    Red Bean and Mangetout Tartlets
        145
    Roasted Butternut and Corn
        Salad 109
    Roasted Vegetables 144
    Spiced Semolina Wedges with
        Oriental Vegetables 68
    Spinach with Peanuts 143
    Stir-Fried Fine Greens 27
    Terrine of Tomatoes, Red Pepper
        and Basil with Sultana and
        Caper Dressing 55
    Vegetable Tower Topped with
        Camembert and Red Pepper
        Sauce 132
    Watercress Gnocchi 141
    Wild Rice Pilaf 143
    Yellow Rice with Raisins 143
Venison
    on Red Cabbage with
        Black Currant and
        Apple Sauce 22
    Pie 96
    Roasted Springbok Fillet, Sweet
        Potato Tatin and Pickled
        Beetroot 54
    Springbok Steaks with Chilli-
        Roasted Onions 43
    Steaks with Cranberry Apricot
        Chutney 33
    Stock 134
Vetkoek Schwarmas,
    Karoo 110
Vinaigrette 137
    Mustard Seed 137
    Pine Nut 137
    Sun-Dried Tomato 138

W
Warm Beef Salad with Bacon and
    Blue Cheese Dressing 108
Watercress Gnocchi 141
Wild Rice Pilaf 143
Wine Jelly 79

Y
Yellow Rice with
    Raisins 143
Yorkshire Pudding 123

Z
Zhug 139